A QUEER HISTORY OF FLAMENCO

A QUEER HISTORY OF FLAMENCO

*Diversions, Transitions, and Returns
in Flamenco Dance (1808–2018)*

Fernando López Rodríguez

Translated from Spanish by Ryan Rockmore

UNIVERSITY OF MICHIGAN PRESS
Ann Arbor

Originally published as *Historia queer del flamenco* by Editorial Egales, S.L., Spain, 2020, © Fernando López Rodríguez

English language edition © University of Michigan Press, 2024
All rights reserved

For questions or permissions, please contact um.press.perms@umich.edu

Published in the United States of America by the
University of Michigan Press
Manufactured in the United States of America
Printed on acid-free paper
First published November 2024

A CIP catalog record for this book is available from the British Library.

Library of Congress Cataloging-in-Publication Data

Names: López Rodríguez, Fernando, author. | Rockmore, Ryan., translator. | Michigan Publishing (University of Michigan), publisher.
Title: Flamenco's queer history : diversions, transitions, and returns in flamenco dance (1808–2018) / Fernando López Rodríguez; translated from the Spanish by Ryan Rockmore.
Other titles: Historia queer del flamenco. English | Running title: A Queer history of flamenco
Description: Ann Arbor [Michigan] : University of Michigan Press, 2024. | "Originally published as Historia queer del flamenco by Editorial Egalse, S.L., Spain, 2020"—Title page verso. | Includes bibliographical references (pages 191–203).
Identifiers: LCCN 2024028340 (print) | LCCN 2024028341 (ebook) | ISBN 9780472077120 (hardcover) | ISBN 9780472057122 (paperback) | ISBN 9780472221912 (ebook)
Subjects: LCSH: Flamenco--Spain--History. | Homosexuality—Spain—History. | Flamenco dancers—Spain. | Gender identity in dance.
Classification: LCC GV1796.F55 L6513 2024 (print) | LCC GV1796.F55 (ebook) | DDC 793.3/1946—dc23/eng/20240715
LC record available at https://lccn.loc.gov/2024028340
LC ebook record available at https://lccn.loc.gov/2024028341

DOI: https://doi.org/10.3998/mpub.12690077

Support for the translation of this book was provided by Acción Cultural Española, AC/E.

To those who know and to those who understand.

Contents

Opening Questions	ix
Epigraph	xi
Translator's Note	xiii
Introduction	1
ONE. The Emergence and Diversions of Gender (1808–1975)	6
TWO. Transitions and New Identities (1975–2008)	77
THREE. The Reactivation and Circulation of the *Tablao* in Times of Crisis (2008–2018)	107
Conclusion: A Revolution?	163
Notes	167
Bibliography	191
Acknowledgments	205
Index	207

Figures follow page 106.

Digital materials related to this title can be found on the Fulcrum platform via the following citable URL: https://doi.org/10.3998/mpub.12690077

Opening Questions

Is flamenco a desire?
Is flamenco a satisfaction?
Is flamenco a sublimation?
Is flamenco a neurosis?
Is flamenco a sexual problem?
Is flamenco a symbolic language?
Is flamenco a religious phenomenon?
Is flamenco a sensation?
Is flamenco an illusion?
Is flamenco a reflection?
Is flamenco an awareness of oneself?
Is flamenco a concept?
Is flamenco an expression?
Is flamenco an ideological production?
Is flamenco a political reflection?
Is flamenco a specific language?
Is flamenco a marketable good?
Is flamenco a mystification?
Is flamenco a system of communication?
Is flamenco a sensitive perception?
Is flamenco a spectral production?
Is flamenco a symptom?

Interrogaciones sobre el flamenco (Fernando López, 2018)
Citing *Interrogations sur l'art* (Léa Lublin, 1975)

"If I can't revolt, I don't want to be in your dance"
  —Quotation by Emma Goldman (1869–1940),
    inverted by Fernando López

Translator's Note

"The translator must surrender to the text [. . .]
Translation is the most intimate act of reading."
—Gayatri Chakravorty Spivak[1]

I did not approach this work as a translator, per se.

It was February 2019, and I was in Madrid, on a cheap weekend jaunt from New York, to see the world premiere of dancer-choreographer Manuel Liñan's ¡Viva! It was my first time meeting Fernando López Rodríguez in person, bouncing around gay bars and flamenco hangouts after the performance. We spoke casually over drinks, along with guitarist Jero Férec, about the need to center queer flamenco voices in scholarship and disseminate contemporary flamenco research from Spain to English users. Throughout this project, I have thought fondly of how this translation queerly came about that weekend with them and everything that has enabled me to approach this text.

Without any formal training in translation theory or long-form practice, I had to learn "on the job" and lean on other life experiences: my life as a professional flamenco dancer, high school Spanish teacher, queer person, flamenco dance researcher, resident of Spain for two years, and speaker of the *andaluz* (Andalusian) dialect, among others. Far beyond mere knowledge of the Spanish language, my *intimate* connection to the text carried me through. The songs and lyrics that Fernando cites transported me back to late-night *juergas* and gatherings in Madrid and Seville. The videos he references were the ones I watched, always with a cigarette hanging from my mouth, between flamenco classes as I developed my artistic craft. The interviews he transcribed, many of them ringing with the andaluz dialect, sent me back to hours-long conversations with friends in Seville over a warm *puchero*. And the *tablaos* he analyzes were the very locales I frequented, some of them now unfortunately closed forever. In these ways, and many more, *surrendering* to the text was the easiest part of the process.

The primary purpose of this translation is to bring queer histories, theories, and artists of flamenco to an English readership. In this transfer from one linguistic terrain to another, I have tried to remain faithful to the literal meaning of Fernando's words and phrasings and to avoid taking creative liberties. While the contemporary translators' tools are many–including WordReference, the Royal Spanish Academy's dictionary, Google Translate, ChatGPT, Grammarly, and one's command of the language–the task of a translation of this size is first and foremost a human, personal endeavor. In this day and age, with artificial intelligence and automated translators all around us, it feels necessary, political perhaps, to say it has been a pleasure to choose every word of every sentence of every page you are about to read. Honoring the many translators before me, I have also incorporated, with designations in the endnotes, existing English-language translations or original passages in English of works that the author cites whenever possible. Otherwise, as the phrase often goes in these endeavors, "my translation."

I would like to address a few challenges I encountered along the way. The first relates to the andaluz dialect present in some of Fernando's interview transcriptions. In the Spanish-language version, particularly with Enrique "el Cojo," we see phonetic representations common in the dialect with words sometimes missing final syllables or letters: for example, "*mu*" instead of "*muy*" (very) or "*tor mundo*" instead of "*todo el mundo*" (everyone). I have chosen contractions–like "I'm" or "it's"–to denote a level of informality or relaxed, casual nature, rather than linking these speakers to a marginalized dialect of the English language and further reifying hierarchical and demeaning views of non-Standard regional dialects. Secondly, although writers often avoid the passive voice in English, it is far more common and accepted in Spanish. I have attempted to maintain a palatable balance of active and passive voice throughout the text in order to maintain some of Fernando's style. Last, knowledge of a language has its limits for any non-heritage speaker. Therefore, upon those encounters with words that were beyond the help of any resource or my own memory (especially those at the idiosyncratic intersection of queer, flamenco, and/or andaluz parlance in Spain), I am incredibly grateful that I was able to turn to Fernando in times of need.

I also chose to keep particular words in their original Spanish for this translation. Throughout the text, these words appear first in italics and then non-italicized thereafter. Even though I have tried to make their meanings understandable with context, English equivalents, or endnotes, I will address some of them here:

While flamenco is understood as a musical and dance genre, it actually comprises many different musical-rhythmic styles called *palos*. For example, while an *alegría* and *farruca* might both exist within the flamenco family tree, their differences (in chords, counts, and accents) outweigh their similarities. There are plentiful resources online to find the specific characteristics of the dozens of palos. In the text, palos can be recognized in lowercase by the lack of English equivalent and association with an artistic performance. I have also decided to leave the *apodos* (aliases or nicknames) of artists untranslated and between quotation marks, except for a selection toward the end of the text where English translations felt appropriate.

Gitano is often literally translated as "Roma" or "gypsy" (the latter broadly understood to be derogatory), representing the historically-persecuted and marginalized group of Spanish Roma. Following conventions established by leading flamenco scholars, I have chosen to retain the borrowed Spanish term that prioritizes how this community refers to themselves, particularly in the flamenco context.[2] Capitalization of the term, in English, also recognizes their social identity in the same way we do for other nationalities and ethnicities.

Fernando employs a number of terms that relate to, what we would call in English, queer identity and performance. These terms include, with their literal translations: *travesti* (transvestite, trans, particularly "people assigned male sex at birth and who feminize their bodies, dress, and behavior"),[3] *transformista* (cross-dresser, drag queen/king), *marica* (faggot), and *travestismo/transformismo* (cross-dressing). However, to replace all of these words with one English equivalent dilutes their social, political, and cultural complexity. I have chosen, for the most part, to introduce these words in italics with a close equivalent in English and then continue with the Spanish-language term. This choice keeps with current trends in queer studies of the Spanish-speaking world.[4] I have immense gratitude to Professor Lawrence La Fountain-Stokes and his guidance on this topic.

The final word I would like to address here is *tullido* (cripped/crip). Fernando points out in his text that the artists' own use of the word is to transform, or reclaim, a "*potenticial insulto*" (potential insult). Based upon relationships over the years with disabled artists and my familiarity with disability/crip studies, the term "cripped/crip," although pejorative in origin, felt appropriate in this context.[5]

Although this is the first Spanish-to-English translation of a full-length scholarly work on flamenco, I hope it is far from the last. It joins the English-to-Spanish translation project *Sonidos negros: Sobre la negritud del flamenco* (Sonidos Negros: On the Blackness of Flamenco), just released in 2022 by K. Meira Goldberg and Kiko Mora, as academic works that seek to unearth hidden, silenced histories and bridge the scholarly gap in flamenco studies between Spanish and English.[6] My sincere hope is that scholars continue to explore, through international and interlinguistic partnership, the threads of historically-marginalized voices in flamenco.

This note would not be complete without expressing my immense appreciation for LeAnn Fields and her editorial team at University of Michigan Press; their patience and support have been invaluable throughout this process. Of course, Fernando López Rodríguez deserves more thanks than I can convey for gifting us his original work. I would be remiss not to offer gratitude to my loving partner, Aaron Mason, who had to hear "Does this make sense?" more times than I can remember. And last, but far from least, the women who have helped me hone the skills that made this translation possible: K. Meira Goldberg, for ushering me into the world of flamenco studies and offering us so much through her research; Ninotchka Bennahum and Michelle Heffner Hayes, for helping my first scholarly publications simply make sense; the late Andrée Grau, for exposing me to the rich field of dance anthropology; Susan Leigh Foster and Anurima Banerji for teaching me that writing truly is a craft and a process; and Teresita Barcia-Varno, my high school Spanish teacher, for instilling in me an unwavering love for the Spanish language and cultural manifestations of the Spanish-speaking world.

Introduction

I started dancing and writing at the same moment, although I was already watching dance and reading for many years before that. I was a reader and spectator before a writer and dancer. At eleven years old, in the middle of a premature existential crisis, I decided to get over the "internalized gender barriers" and join the dance academy where my older sister had been studying from age three. The academy was right below my paternal grandparents' house, where you could hear the echoes of piano chords, jumps, castanets, and footwork patterns. I wanted to belong to that world, at whatever cost, and I did it, losing "friends" and on the receiving end of laughs, nicknames, and insults along the way: dancing was for girls and faggots (*maricones*), and by doing it, I became one of them. In a way, I had to come out of the closet twice, and this was the first time, perhaps too early for a young boy.

I continued dancing, decided to specialize in flamenco, passed the exams for all five years of the flamenco dance major from the Asociación de Profesores de Danza Española, Clásica, Flamenco y Moderno and the Cátedra de Flamencología de Jerez, attended the Universidad Complutense as a philosophy student, and right away started to take part in its Grupo de Danza Española. I made my way to Paris and kept dancing. I discovered in a much more intimate and profound way what contemporary dance, improvisation, experimentation, and performance were; I am not sure if that was a response to a certain boredom and disappointment that I came to feel with flamenco or if it was instead on the contrary. The discovery of that latest lover made me feel that I no longer wanted to—that I could no longer—dance as I had until then. I jumped from the philosophy department to dance studies and stayed in Paris. I kept dancing, crossing and constructing bridges between disciplines wherever they did not exist, even in precarious ways. Sometimes, I could not erect the smallest of structures, leaving me on one shore and looking from afar at what was happening on the other side, trying to communicate at the top of my lungs with those over there. I returned to Spain and kept dancing. I returned to Paris as a doctoral student in aesthetics, sciences, and technologies of the arts, specializing in dance and gestural arts. And, as I was dancing, I wrote the dissertation that gave rise to this book, which I defended in November 2019 at the University of Paris VIII, entitled "Mutaciones del deseo en danza: Tablao y flamenco contemporáneo. Género, contextos de producción y categorías estéticas en España (1808–2018)."

A thesis carried out in order to explain myself, to explain ourselves, to explain myself *in the "we"* and one that perhaps I should have thought about writing when I had reached old age, from a position of greater temporal distance, perhaps more objective but perhaps too condescending so that, as Deleuze and Guattari affirm, "all the parts of the machine come together to send into the future a feature that cuts across all ages."[1] I wanted to avoid dancing that condescendance (*condescendanza*) of those who have already stopped dancing and observe bodies from the outside in order to harvest the fruits of knowledge before they become too ripe for consumption, as described in a lovely way by Giorgio Agamben:

> This is the reason why it is said that the supreme knowledge is that which comes too late, when we no longer have any use for it. This knowledge, which has survived our works, is the last and most precious fruit of our lives, though somehow it no longer concerns us, like the geography of a country that we are about to leave behind.[2]

That dissertation, a kind of three-headed hydra, contained not only a scientific text but also the choreographic creation of *Pensaor, un filósofo en el tablao*—alongside singer Álvaro Romero, guitarist Jero Férec, and lighting/audiovisual designer Jorge Pascual—in which I reused some of the elements discovered during my research, and the documentary *¿Funcionarios del arte? Los tablaos en Madrid*, which I showed at the Teatro de la Zarzuela, in 2018, including videos of some of the interviews conducted with dancers and producers and archival images of *tablaos* [flamenco nightclubs] in Madrid from the 1950s to 1980s.

Several things have changed from the dissertation text to this book, given that I have broken up the dissertation into numerous articles and published them in different contexts, especially surrounding the question of "contemporary flamenco" and the analysis of my choreographic works, created in direct relation to my research work. Additionally, the process of self-translation from French to Spanish and the rewriting of the text have allowed me to sort out some unresolved doubts that I had only touched upon at a glance in the dissertation and to answer some of the questions generously posed by my committee members on the day of my defense.

If this book is titled *A Queer History of Flamenco*, it is for at least two reasons. The first is that one of my essential motivations as a researcher and artist has been to look for, analyze, and reclaim key marginalized spaces and figures in flamenco that did not show up in the typical manuals of this art form and whose absence, to my understanding, has provided a distorted image about those who have done flamenco—along with where, how, and why—throughout its recent history. This group of "weird" people includes feminists, *travestis*,[3] butches, and camp queens, but also *Gitanos*,[4] disabled people, *guiris* [foreign tourists], and "incomprehensible" artists who insisted on doing things "in another way" without abandoning the category of flamenco.

Second, the queerness of this History is my gaze. In the same way that the categories of "traditional flamenco" and "contemporary flamenco" have existed—similar to the politics from which they are derived—so has a traditional History about flamenco that comes from a type of gaze that I try to divert here. Diverting the gaze in order to talk about the body and from the body—abandoning pointless debates about purities and impurities; anecdotes about the lives of artists that are completely separate from creative processes; mythologies about "geniuses" who seem more like prophets than artists and seem to make art in solitude, completely isolated from their collaborators and the historical, social, economic, and artistic moment in which they lived. Diverting the gaze to talk less *about* the shadows of flamenco (alcohol, sex work, drugs, child labor) and to talk more *from within* the shadows; trying to, as Spinoza would say, understand without judging; adding small tiles to a complex mosaic that obliges us, in order to see it, to wink both eyes, to come and go between the gaze with a magnifying glass, which caresses the details, and the scenic gaze, which encompasses the whole of the parts. Of course, the ability to see other things and, above all, another way requires us to close our eyes and let the seconds pass with our mind faded to black, which turns into absences that flamenco experts will note in this work: there are themes here that evidently are not spoken about or are only observed out of the corner of one eye. On the other hand, the "diverted gaze" that I propose assumes a slight squint on certain questions that I formulate for the first time and for which ongoing focal adjustments will surely be necessary to explain them accurately.

In the first chapter, playing on the double meaning of the word *género* [gender/genre], I attempt to analyze the emergence of flamenco along with the simultaneous diversions of "género" that appear in the establishment of certain normative clauses. Respecting chronological and thematic axes at the same time, I intend to resolve the (dis)continuities between two "intimate" spaces where "traditional" flamenco takes refuge: the *cafés cantantes* [nighttime performance venues specializing in flamenco] of 1850–1920 and the tablaos, focusing in this chapter between their emergence in the 1950s and 1975. I tackle issues ranging from the artistic, like the movement codes for men and women or the distribution of roles between musicians and *bailaoras* [female flamenco dancers], to the social, such as job insecurity, the objectification of the female body, sex work, the consumption of drugs and alcohol, child labor, the barely hidden flirtation between the world of flamenco and the elites of the Franco regime, and the development of "gender-based dissent" (drag [*transformismo*] and song lyrics with feminist content, to name a couple) before and after the Civil War [1936–1939].

Chapter 2 places the focus on three types of "transition." The first is politics, as it relates to the new "socially committed" flamenco artists. The second is aesthetics, through the appearance of the soon-to-be-called "contemporary flamenco dance" and a connection to the different factors that, as I will explain, favored its emergence between 1975 and 1990. Finally, the third is the transition of gender that was already heralded years before the dictator's death but truly exploded during the 1970s and 1980s. In this chapter, Gitano activists, leftist singers, travestis, and transsexuals are on a date with one another, united by a dual desire for individual and collective freedom.

In the third chapter, focusing on a much shorter period between 2008 and 2018, which also corresponds to the period lived by me in the first person as an artist and researcher, I try to show the effects that the economic crisis of 2008 had on the flamenco universe and how artists had to develop various survival strategies in order to keep working. If the first chapter spoke about *diversions* (adjacent to) from the norm and the second about *transitions*, this final chapter addresses *crisis*, as well as *crises*: economic, political, and gender based, all of them growing in the flamenco world and which, even in broad strokes, I will barely manage to map.

Three *furreteos* close this book. In the flamenco world, *furretearse*—or *folletearse*—means to go out of *compás* [rhythmic structure in flamenco], make a mistake while doing footwork, end at the wrong time, or make a mess (of yourself) rhythmically. Folletearse is, ultimately, a "queer art of flamenco failure"[5] that I wanted to use as a space of possibility to graft various reflections that divert attention from the central theme in order to "go out on a necessary limb" of themes about Gitanos and the blueprint of what a cripped (*tullida*) History and a foreigner History of flamenco would have to be; these reflections will come to round out, amplify, and dispute the parameters within which I have written this work and some of the general conclusions that I have reached.

I would like to conclude this introduction with a simple image that might summarize how I am conceiving of this book as the product of someone who has learned to look at flamenco—and all that this entails directly and indirectly—*shoulder to shoulder* with researchers and artists who, before me, have done invaluable work without which this book would not have been imaginable. Like a young boy at a parade packed with people, I have scaled the bodies of different researchers and artists in order to, once perched above, see something that alone or from down below I could not see, something that they could only glimpse, since my eyes, elevated by their backs, reached further. Getting on another's shoulders does not happen without shaking, trembling, and dizziness, for the climber or muscle aches for the person at the base. This act involves trust by the person who climbs and generosity by the person who offers their body so that the other can extend their gaze. The following is what I desire for my reader: that they climb onto my shoulders to look further and see more than I can, *by way of me, beyond me*. We will see each other at the end of the footwork section . . . Have a good trip.

Abu Dhabi–Madrid–Jerez de la Frontera
February 2020

ONE

The Emergence and Diversions of Gender (1808–1975)

Flamenco: National Identity, Gender Identity, and Aesthetic Identity

Flamenco Was Born Male

The term *flamenco*, to designate a distinct musical and choreographic style, was first written and preserved in 1847. Its initial appearance was in an article titled "Un cantante flamenco" [A flamenco singer], published on June 6 in the Madrid-based newspaper *El espectador*:

VARIETY ACTS. Madrid Lifestyle Section.

A FLAMENCO SINGER. A few days ago, Lázaro Quintana, the famous singer of the Gitano genre, arrived at this Court. As assured by our sources, he intends to reside here for some time. Anyone who has traveled through Andalusia and attended some of the functions frequently held in the capitals of Cádiz or Seville, among the people affected by those entertainments, will have at least heard the respect that his name deserves among the singers of this genre. Enthusiastic about Spanish customs and mainly about those of Andalusian origin, whose poetry interests everyone and delights many, we attended a gathering where he and the never-well-regarded Dolores "La Gitanilla," already known in this country for her dances and singing, were expected to attend. We listened a considerable amount to both of them. More than once, the heartfelt flamenco songs we heard touched our hearts, as typical of midday as they were adapted to those poetic imaginations that the children of that land regularly possess.

We see in this birth certificate that flamenco is born as a spectacle, in a café, gendered, and masculinized. As a Spanish cultural phenomenon, flamenco differs from foreign artistic forms that are considered effeminate. As José Álvarez Junco explains, the Spanish War of Independence (1808–1814), caused by the invasion of Napoleon I's navy, sparked the need in Spanish society to create a national identity against the invading enemy—meaning France—and against the intellectual, social, and political movement of the Enlightenment, with which said enemy identified:

> Starting in 1808, one can speak of nationalism in Spain: ethnic patriotism became fully national, at least among the elites. And this was the indisputable work of the liberals. The modernizing elites took advantage of the occasion to try to impose a program of social and political changes. Their modus operandi was to launch the revolutionary idea of the nation as the holder of sovereignty. The national myth was a mobilizer against a foreign army and Joseph Bonaparte's collaborators, as long as they were not (French-allied) Spaniards. The Spanish liberals resorted to the affinity between patriotism and the defense of liberty. As the Asturian deputy Agustín Argüelles declared when presenting the Constitution of 1812, "Spaniards, now you have a homeland."[1]

This anti-Enlightenment positioning of identity then contaminated all spheres of Spanish society in the nineteenth century, including the cultural and artistic spheres in which flamenco was at full term, already giving its first kicks inside the womb of the motherland. Accordingly, flamenco is born in an environment that is going to make the values of the French Enlightenment its countervalues, placing the truth of its passion and spontaneous character in opposition to the cold rationality of the Enlightenment, whose reflective character will have to be considered a lack of spontaneity and, therefore, false. As the anthropologist Julio Caro Baroja explains in his work *Temas castizos*:

> At the same time, that of Carlos III [1716–1788], enlightened society produced the coldest neoclassicism, the most abstract legislation, the attempts at regulating the Economy, Religion, the most utopian public spectacles. All the while, the *people* oppose and continue clinging to their tastes for old theater, *romances de ciego* [blind man's ballads], and gruesome stories of saints and sinners of the

Baroque. Society gets swept up in violence and can turn a convict into a hero. It values youth based on the elegance and bravura of men and women, these qualities needing to be perceived in their way of dressing, singing, dancing, and making love.[2]

The anti-Enlightenment values adopted as a sign of Spanishness (*españolidad*) or *casticismo* ["Castillian national essence"][3] will be questioned and criticized by a good number of intellectuals of the time, such as the writer Jovellanos, for example, who wonders: "What else are our popular dances than a miserable imitation of the free and indecent dances of the negligible plebs? Other nations bring the gods and nymphs to dance on the tables; we bring the workers and greengrocers from Madrid." Despite the criticism of these intellectuals, pejoratively called "Frenchified," the anti-Enlightenment values and the aesthetic that emerges from them become law, as flamencologist José Luis Navarro indicates:

> The nineteenth century will see many things change in the Andalusian dance scene. It begins with the implementation of a political measure: the Royal Order of December 28, 1799 [repealed in 1821], which prohibits actors, dancers, and singers from other nations from being represented throughout Spain [nor may they "perform, sing, or dance pieces that are not in the Spanish language," according to the General Regulations for the Management and Reform of Theaters, drawn up in 1807 by the Madrid City Council]. With it, the intention is to combat the growing monopoly of Italian companies and dancers, especially in opera.[4]

In summary, flamenco identity, like Spanish national identity throughout the nineteenth century, seems to be born in a context in which economic status, intellectual training, and gender identity are inescapably intertwined: the fight against the foreign enemy, bourgeois and enlightened, does not provoke an effort to excel by a good part of Spanish society, but rather an inversion of values. This axiological inversion, making the popular that which is considered the most valuable, runs parallel to the establishment of disdain, with a gendered tone, in considering Enlightenment values as inferior and, therefore, effeminate (or vice versa). The explanatory theory of French sociologist Pierre Bourdieu can clarify this *testosteronization* of Spanish identity, as he writes:

The cult of virility, i.e., of harshness, physical strength, and surly coarseness, established as a chosen refusal of effeminate refinement, is one of the most effective ways of struggling against the cultural inferiority which unites all those who feel deprived of cultural capital, whether or not they might be rich in economic capital, like shopkeepers.[5]

In the case of flamenco dancing, this manliness translates into a work "of effort and release, in which tension is the result of concentration and suspension, of sound and silence."[6] In order to analyze this expressive palette, I will use flamenco, as it has come to my body, and the Effort model created by the movement analyst Rudolf von Laban (1879–1958) at the end of his life.

Laban distinguishes four *motion factors*: time, space, weight, and flow. Each one of these factors has two opposite poles between which, to different degrees, the different *effort elements* oscillate: time is divided into sustained and sudden; space—or rather, the perception we have of it—can be direct or flexible; weight, firm or gentle; and flow or energy, free or bound. None of these poles of movement is completely excluded in flamenco, although it is true that some of them occupy only a secondary role, like colors that are added to the gesture to nuance it. This is the case of flexible space, free flow, and gentle weight.[7] The privileged gestural colors in flamenco movement include firm weight and bound flow and correspond, following the list of the eight action verbs proposed by Laban, with the following actions: *punch, press, wring, slash,* and *dab*.[8] The *bailaores* [flamenco dancers] *punch* with their feet when performing footwork and with their hands when clapping, as well as hitting their chests or thighs to create rhythms. The *pressing* action is visible when dancers raise or lower their arms with their hands open as if they were flapping against the air and even when they walk, doing so not so much *in the space* as *against it*. The *wringing* action is recognizable in movement performed with the wrists and fingers, be it concentric or eccentric, and also in flamenco-specific turns—which have little or nothing to do with the gravitational challenge of pirouettes—like the so-called *vueltas de pecho* and *vueltas quebradas* (both turns inclined at the waist with the upper body rotating at an angle to the lower body). The *slashing* action is visible in the shapes created with the arms where the elbow is extended (diagonally upward, forming a V, crossed in front of the chest). Finally, the *dabbing* action is visible in a step precisely called *látigo*[9] and in certain movements performed with the *mantón de Manila* [fringed shawl].

Flamenco is born in opposition or born to resist, and, therefore, it must show itself to be strong, leaving aside the lightest, softest, or most flexible actions, such as drumming, brushing, sliding, or floating, actions that, on the other hand, will be considered "effeminate," with all the negative weight that it implies. How, then, do we define an aesthetic universe in which the fundamental actions, although there are other possibilities, include hitting, pressing, wringing, slashing, and dabbing? What type of dance and dancers does this aesthetic universe produce? Which sensations, emotions, and concepts can be expressed through it? What kind of energy does it emit? With which possible images is it associated? What kind of aesthetic experience is transmitted to the spectator? If, as the philosopher Ludwig Wittgenstein rightly affirms, "The limits of my language mean the limits of my world,"[10] what is excluded from that artistic universe? What is impossible to say inside of it? In what way does the establishment of these aesthetic borders, more or less porous, which define as much as they exclude (Spinoza already says that "all determination is negation"), not already anticipate something that will end up happening much later when the flamenco artists themselves begin to feel the constraints of these aesthetic limits? Laban himself defends it as follows:

> After each discovery of a new effort combination which for a period is cherished as the perfection of movement habit, a temporary return to more primitive forms sets in because it is realised that specialisation in a restricted number of effort qualities has its dangers. . . . New dances and new ideals of behaviour arise by a process of compensation in which a more or less conscious attempt is made to regain the use of lost or neglected effort patterns.[11]

According to this Labanian analysis of the History of gestures, "in terms of transhistorical symbolic actions," as the dance historian Isabelle Launay[12] calls it, the complaint that flamenco artists will express, especially from the 1990s and very often in relation to the roughness of flamenco, will be nothing more than the emanation of a need to reintegrate weak weight as a movement factor whose exclusion has defined the contours of this aesthetic universe since its creation.

The Feminization of Dance in Spain at the End of the
Nineteenth Century

Despite the launch of a poetics of gesture that we could consider entirely masculine, flamenco dancing, which started to become codified as such during the second half of the nineteenth century, began to be perceived as a, strictly speaking, feminine activity. An example of this, mentioned by José Luis Ortiz Nuevo, is the following newspaper review:

> What prevails today at the court is what has come to be called the flamenco genre.... The most sophisticated and select people of Madrid's high life are dying to hear the cries of the *cante jondo* [deep flamenco singing] and see the dances of the Gitanos and men of dubious sex.[13]

The appearance of a "doubt" about the gender of men who dance—and which is not, indeed, a genuine doubt in the sense of an epistemological hesitation, but rather a performative act of language that, by its very manifestation, declares the unfortunate character of a behavior—indicates that dance was already perceived at that time as something strictly feminine. As I argued in *De puertas para adentro: Disidencia sexual y disconformidad de género en la tradición flamenca*,[14] this feminization of dance could be explained historically as relating to a change in the regimes of perception of the body due to the loss, in 1898, of the last overseas colonies (Cuba, Puerto Rico, and the Philippines).

As Alberto Mira,[15] Richard Cleminson, and Francisco Vásquez García[16] have observed, a crisis of masculinity in Spain and a search for the lost national virility accompanied the national catastrophe and period of decline with which Spain ended the nineteenth century. We found ourselves in a state of anxious pursuit of the type of man who would be capable of cleansing the country of its international humiliation. In their text *Sexo y razón*, Andrés Moreno and Francisco Vázquez García describe this era as follows:

> It is about reclaiming the force of a nation stripped of its colonial empire, delayed and disrupted in its industrialization process, and corrupted and archaic in its political organization, social structure,

and ways of life. Politicians and intellectuals often understood the national decline in biological terms, and the act of regeneration, viewed as a living being, as a species, as a race, guided the country and its population. The Spanish physical build had irreversibly degenerated, and it was essential to reinvigorate it.[17]

The physical build they searched for—strong, courageous, and productive—did not seem compatible with certain art forms, like dance, in which the body is exposed and displayed in direct relation to its sensitivity and emotional expressivity. The first consequence of this national concern with manliness was the gradual disappearance of male dancers, as the Sevillian dance master José Otero tells us in his *Tratado de bailes* in 1912. In the middle of a passage during which Otero is explaining the partnering positions in *sevillanas* [popular dance from Seville], we find the following statement:

> It is also true that, now, few boys dance; almost all of them are girls . . . but twenty-five years ago, two young girls never danced together, since many of you will remember that while two girls would go out to dance Sevillanas together, the following verse would be sung continuously:
>
> > Why do so many peeping Toms go to the ball
> > if two young women dance together for lack of men?
> > Long live humor,
> > and if you do not have it, come to this house.[18]

The nostalgia that Otero feels for his youth, a time when as many men as women went out to dance, "although they did not have much money to spend,"[19] is a testament to how perceptions of the male body can shift within a particular historical circumstance, especially one in which it becomes increasingly necessary to convey a sense of strength and power. Nevertheless, another body exposed to the spectator's gaze maintains this impression of virility that the male dancer's body appears to lack: the bullfighter. As historians Cleminson and Vázquez García confirm, based on the writings of various intellectuals of the era:[20]

> The expansion of *"flamenquismo"*[21] appears as a symptom of the national decadence and, thus, of effeminacy. The condemnation that follows appears associated with the repudiation of the Gitano

people, considered an image of laziness. . . . Curiously, this negative association between flamenquismo and the idleness of Roma people was not evoked when it came to the world of bullfighting, which is closely related to "flamenco customs." Flamenco was seen to effeminize because it brought to bear the influence of Gitanos; bullfighting virilized because it transformed sloth into energy.[22]

What happened throughout the nineteenth century so that in different parts of Europe a crisis of gender and sexuality was produced, with tremendous repercussions for the field of dance? What brings the critic Jules Janin to refer to a male dancer as "a horrendous ballerina of the male sex" in 1840?[23] Research by Hélène Marquié shows how the professionalization of male dancers in the French opera and the introduction of the spectator figure—who does not participate in dancing but merely watches—produces a profound rift in terms of gender: dancing a social dance, in which everyone dances, is not the same as getting onstage and letting nondancers stare, admire, or desire you.

> The rupture between theatrical dance and social dances, starting with professionalization, is finalized entirely by the end of the 1820s. Dancers no longer inspire young people enough to [imitate them] in social dances, and the techniques and costuming diverge radically. While ballet will transform more toward a feminized activity, social dances will continue to be practiced by both sexes. . . .
> As of the 1830s, ballet is considered within the woman's realm, with theatrical dance serving as an art form of the feminine essence. Male dancers, critiqued repeatedly, are gradually excluded from the stage, beginning with the Paris Opera. From the pen of critic Jules Janin in 1832, we read: "I do not recognize the right of a man to dance in public." This is reasserted in 1833: "A man does not have the right to dance."[24]

If we move further toward the end of the nineteenth century, we find a new surprise that seems to reinforce this link between dance as a feminine activity and, accordingly, in the case of men, between dance and homosexuality. In the description that Karl Heinrich Ulrichs provides of the "Uranians"—a sexual category created by Plato that accounts for homosexuals as a "third sex," with an amalgam of bodily and psychological characteristics from both sexes—Ulrichs states:

The muscles of the Uranian are weaker than those of men. As a result, in most cases, there is a natural tendency toward calm movements (strolls, hikes, mountain sports, cycling, swimming, and dancing). While the bodily musculature leaves much to be desired, the lingual musculature denotes customary activity. Because of that, we consider Uranians, like women, to be extremely loquacious.

They frequently appreciate small steps, dancing about, seemingly moving with somewhat elastic strides. Their way of walking is so characteristic that I could very often recognize a Uranian from my office just by their stride as they entered from the waiting room.

Also, the arm movements of Uranians are by and large customary, especially those movements from which writing is derived.[25]

This description, as Javier Sáez points out well,[26] was contested by other Uranians of the time, like Hans Blüher (Wandervögel, or "Wandering Bird," Movement), Adolf Brand (Gemeinschaft der Eigenen, or Community of Free Spirits), and Friedrich Radsuweit (Bund für Menschenrecht, or League for Human Rights). He finds it curious that homosexuality is linked to languid musculature and associated with activities like dancing, hiking, swimming, or cycling, which constitute intense muscular exertion. Likewise, the attempt at "movement analysis" of the Uranian walking style is humorous because of the stereotypes, albeit undoubtedly interesting, in which he distinguishes a changing rhythm of beats and a proliferation of finger, hand, and arm gestures.

Returning to the flamenco world alongside the feminization of dance and, hence, of flamenco dance, a masculinization of bullfighting and the gradual disappearance of female bullfighters begin to occur. Female bullfighters have had a constant presence in Spanish bullfights since 1654, when the name of a female bullfighter appears in a document from the Council of Castille on June 25.[27] Toward the end of the nineteenth century, however, bullfights performed by women started to be disparaged and, eventually, prohibited by Juan de la Cierva, a minister in Antonio Maura's administration, on June 2, 1908. Within this prohibitive context—which makes me ask myself if men were also possibly banned from dancing—unbelievable situations begin to occur, such as when female bullfighter "La Reverte" changed her feminine name to the more masculine Agustín Rodríguez in order to keep working. The arrival of the Second Republic in 1931 and legislation introduced by minister Rafael Salazar Alonso in 1934 will finally lead to the rehabilitation of female bullfighting.[28]

The Café Cantante as Ancestor of the Tablao (1850–1920)

The first public showings of flamenco dance took place starting in the second half of the nineteenth century, as confirmed by an 1847 review in *El espectador*, in which the word *flamenco* appears in the variety acts section of the newspaper. If we stretch the "midwife" metaphor some more, we would have to say that flamenco dancing, beyond the hint of its first intrauterine movements, is already born onstage and in front of the audience. Other researchers have dealt with this prestaged flamenco, which, using Marxist terminology, has come to be called "use flamenco" (*flamenco de uso*). This term characterizes it as the flamenco made *between* and *for us* and conterposes it to a "flamenco of exchange" (*flamenco de cambio*), an artistic-staged phenomenon, decentered from subjective and/or community pleasure and carried out *for others*, spectators outside the community.

The truth is that this categorical differentiation is, at least in the case of dance, inadequate to the extent that there is always already a staging of the body and movements themselves in the dance that we perform *among and for ourselves*, which makes the study of flamenco *juergas* [flamenco parties] and private functions from the prism of aesthetics relevant, not resorting only to theoretical tools from anthropology and ethnology. In the same way, the flamenco that is performed in theatrical spaces and occupies the entire project presented here is not only performed *for others* but also among the artists themselves and for their pleasure, creating theatrical communities, gatherings, and coexistence within the artistic and labor framework. Where the use of the fundamentals of analysis from the philosophy of art (the scene) might seem more appropriate, it is essential to make an epistemological stew in which the gnoseological values, analytical tools, and perspectives of anthropology are also present.

When flamenco dancing first sees the world's light, someone is already watching in front of it. Thanks to the appearance of these cafés cantantes, inspired by the *cafés-concerts* in vogue in Paris, Vienna, and other large European cities, flamenco begins to truly develop as a commercial art, forming part of variety shows in which other music, dances, and artistic forms were also scheduled (silent movies, circus, stand-up comedians, short plays, *zarzuela*). Between 1850 and 1920, the cafés cantantes were enormously successful in Spain, especially in large cities like Seville, Málaga, Cádiz, Barcelona, and, above all, Madrid, where Blas Vega lists more than eighty-five establishments.[29] However, they also existed in areas linked to mining, such as La Unión, Cartagena, and Jaén. The cafés cantantes, which will socially connote places with violence, theft, alcohol consumption, and prostitution as their backdrop, are going to welcome flamenco as if it had found its *natural place* there: a working-class nightlife space, in which the distance between the stage and the hall is minimal and the singing, guitar, and dance can mix with other "masculine" passions.

A good description of this aesthetic adaptation between flamenco and the café cantante—which would continue with the tablao a century later—is provided in a newspaper article from 1870 in the following terms:

> Flamenco dancing will be as remarkable as its admirers say, but it is not typical of a theater, whatever its conditions. Its place is in the cafés on Mesón de Paredes Street, but in the Alhambra Theater, where the audience is different, it is impossible to please. Outside of this, everything done there pleasantly entertains the audience, who will find a suitable place to spend their summer nights. I am going to say, in closing, two words to the gentlemen, but quickly so that the wives do not hear it—of those men who have them, of course. In the Alhambra, their can-can goes way up to . . . there, and *live groups* with girls are advertised that will go . . . far beyond. So I will not say more.[30]

As can be seen in this short text, the consanguinity between flamenco and the café cantante has the negative consequence of excluding the flamenco genre from theatrical spaces since, although the author of the text grants it a particular value, he considers it inappropriate for the theater, a place reserved for other artistic forms probably considered more refined. Beyond the aesthetic and class biases expressed here, it is still true that all stage spaces are not the same and that the distance between the spectators and the performers definitively determines the type of aesthetic experience that is produced there, as well as the possibility of energetic contamination between the artists and the audience. In a type of dance like flamenco, less dependent on the visual form than other dance styles and much more based on the "kinesthetic contagion" of the feelings and emotions experienced by the dancers, proximity and the reduction of space constitute a better breeding ground for the artistic experience to flourish in.

Two Divisions of Gender in the Café Cantante

Navarro García indicates that the choreographic flamenco repertoire was quite small at the time of the cafés cantantes.[31] The acts, much shorter than those performed later in the tablaos, had as their fundamental objective to show the individual personality of each dancer. This objective made the repetition of the same song possible—for example, *alegrías*—throughout the entire show since each one of the artists offered her personal choreographic interpretation.[32] A competitive dynamic among artists and a logic of competition were already germinating in the show's very structure. The repertoire comprised alegrías, a singing style with its origins in Cádiz, in which bailaoras could sing a little and display their relaxed character; *tangos*, which according to Cruces Roldán could sometimes be danced with a fringed shawl and wide-brimmed hat;[33] *soleares*, the *jondo* [deep/flamenco] counterpoint of the show, also danced by women;[34] and *zapateados*,[35] a dance performed by men and featuring rhythmic footwork.

The distribution of the repertoire—zapateados and *jaleos* for men; soleares, alegrías, and *tientos* for women—illustrates the establishment of a first gender divide in the cafés cantantes within flamenco dance itself. Dominated by a drive for binary categorization in terms of gender, we no longer have representation only of a masculine aesthetic universe—flamenco—that differs from other styles considered feminine and effeminate. We also have, within flamenco, a distribution of tasks according to which dancing is properly feminine while singing and guitar playing are considered more typical of men. Last, within dancing—considered a "feminine" task—there is a division between "manly dancing" (*baile de hombre*) and "womanly dancing" (*baile de mujer*), not only in terms of the type of songs to which each of them can dance but also in terms of movement codes, whose differentiation, according to Navarro García[36] and Gamboa,[37] would have been a consequence of the staging of flamenco in cafés cantantes. According to Blas Vega, along with the staging of flamenco dancing in the cafés cantantes, the *bata de cola* (dress or skirt with a long train) appears on the scene, initiating a new wardrobe utterly different from that of previous *bolero* dancers and also complemented by the fringed shawl and wide-brimmed hat.

At this point, manly dancing—centered on the use of the lower part of the body ("from the waist down") and displaying virtuoso footwork—starts to be distinguished from womanly dancing—judged more by its expressivity and focused on the upper body ("from the waist up") with movements of the torso, arms, hands, and head. Cruces Roldán has analyzed how this binary affects the different parts of the body (legs, belly, arms) and has proposed a series of general characteristics of manly dancing and womanly dancing, metaphorically opposing the softness of the woman's flesh to the rigidity of the man's bones.[38] The verticality of posture, straightness of the lines of movement, strength, precision, and austerity (*punching* and *slashing*, in Labanian terms) could be characteristic of manly dancing. Womanly dancing could be distinguished by waviness in the movement (*twisting*, in Labanian terms), insinuation (provocative gaze, smile, use of the skirt to play with the offering and hiding of legs), and the use of accessories (shawl, bata de cola, hat, fan).

In the same way that there were men who danced even though that dance was considered a feminine activity, there were women who sang and played guitar despite those being more masculine activities. This sharp distinction between Cruces Roldán's description of manly dancing and womanly dancing, which would make us unable to speak of complete flamenco bodies and force us to deal with bodies that are poetically severed at the waist, should not be understood as an unavoidable boundary that would prevent the existence of intermediate aesthetics that could be considered exceptions or counterexamples. Instead, we should understand them as a general sketch of the choreographic practices of bailaores and bailaoras, beginning with the staging of flamenco in cafés cantantes. The authenticity of this sketch, with undoubtedly emphasized features, can be verified by analyzing the descriptions of the musical-choreographic repertoire performed by men and women, as well as taking into account what can and cannot be done by dressing in the costumes and accessories worn by some and by others.

In effect, fast-paced, percussive dances and choreography based on complex foot exercises comprise the masculine repertoire (jaleos and zapateados). These exercises force the dancer to stabilize his spine, which almost completely eliminates the possibility of stooping forward or backward, often found in the feminine style. They also minimize the work of the upper body and limbs (arms and hands), which will have to acquiesce to being elements that accompany the footwork due to both the need to stabilize the spine and the difficulty of coordination between the upper and lower parts of the body. The men's tight clothing also reinforces this rectilinear aesthetic, given the type of pants, their rigid fabric, and the covering of the belly up to the ribs, which makes twisting even more difficult. The jacket, rigid as well, prevents the dancers not only from twisting their spine but also from raising their arms above their head.

On the other hand, the women's repertoire draws on slower musical styles (soleares, tientos, and alegrías) with much less rhythmic impact—often without the hand clapping (*palmas*), as is the case with the *soleá*—and with more melismatic melodies. These musical qualities lead to the creation of long choreographic passages in which the dancers work with their torso, arms, and hands to decorate the pattern of the long melodic lines while using accessories that fill the space, both toward the sky (the shawl, for example) and the ground (the walks with the bata de cola).

The categories of "dancing from the waist up" and "dancing from the waist down," despite their old-fashioned character, continue to produce concrete effects in the daily practice of flamenco dance since they are reproduced in the areas of pedagogy and artistic production. In this way, they serve to evaluate the performances of artists by measuring the distance they maintain with a gender schism that has become, in the imagination of aficionados, an aesthetic ideal always "on the verge of being lost," perhaps precisely because, as an abstract model, no one has ever been able to fully embody it. The lack of existence of this ideal impedes neither its efficacy, which translates into more or less symbolic sanctions when the distance between the ideal and in practice is perceived as too great (the absence of applause or shouts of encouragement [*jaleos*], bad reviews, lack of consideration by producers), nor its persistence over time.

From Voyeurism to the Scopic Drive

One of the significant changes produced by the café cantante as a theatrical device, which could partly explain the differentiation between men's and women's dancing, is the conversion of flamenco dances into one-person or solo dances.

The passage from couples dances—which continued to be present in cafés cantantes thanks to bolero dances—to solos produces a change in the perceptual regime of the dancers' bodies that, from then on, are going to be observed facing the audience, fully exposed to its gaze, rather than in profile, face-to-face with their dance partner. Each dancer will cease to be a mere member of an artistic pairing to become an independent figure.

The fact of not seeing a couple made up of a man and a woman onstage seemed to turn solo dancers into single dancers available in the sexual market. As Ramón Martínez argues in his book *La cultura de la homofobia y cómo acabar con ella*,[39] inspired by Monique Wittig's *The Straight Mind*,[40] heterosexuality should not be considered only as a sexual and/or affective option, but above everything else as an embodied ideology in the body, in kinesthetic practices, and in the perception of oneself and other bodies. According to this, the "heterosexual couple" would epistemologically precede the individual so that we would not conceive of the link between two bodies as the union between two differentiated individuals but the other way around. The individual is perceived from the notion of a couple, or its absence, as an unpaired element. In this way, no matter how much the couples dances disappear from the stage, they continue to be the model of interpretation for the solo body in such a way that we could say that the choreographic form of the solo is a "single dance" that invites us to think about the body of the solo dancer as sexually available to the spectators for whom they dance. The dancer forms a partnership with the spectator, who no longer occupies the place of the voyeur aroused by the sight of an erotic dance that represents a relationship of desire between a man and a woman (as was the case in many of the couples dances, like the *fandango*, *seguidillas*, and the bolero,[41] all of them considered "lascivious" dances). Instead, the spectator becomes one side of the observer-observed/desirer-desired relationship.[42]

Likewise, given that the cafés cantantes are fundamentally places frequented by men, the male dancer-female spectator (man-woman) pairing is practically anecdotal compared to the female dancer-male spectator (woman-man) pairing. This explains why in the cafés cantantes, now considered libidinal devices, the proportion of female artists was much higher than that of men: one man for every seven women.[43] The article "The Dancers of Spain," written by Edward G. Kendrew and published on December 20, 1912, in *Variety* magazine, points to this situation:

> In a few large towns of the Peninsula are the cafe concerts of the French type, but with several numbers devoted to Spanish dancers, and this form of entertainment (apart from the bull fights and the invading cinematograph) is the most popular among the people at the present time. However, the working classes do not have much to spend on amusements, and there is little opportunity for such an enterprise on a large scale. . . .
>
> Spain is not the land of gaiety we imagine. The happy street crowd, attired in bright costumes such as we see in comic opera, is a fallacy. On the days of the corrida, or bull fights in the various cities—which is a local fete,—the women appear in colored mantons or shawls, but for the remainder of the year they are invariably cheerless and dressed in black. This is particularly remarkable in the sunny south. The highly paid Spanish beauties, full of fire and ginger, are found mainly in foreign music halls. There is little scope for them at home. Those who dance in Madrid, Seville and Barce-

lona dream of a foreign engagement, for the actual salaries paid in the dancing cafes are, with few exceptions, ridiculously low. In the smaller places the dancers do not anticipate better conditions. They are chiefly Gitanas, or gypsies [sic] of Moorish extraction, reared with illiterate and rudimentary ideas of life.

These girls find the low salaries paid in the cafes sufficient, and a welcome change from home drudgery. . . . The Spanish girls, however, are not unique in this respect. It is only within the past few years that the typical singers of the French cafe chantants in garrison towns were compelled by the owners to mix with the audience and make collections in the body of the hall. Even now the system is still practiced illicitly. In Spain it remains a regular custom.

And yet many of these Spanish girls are clever artistes, showing real talent, which (unlike her French sister, the chanteuse) is only acquired after years of hard apprenticeship. Dancing has to be learned, even when the pupil has a natural aptitude, whereas the singers are frequently launched out with little preliminary preparation. There are many schools for dancing in Spain. One in Seville, managed by a man called Otero . . . , is quite famous. . . .

It is in this part of the Peninsula that the typical dance cafes are to be found. The evening's show is divided into four sections, from 8 to after midnight, and although admission is free it is necessary to order a fresh drink for each section. The Spaniard is nocturnal, and in the city he goes to bed very late. Dancing is the main, and often the sole feature of the program. The dancers are accompanied by a small band of guitar and mandolin players, seated at the back of the platform, which cannot be termed a stage. Some are accompanied by a pianist, who seems to have one air for all. The last section is the most vivacious, and in some of the traditional cafes at least one girl will leave the "stage" and dance on a table in the middle of the hall, often in very light attire. . . .

Notwithstanding the cinema houses and cafe concerts do not include vaudeville acts, they accept women singers, more or less talented, when good-looking and of agreeable physique. A man appearing along on the stage is often met with noisy opposition unless he is known or presents an exceptionally good act. Unlike South America, a woman is safe in going to Spain, and is not obliged to mix with the audience, as the native dancers do. So long as she is pretty she will earn applause. But there is a decided tendency for suggestiveness, and the girl who is the most risque takes the cake. Artistes are sometimes booked by impresarii from their appearance on the lithos or picture post cards, and if the original does not come up to the portrait the engagement is soon finished by the cancellation clause in the contract. The preliminary engagement is for ten days, with a clause that it can be cancelled on the third day. If the girl is prepossessing, and has a little talent, there is a rush for her services, though it cannot be said the managers fall over each other in making big offers. Few acts are really well paid.[44]

In this article, Kendrew not only elaborates on the low salaries and the eroticization of the dancers' bodies in the cafés cantantes, but also gives clues about the very structure of the shows. There are pauses between the different artistic numbers to force viewers to drink, and the shows follow a crescendoing erotic logic. The artists seem to be aware of the extent to which the success of their acts depends on the type of clothing they wear, the proximity to the audience, and their cunning or provocative gestures, which could later end with a sexual act, as demonstrated by certain artists of the time. Singer "Tía Anica la Piriñaca" (1899–1987) spoke about the period of the cafés cantantes in the following way:

But there are, there are bad women, but not like before. They used to be a dime a dozen, but there were many women. Women like these were very funny, knew a lot about flamenco, danced, and sang, and everything, and were very likable. You arrived and you were single and you liked them and that was that. You got involved with them and spent everything. . . . Other men have married those women who are actually married. By that man's side, now those women are good, of course, so . . . But before? Oof! They used to go to a juerga, and everyone was on cloud nine because of their playfulness. They danced and sang; there were so many of them, so many of them, there were so many of them.[45]

One exceptional example of the artistic representation of prostitution in the flamenco world during the era of the cafés cantantes was *Woman and Puppet* (*La femme et le pantin*), a novel written by the French Pierre Louÿs in 1898 that has been adapted into several films: *The Woman and the Puppet*, an American film by Reginald Barker (1920); *La femme et le pantin*, a French film by Jacques de Baroncelli (1929); *The Devil Is a Woman*, an

American film by Josef von Sternberg (1935) with Marlene Dietrich playing the role of the dancer; *Laabet el Sitt*, an Egyptian film by Wali Eddine Sameh (1946); a newer French version directed by Julien Duvivier and with Brigitte Bardot in the role of the dancer (1959); *Ese oscuro objeto de deseo*, a French-Spanish film by Luis Buñuel (1977); and the made-for-TV movies by Mario Camus (1990) and by Alain Schwartzstein (2007) for Spain and France.

Concha Pérez, the female object of desire in *Woman and Puppet*, is a flamenco dancer who works in a café cantante and does private shows for groups of men in private rooms of the venue. In the novel, Louÿs describes the scene as follows:

> Her greatest triumph was the flamenco. What a dance, monsieur! What a tragedy! It combines all passions in three acts: desire, seduction and enjoyment. No dramatic work expresses feminine love with the intensity, the grace and the fury of the three successive scenes. Concha was incomparable in it. Do you really understand the drama which is played therein? To one who had not seen it I would have to explain it a thousand times. It is said that it takes eight years to make a *flamenca* [female flamenco artist], which means that, with the precocious maturity of our women, they have lost their beauty by the time they have learned to dance it. But Concha was born a flamenca; she had no experience but she had intuition. You know how they dance it in Seville. You have seen our best ballerinas; not one is perfect, for this exhausting dance (twelve minutes! Can you find an Opera dancer who can dance a variation of twelve minutes!) has in it three unrelated roles: the lover, the ingénue and the tragedian. One must be sixteen years old to act the second part wherein Lola Sanchez now realizes marvels of sinuous gestures and light attitudes. One must be thirty years old to play the end of the drama, wherein the Rubia, in spite of her wrinkles, is still excellent every night....
>
> A moment later, I was alone on the balcony of an interior court and, through the French window, I saw, monsieur, a scene from hell. There was a second dancing hall, smaller, well lighted, with a platform and two guitar players. In the center was Concha, naked, with three other nude women, dancing a mad *jota* before two Englishmen sitting in the back.... I said naked; she was more than naked. Black stockings, as long as dancers tights, reached up to her

thighs, and she wore noisy little shoes which snapped on the floor. I dared not interrupt. I was afraid I would kill her. Alas! My God! Never had I seen her so beautiful! It was no longer a question of her eyes or her fingers; all her body was as expressive as a face, more than a face; and her head, enveloped in hair, rested on her shoulders like a useless thing. There were smiles in the folds of her hips, blushing cheeks when she turned her flanks; her breasts seemed to look forward through two great eyes, fixed and dark. Never have I seen her so beautiful. The false folds of a dress change the expression of the dancer, deviate absurdly the exterior line of her grace; but there, by a revelation, I saw the gestures, the shivers, the movements of the arms, the legs, of the supple body and the muscular loins, born indefinitely from a visible source, the very center of her dance, her little brown belly.[46]

In the different versions of the film, however, the naked dancer does not appear accompanied by other women and does not dance a jota but something similar to flamenco.[47] Guitar music accompanies her, and she plays with a Manila shawl that allows her to alternately show and hide her breasts, buttocks, and sex.

In the flamenco sphere, an adaptation was brought to the stage in 2004 by Isabel Bayón's company, in which the Sevillian dances, to tangos, the emblematic scene of the half-naked person wearing transparent black stockings that reach up to mid-thigh, white panties, and a salmon-colored corset.[48] Despite this, *Woman and Puppet* has not achieved the same success as another romantic French novel, *Carmen*, by Mérimée, which we will discuss later. Perhaps it is partly due to the musical adaptation created by Bizet, which facilitates the transition between text and gesture. However, perhaps it also has to do with a narrative difference that, from the perspective of gender, is not at all inconsequential. Concha Pérez and Carmen share the same personalities as free and seductive women, but the final destiny of both is not the same. While Concha dedicates herself to seducing Don Mateo without ever sleeping with him and comes out unscathed by the flirtation, Carmen will be murdered in a quasi-moralizing scene during which the reader—or, rather, the female reader—is warned of the fate of those women who live their sexual-affective lives freely and do not meet the expectations of the man on duty. The punishment of death for Carmen also has a compensatory effect on the man, who somehow recovers his honor by murdering the one who had supposedly questioned him. Does this dramatic ending have anything to do with the success of one novel over the other? Are the woman's death and the man's recovered honor in *Carmen* more acceptable for the reader than the unscathed woman and the dominated man in *Woman and Puppet*?

Male Prostitution in the Cafés Cantantes

In certain cafés cantantes of big cities, prostitution was not only done by women but also by men and homosexuals. Sal de Velilla, an author from the beginning of the twentieth century, testifies to this: "Adolescents who sing and dance trying to arouse lascivious desires, which they later appease with abnormal councils, are replacing the beauties of our music halls and cafés cantantes."[49]

The historians Vázquez García and Cleminson declare that cafés cantantes should be considered not "gay institutions" but places where "all sorts of erotic whims" were allowed. They also insist that this type of prostitution existed in certain cafés in Barcelona's Barri Xinès (Chinese Quarter), the El Polinario café on Calle Real in Granada, and Madrid's Café del Vapor, located at number 2 Calle Mesón de Paredes, next to the current Tirso de Molina plaza in the Lavapiés neighborhood. This last one was frequented by, among others, the journalist and writer Pedro de Répide (1882–1948), "a laidback homosexual [who] smelled of cheap perfume and powdered his face,"[50] and the aristocrat Antonio de Hoyos y Vinent, accompanied by his cousin Gloria Laguna,[51] his "page" Luisito Pomes, and his "friend," the designer José Zamora (1889–1971).[52] Vinent also frequented other cafés, such as the Café de Levante in Madrid, which had different locations and was decorated with paintings by the Romantic painter Leonardo Alenza.[53] Litvak, a contemporary writer of Vinent, describes him as follows: "The aristocrat with the sport coat, high-heeled shoe, and monocle frequented the Café de Levante, where he flirted with bullfighters. Youngsters from the shadows and people from high society passed through his halls searching for perverse feelings."[54]

Multidisciplinary and Hybrid Artists

Except in a small number of cafés cantantes dedicated exclusively to flamenco singing, as was the case with the famous Café de Silverio, opened in 1881 by singer Silverio Franconetti on Calle Rosario in Seville, in most cafés, especially in Madrid, a diversity of artistic genres performed onstage was the norm. The flamenco historian Blas Vega describes it as follows:

> Villa Rosa represents in the happy and crazy 1920s what Los Gabrieles did in the 1910s. It will become the center of Madrid's nightlife, of a society that began with the century, frivolous, fanciful, and avid for sensations and exoticism, and that, seeking the recipe for having fun, will motivate the importation into—fashionable—Europe of abundant places like *cabarets*, the *rouleta*, the *the*, the *soupertango*, the *cocots*, the *dancing* . . . leaving flamenco, the distinguished juerga, as a note of contrast, of traditionalism, of something authentic and picturesque.[55]

The flamenco artists who worked in cafés cantantes often had a profile close to that of variety artists since they could sing, dance, and perform stand-up comedy. Poet and writer Luis Rosales (1910–1992) describes a vivid scene in a cabaret in which, at that time, all boundaries, including the one that separates the stage from the public, were absolutely porous:

> I can remember, and I will never forget, that one day when I was in a cabaret in Madrid, there came a time when the cabaret women began to dance on the tables [of the spectators]. I remember that one of the girls began to dance, reciting the *Romance de Antoñito el Camborio* [by Federico García Lorca]. That was in 1935.[56]

In addition to their multidisciplinary side, some artists danced and sang not only flamenco but also other musical styles, such as the *cuplé*, the mischievous and even erotic musical genre whose origin seems to be found in the Spanish translation of the French song "La puce" (The flea), which was sung for the first time in 1893 by Aurora Bergès. We find among these multidisciplinary and hybrid artists certain paradigmatic cases, such as that of singer Amalia Molina (1881–1956) or that of the singing dancers Encarnación López, "La Argentinita" (1898–1945), and Pastora Rojas Monje, "Pastora Imperio" (1889–1979), who will, in turn, be imitated with enormous success by the cross-dresser (*transformista*) Edmond de Bries—of whom I will speak in more detail later—in two numbers of his repertoire: the song "¡Vaya usted con Dios!" (lyrics by Salvador Valverde and music by Manuel Font) and "Mi canción a España" (lyrics by Ricardo Rada and music by Álvaro Retana).[57]

Far from being a technical richness possessed by artists, aficionados of the time considered the ability to sing styles of music other than flamenco to be a sign of a lack of flamenco talent. Historian Antonio Escribano, for example, tells how Amalia Molina, despite her success, was described as "short" ("limited in her flamenco register") because she only performed a handful of song styles: *marianas*, soleares, and tientos-tangos. The same thing happened to Pastora Imperio, who, in the beginning, "danced little and got lost," and whose strong dances included alegrías, soleares, and tanguillos.[58] On the opposite side of this point of view, the Granada-born philologist José Javier León stresses, concerning Encarnación López, "La Argentinita," the importance of stylistic hybridization and denies the incompatibility between flamenco and the so-called negligible genre.

> Since we are talking about shows, it is noteworthy that "La Argentinita" feels a crazy, resolute passion for the kind she cultivates, that of variety shows, which she defends from those ridiculous names of insignificance and other, worse ones with which others intend to denigrate or downplay them. She has good taste in believing that the *couplet*, when refined and intentional, deserves respect and artistic praise.[59]

This extract from 1914 points in the same direction as a statement made by the artist herself, collected in an interview from 1925, in which the interviewer asked if she preferred to sing cuplés, perform monologues, or dance:

> In short, I do not know. What I can assure you is that I love all things theater. I interpret a dance or a cuplé with the same enthusiasm and the same interest as I recite the monologue "Una mujer sensible," by Martínez Sierra, or "¡Ay que se me cae!," written expressly for me by Muñoz Seca, in both of which I am delectable, according to the graphic expression of a distinguished cannibalistic friend.[60]

As León argues, it is precisely thanks to this stylistic hybridization that someone like Encarnación López was successful, given that "in the golden years of the variety shows, the place of honor was the final number and always corresponded to the cuplé singer, and the second-to-last number was for the dancer.[61] Her success consisted of interpreting songs and embellishing them with the proper choreography. In that way, she ensured honor and applause for herself while she innovated."[62]

Women, Artists, and "Feminists"

The mixture of genres seems to take place not only in terms of stylistic hybridization and stage techniques (song, dance, and dramatic interpretation). Some women, like Adela Cubas, assume the role of guitarist, normally occupied by men at that time, which will not exempt them from facing the same chauvinist problems as dancers in terms of the need to have a beautiful body and face to work as artists. Even though the guitar stands between the performer's body and the viewer's gaze, and although the guitarist only shows her body sitting and semi-hidden behind the musical instrument, the spectator wants to see a pretty face and a voluptuous silhouette "behind the melody." As stated in a 1911 interview conducted by the flamenco historian Eulalia Pablo in her work *Mujeres guitarristas*, Adela Cubas, who often worked with the aforementioned hybrid artist Amalia Molina, had numerous issues finding work due to her lack of beauty:

> "I am very ugly, and ugly women in the theater are not lucky, no matter how artistic they are. No one promotes them, neither journalists nor businessmen. And without the benefit of publicity, they won't get beyond mediocrity or achieve the heights of fame. . . . I have been hired twice to go to America, and both times I have failed. The first was because the businessman found me so horrible that he told me he would hire me if he could go onstage with his back turned. The second contract was taken from me by a dog . . . , a really marvelous little dog that does math and plays dominoes remarkably well. So much so that if they change a tile, he barks and rejects it. . . . I know that I am ugly, but I don't care. I even get some moral advantage out of my ugliness. An ugly woman sees things more clearly, more realistically. She lives less deceived. She can have more confidence in the affection she evokes."
>
> "So why do you complain about what they call your ugliness?"
>
> "Because of how it makes the artistic path in life difficult for me. Any cuplé singer earns more than I do, even if she was just an utter disaster."[63]

Despite the difficulties, these female artists continue to fight for their right to work, and even if some of them do not consider themselves feminists "in the invasive sense of the word," like Molina, they will remain active in terms of political revendication:

I don't consider myself a feminist in the invasive sense of the word. . . . I think men are very vain and quite selfish. They control the rights of the woman they love without making the slightest concession in their ways or relief from their behavior in exchange for this privilege. On the contrary, while the little angels have fun and enjoy life without the slightest remorse, the tyrants demand that we stay quiet at home without seeing or speaking to anyone. And some even get uncomfortable if we go to bed without waiting for them.[64]

This activism will translate both into negotiations over working conditions, which every source indicates were quite awful for female artists,[65] and into onstage performance of explicitly feminist and republican songs like "La diputada" (by Carrere and Font de Anta, 1932). In this interesting paso doble and fandango, in which a musical passage from the "Himno de riego" [the anthem of the Second Spanish Republic (1931–1939)] can be recognized, the lyrics say:

The time for feminism arrived / and as always, I was sharp / and I took something with me everywhere / I brought the election certificate. / In congress with Luis de Tapía / I am acting as a leader / Long live divorce! Long live my hands! / that have not yet sewn, not even a sock!

[Read aloud]: *And even at the hairdresser's, / they call me "Your Grace" / And as Victoria Kent / I travel for free on the train. / Yes, gentlemen deputies / we must put an end to Bolshevism / and to laziness, which is the same: / here he who doesn't work doesn't eat, / starting with the wirepullers.*

The day the president / lets me speak / they'll have to take me out / on their shoulders through the street. The poor Count of Romanones / who does not even have a *peseta* [former Spanish currency] / told me last night: Well, it suits me / to be a representative and on a diet! / Well, yes, during these times, / in which there are no friends in high places for a servant, / I can waste time with some pesetas. / Oh, what a dream!

[Read aloud]: *And although I have a house in Madrid / and a small farm, / it's been seized, and I lost it. / Light up the powder keg! / I believe that everything will be fixed / including the anthem! / because I plan to ask / Don Fernando de los Ríos / who is very flamenco / for it to be the greatest fandanguillo.*

Estanislao's wife / has had four children / Estanislao's wife / and then people say / that he's an unemployed worker / he's had four children. Olé! Long live flamenco and bullfighting![66]

This song showcases a whole series of characters from the time of the Second Spanish Republic: the Count of Romanones (1863–1950), a Liberal Party politician and businessman; Victoria Kent (1891–1987), lawyer and politician of the Socialist Radical Republican Party; and poet, journalist, and satirical writer Luis de Tapia (1871–1937). The latter has been the author of another song with feminist content, "Soy mujer," recorded by Encarnación López, "La Argentinita," in 1935. The lyrics paint a picture, ironically and critically, of a traditional Spanish woman who is a reader of Romantic authors and unhappy yet satisfied with continuing to be a woman "as God intended":

> I am the model woman,
> I know how to embroider and sew,
> I haven't cut my hair,
> I am still a woman.
> [Read aloud]:
> I don't like the current meager fashion,
> I am simply an old-fashioned woman.
> I'm not a hoyden, I don't have long hair,
> But I have a great head of hair.
> I don't waste on a short skirt for a dress,
> I keep the legs for my husband.
> I don't dance the swing, I don't dance the foxtrot,
> And smoking? Ugh, yuck! It makes me cough.
> I am unhappy
> But I am a woman
> But I am a woman.
> As you already know
> I am the woman of yesterday.
> I don't drive a Mercedes,
> I am still a woman.
> [Read aloud]:
> Playing tennis does not fulfill me.
> I am not Lenglen, nor do I need to be.
> Yachts and waves I do not captain,
> it is only in stores that haggle.

The ice ballet was not done for me,
I don't use skates, I don't slide anymore.
In the automotive
I do not play the role of chauffeur.
I am unhappy,
But I am a woman, But I am a woman.
I go on being a strange character
in matters of love,
I do not commit to a boyfriend,
I remain a woman.
In matters of love, my body does not wait
for some spiv to annoy me.
I like compliments, but I never want
some vulgar nobody to degrade me.
I am excited by love letters
bashful and written on pink paper.
And Bécquer, Espronceda, Larra, and Campoamor
are my authors of amorous phrases.
I love the foul
fights of yesterday
I am unhappy,
But I am a woman,
But I am a woman.[67]

As we can see in both "La diputada" and "Soy mujer" and beyond the content of the lyrics, this type of song always included a moment or recitation in which the singer performed a fragment of text as an actress, but within the structure of the same song. The act of combining moments of music, fragments of monologues, and choreography in the same show, therefore, not only produces the hybridization and hodgepodge of artistic genres, but also "attacks" each of the artistic cells of the show, making them internally hybrid.

"Soy mujer" is not the only song with feminist content performed by La Argentinita. In 1921, the artist also sang a cuplé by Haro Teglen, "¡Venga alegría!," which tells the story of a woman ignored by her husband, or "Todo al revés," from 1922, whose lyrics say:

Continuing like this
The same as things are now

Women will suffer very soon
At the hands of men
Then we'll see
The world upside down
And roles changed
Man will be woman.
Man will be woman!

[Read aloud]: And then men will have to see—as women will, therefore, do as men do—when they ask a girl: "Where are you going, doll?" And she says: "To wait for the male dressmakers. There is a teenage blond guy with bobbed hair who has got me dazed. He has big, beautiful eyes. The other day I took him to the new cinema they've built . . . and if you saw how innocent he was. All he did was sigh and ask me for sandwiches. With that, I told him, 'Do you have a tapeworm, sweetie?' And he answered me with candor . . . : 'No, it's just that I couldn't go eat because I just finished sewing some trousers.'"

Although to some, it seems
That I am a drama queen
With femi-feminism
All of that will come to be.
The lonely chicken
Will go out with his dad,
Or with guns,
And then he will know.
And if he is married
Good boy and . . .
He will go looking at the ground,
She will go like a mastiff.
She will go like a mastiff!

[Read aloud]: And since women will do as men do, there will be scenes like this one: "Please, vamp, go away. I'm married." "With whom?" "With a gob from the municipal band." "Well, take this." "Oh, no, no, I can't accept gifts." "Take them! I'm telling you. And tomorrow I'll buy you a scarf. Come on, darling, get in the car." "Oh, go away, for God's sake." "'Get in,' I said. You've got me crazy." "I'll get in, but what will you think of me? Oh, I'm a gigolo."

Although to some, it seems
That I am a drama queen
With femi-feminism
All of that will come to be.
[Read aloud]: Oh, what a teenager I see over there. Go away, posh
  boy, or buy me a trench coat.⁶⁸

It is, perhaps, curious to see the extent to which the word *feminism* was already circulating socially with enough fluency to appear in song lyrics by well-known artists of the time. However, it is vital to remember that the origin of this word dates back to 1871, when a medical student, Ferdinand-Valérie Fanneau de la Cour, used it in his dissertation, "Du féminisme et de l'infantilisme chez les tuberculeux" (On feminism and infantilism among tuberculosis patients). In this first context of its use, the term refers to a pathology suffered by men with tuberculosis by which their bodies weaken and begin to present feminine characteristics. Months later, in 1872, Alexandre Dumas fils used the term in his pamphlet "Man-Woman," critically and contemptuously, to allude to men who supported women's movements fighting for their civil rights. It was not until 1880 that this term, used by the French suffragette Hubertine Auclert, came to positively describe women's social movements in and of themselves. In the Spanish context, the *Diccionario de la lengua española* adopted the neologism in 1914, a few years after appearing in the interviews gathered here but before moving into song lyrics of the 1920s.

Transformistas and "Gender Fluid" Artists

This love for diversity occurs not only with respect to stage styles and techniques but also in terms of "gender." It is true, however, that if we stick to the terms used in that era, we should speak instead of *sexes* rather than *genders*. Contrary to the notion of *feminism* already in place, as we have seen in common parlance since the end of the nineteenth century, the notion of gender does not appear until the 1950s. The term itself was coined in 1955, different from the idea of "grammatical gender," by controversial psychologist John Money in "Hermaphroditism, Gender, and Precocity in Hyperadrenocorticism: Psychologic Findings."⁶⁹ In his work and again in a psychomedical context,⁷⁰ the notion of gender is dissociated from that of biological sex to refer to the behaviors associated with masculine and feminine identities, in which sociocultural factors would also intervene:

> The expression gender role is used to signify all those things that a person says or does to disclose himself or herself as having the status of boy or man, girl or woman, respectively. It includes but is not restricted to sexuality in the sense of eroticism.[71]

In the flamenco world, at the same time that gender norms are manufactured and put in place, due to repetition in the bodies, certain strategies of dissidence appear. Among these, it is worth highlighting both masculine and feminine *transformismo* (cross-dressing).[72] I use the notion of cross-dressing, or drag, and not *travestismo* (transvestism), since the latter does not appear until 1910, the year in which the German doctor, sociologist, and sexologist Magnus Hirschfeld (1868–1935) coins it in his work *Die Transvestiten: Eine Untersuchung über den erotischen Verkleidungstrieb* (Transvestites: The erotic drive to cross-dress).[73] The emergence of this category, to which Hirschfeld assigns people who dress in outfits normally assigned to the opposite gender, is also linked to the psychomedical field and the notion of erotic desire. This emergence did not happen with the category of cross-dressing, used until then to designate those who dressed up, mainly in theatrical spaces, to cross-dress into another person of the opposite gender, conceiving of the process from the paradigms of imitation and artistic "alchemy," rather than from the framework of libidinal dynamics.

Following the principles of the most basic gender binary, I distinguish here two branches of transformismo: that of men who dress as women and that of women who dress as men. This second branch seems to have received a greater social and artistic acceptance, for reasons that I will try to analyze later, an argument that leads me to analyze the two branches of transformismo separately to try to understand their specificities.

Women Dressed as Men

First, we must name Trinidad Huertas, "La Cuenca" (Málaga, 1855—Havana, 1890), for her pioneering character and imprint on the flamenco world. La Cuenca debuted in the cafés cantantes of her hometown around 1877, and she achieved great success with a staged number based on bullfights, in which she embodied the role of the bullfighter. In an interview entitled "Queen of the Ring" for the American newspaper *Cleveland Plain Dealer*, given in 1888 following a tour of the United States, La Cuenca recounts:

I was born in Málaga, and at the age of five evinced a passionate fondness for all kind of sport. I would even, at that early age, imagine I was a famous matador and go through with mock encounters. My parents objected to my fondness for the sports of the arena, but they did not deny me the privilege of attending bullfights. I would clap my hands in great glee and enjoy the slaughter like an American girl would a very entertaining comedy or pantomime.[74]

Although it is not the purpose of this research to analyze the reception of La Cuenca's dances in stage contexts different from those in which the Malagueñan artist worked, I would like to offer a hint in order to understand the historical context of the United States concerning the question of cross-dressing when she took part in this interview. Starting in 1848, different states in the United States began enacting laws that prohibited dressing in clothes "of the opposite sex." This was not the case in New York City, where La Cuenca performed, but it was in a nearby city, Newark, New Jersey. As Susan Stryker underscores, this situation seems to indicate that cross-dressing was already a problematic issue in the United States at that time.[75] Despite this, Kiko Mora argues, in relation to how spectators perceived La Cuenca's cross-dressing numbers, that

> La Cuenca's number lent itself less "to the world of the post-Romantic ballet transvestite" than to the parodic forms of flamenco and bolero that the carnivalesque contaminates, that is to say, in that hybrid (and commercialized) space between flamenco and bullfights which occurs in masquerades. This environment was where Leavitt found the artist in the show *La Foire de Séville* (the Seville Fair) from the Nouveau Cirque de París. And I think the reason it was chosen was that the impresario was aware that a masquerade show would fit the sensibility of "American burlesque," which he knew very well. The new style of La Cuenca, a mixture, according to her, of "bullfighting with dance and other masculine sports," fit the bill perfectly, whether it was presented as a flamenco dance number in which footwork predominated or as a bullfighting pantomime.[76]

Indeed, La Cuenca was successful not only in America. Previously, between 1880 and 1887, she alternated between the Spanish and Parisian stages after performing for the first time in 1879 at the Hippodrome in the French capital.[77] When she returned to Paris eight years later, she did so again dressed as a matador, receiving certain criticism from the press that emphasized the fact that "she dresses, drinks, and smokes like a man."[78]

In February 1887, in the show *La Feria de Sevilla* (The Seville fair) at the Cirque Nouveau in Paris, La Cuenca danced some "sapphic" sevillanas, dressed as a matador, with the bolero dancer Carmen Dauset Moreno (1868–1910) from Almeria, dressed as a woman.[79] Notably, Carmen Dauset—better known as "Carmencita," who is also said to have danced dressed both as a man and a woman[80]—was probably the first dancer filmed in the United States. This footage is preserved in a short film from 1894, directed and produced by William Kennedy Dickson, the Scottish inventor of the motion picture camera and employee of Thomas Edison.[81] In this video, barely twenty-five seconds long, we see a smiling and flexible Carmencita tracing circles with her legs and arms (*ronds-de-jambe*) in front of the camera. In a second moment, before giving a brief bow in the guise of a greeting, the dancer performs three quebrada turns, in which she not only turns backward with her leg raised to ninety degrees but also does so by tilting her chest and head toward the ground with a twisted spine: a "serpentine dance"[82] in which it is the dancer's own body, without the help of other contraptions, that draws figure eights in the air, defying gravity and flowing through space without submitting to the frontality of the camera.

Finally, regarding the reception of these staged bullfights in the Spanish context, two facts about the nineteenth century are worth noting. First, there is the popularity of the bullfighting world, which translates into the proliferation of bullfighting-inspired dances onstage, such as "La malagueña y el torero" or "El vito," both created between the middle and late 1840s.[83] Second, we have the progressive disappearance of women from the bullfighting world. As has already been said, there is evidence of a continuous presence of female bullfighters from at least 1654, when a female bullfighter was referred to in the Council of Castile on June 25. At the end of the nineteenth century, however, bullfights featuring women started to be denigrated. A royal order by Juan de la Cierva y Peñafiel, Antonio Maura's minister of the interior, ultimately banned them on June 2, 1908. Cases like that of La Reverte, who had been branded as a *marimacho* [tomboy], became known when she revealed herself, from that moment on, as Agustín Rodríguez. Her change of sex, real or fictitious, allowed her to continue bullfighting for a while. Nevertheless, she ended up leaving bullfighting due to the pressure she received. Finally, female bullfighting became rehabilitated with the arrival of the Second Spanish

Republic in 1931, with the ban lifted in 1934 by the minister of the interior, Rafael Salazar Alonso.[84]

This series of events accounts for the social and political impact that bullfighting dances could have in each of the historical moments during which they were performed and shows to what extent they responded both to a widespread trend in bullfighting and, in specific historical periods—at least between 1908 and 1934—to a sublimation of what, outside of the theater, women were not allowed to do: bullfighting and doing it dressed as a man, as had been the custom since 1886, when Dolores Sánchez, "La Fragosa," left the short skirt with which women usually fought to the side and dressed in the male bullfighter outfit.[85]

In addition to Trinidad Huertas, we can name "La Estrella de Andalucía" (Bilbao, 1893–unknown), who, according to Ángeles Cruzado,[86] was called by the press the "queen of the zapateado," or, put another way, the queen of a men's dance. In the same way that La Cuenca uses men's clothing to transform into a bullfighter, the Basque artist does it to perform a dance typically considered to be for men:

> La Estrella de Andalucía, dressed as a man, drew all the attention, and her way of executing, above all, the classic flamenco zapateado earned her the honorable title of queen that she proudly holds and walks with through every theater. . . . And if the success obtained by this aristocrat was great in performing her number dressed as a man, now that she really appears dressed in luxurious women's costumes, the excitement is indescribable.[87]

Third, we have to name Antonia Galindo, from Málaga and known as "La Sillera," "La Bella Dora," and "Dora la Gitana." This artist is called a "transformista and variety artist" by the nineteenth-century press, considered a queen and empress of the *garrotín*, and praised for singing cuplés and performing comic monologues.

Finally, we have Salud Rodríguez, "La Hija del Ciego" (Seville, 1876–unknown), whom Fernando "el de Triana" already linked through artistic affiliation to La Cuenca, who apparently was a role model for Salud:

> Dear Salud, being a *ratilla* (little rat), as they say, became fond of male dances and was very young when she appeared at the Café de Silverio with her dandy outfit and some crazy illusions of becoming the second edition of La Cuenca. And she did it! At first she showed

a minor defect in the placement of her arms, which she herself corrected by seeing her great teacher. In the execution of her footwork, she was remarkable, displaying many details of her own creation, which were very difficult to execute.

Once she was put together, she toured all of Spain and triumphed. And when she landed in Madrid, the people of Madrid took her in, and she has never left.[88]

Apart from these four exclusively flamenco figures, we find other transformistas, like Teresita Canesa from Valencia,[89] Carmelita Ferrer,[90] Carmen Diadema,[91] and Las Argentinas (Olimpia d'Avigny from Naples and María Cores from Buenos Aires), about whom Retana states:

> The audience was tickled in viewing Olimpia, so deliciously feminine, with a spicy beauty in her thirties, dancing in extreme incrustation with María Cores, easily mistaken for a comforting young man.... Both performed with costumes acceptable for a funeral, but the choreography was made to bring the dead back to life.[92]

In every case, women dressed as men are associated, both artistically and in their personal lives, with a masculine archetype: onstage as a bullfighter, in their ability to perform dances strictly from the men's repertoire, or as a guitar player; in daily life with actions considered inappropriate for their gender, like smoking, loving men's sports, as was the case with La Cuenca, or the fact of being a single mother and driving her own car, as was the case with Dora.[93]

Female Drag in Zarzuela

Also during the nineteenth and beginning of the twentieth centuries, in the neighboring world of zarzuela, Ramón Regidor Arribas classifies a group of works in which characters of women dressed as men appear: Serafín (*El grumete*, in 1853 by composer Antonio García Gutiérrez), el Vizconde de Vivar (*El vizconde*, in 1855 by composer Francisco Asenjo Barbieri), Federico (*El sargento Federico*, in 1855 by composer Luis de Olona), Colás (*El monaguillo*, in 1891 by composer Miguel Marqués), el Rey (*El rey que rabió*, in 1891 by composer Ruperto Chapí), Roberto (*La tempestad*, in 1882 also by Ruperto Chapí), Darnley (*Mujer y reina*, in 1874 by dramaturg Mariano Pina Domínguez), Gaspar (*El tambor de granade-*

ros, in 1894 by Ruperto Chapí), Carlos (*La viejecita*, in 1897 by composer Manuel Fernández Caballero), Fernando (*El reloj de Lucerna*, in 1884 by dramaturg Marcos Zapata Mañas), Gabrié (*La tempranica*, in 1900 by composer Gerónimo Giménez), el Trompeta (*El gorro frigio*, in 1888 by composer Manuel Nieto), el Vendedor de Pájaros (*Las musas latinas*, in 1914 by composer Manuel Penella), el Pajarero (*La reina mora*, in 1903 by composer José Serrano), Benamor (*Benamor*, in 1923 by composer Pablo Luna), Abel (*La taberna del puerto*, in 1936 by composer Pablo Sorozábal), and Monacillo (*Peñamariana*, in 1944 by composer Guridi). Added to this list is what Regidor Arribas calls "travestismo de ida y vuelta" [round-trip cross-dressing], a phenomenon in which women who play, usually young, female characters dress as women.[94]

Men Dressed as Women

The chronology of men dressed as women is different. According to Juan Carlos Usó, this phenomenon, linked to variety shows imported from Italy and France in which men imitated famous female singers, was practically nonexistent until 1894, when Leopoldo Frégoli, who continued performing in Spain until 1922, came to our country.[95] Frégoli was succeeded by Robert Bertin from France, who debuted at the Teatro de la Zarzuela in 1906, imitating stars of the time, such as Yvette, Guilbert, Consuelo Tamayo, "la Tortajada," Bella Otero, Paulette Darty, Polaire, and Cléo de Mérode. The first Spanish transformista was Ernesto Foliers, who debuted in 1908 and will, in turn, be imitated by other cross-dressers, like Rafael de Arcos, Actis Eliu, Bella Dora, Cav. Pellerano, Luis Esteso y Graells, and others. Besides Foliers, we must highlight Edmont de Bries (Cartagena, 1897–unknown), who achieved enormous success by imitating, among others, the character of the Gitana. In an interview given to the *Cine mundial* magazine that appeared on January 1, 1925, the journalist José Abuerne asked De Bries what his favorite character was, and the Carthaginian replied:

> The Gitano. I feel it to my core. I am possessed by a Gitana woman and I believe I capture her onstage as if I had been a woman, born in the Triana neighborhood and educated among the most famous flamenco artists. But understand this. Elegance, that is, the malleable dignity of my interpretations, flees like the devil from bad taste.[96]

Beyond the theatrical sphere and variety shows, we find an early case of male drag in the flamenco world on October 16, 1886, in a description of a café cantante in the newspaper *El derecho*.[97] In it, we learn of the "prostitution of good habits" and the presence of bearded men dressed as women.[98] Nearly fifty years later, we find a second example, that of a character whom we do not exactly know if he was a *transformista* or an artist who had a fluid gender expression. In his 1935 text, Fernando "el de Triana" speaks about José León, "La Escribana," of whom he confirms that, aside from singing very well in alegrías, he was an artist known for his sense of humor onstage:

> In the artistic *cuadro* [flamenco troupe] that performed in the famous Café del Burrero (subsidiary), next to the Triana Bridge, there were two artists who, although they looked like a man and a woman, called themselves *comadre* [bosom friend].
> One was the extraordinary and very amusing bailaora Concha la Carbonera, and the other woman or the other man, or whatever [they were] (although, I think the only resemblance of a man was the clothing), [José León] was known as La Escribana. . . .
> This couple of comadres, as they publicly called each other, thought about nothing but jokes and having fun as much as possible, cracking themselves up over anything that is an abomination to nature. . . .
> Later, a great troupe dressed as bandits came together, with the same artists from the flamenco cuadro, including standouts like La Serrana, Fernanda Antúnez, her sister Juana, La Carbonera, maestro Pérez, and La Escribana. . . .
> The stage was so large that on more than one occasion, little calves from local livestock were brought to fight, forming a rival cuadro with the same artists. After the fight, the two bosom friends started the amusing dialogue: "How are you so afraid, comadre?" said La Carbonera. "Me, afraid? That's you. You don't even earn enough for soap." "You're so dull! You could see that the bull was going to eat me and you didn't even use a cape to shoo him away!" "That's it: if I used the cape on the bull and the bull put his horns in me, were you going to take him out? No kidding! No way with how afraid you are, which shows on the tips of the few hairs you have left." "What I know is that I'm not feeling well after all the scares from the goddamn bullfighting. I wish I could be like you, taking

everything as a joke, laughing at everything, and not being afraid of anything."[99]

This hybridity of gender is also reflected in the film *La bandera*, by Julien Duvivier (1935), in which the French filmmaker shows us a scene in La Criolla, a café-cabaret in Barcelona whose audience is full of men dressed as flamenco women.[100] In the center of the space, a bailaora covered only in a tasseled thong executes a dance with a transparent veil accompanied by guitar music. The ambiance of this scene seems taken from the novel *La femme et le pantin* (*Woman and Puppet*), written in 1898 by Pierre Louÿs, and about which Duvivier will make his film version in 1959. However, it coincides perfectly with an extended narrative published by José María Aguirre in *Mundo gráfico* on November 29, 1933, in which he describes the environment of La Criolla and which I reproduce here almost in its entirety:

"La Criolla," the Most Typical "Cabaret" in the Chinese Quarter

At dawn, the atmosphere of La Criolla—the most typical cabaret in Barcelona's Chinese Quarter—is loaded with disturbing and bewildering influences. The seven deadly sins, and even more whose existence escaped the anticipation of the sacred lawmakers, have an accomplished settlement in the enclosure. They gasp, like famished canines, for alcohol, lust, and crime. With the conjuring of the equivocal promise of the Celestinesque appearance of cover for nocturnal beings, they come, trembling with unhealthy curiosity, having to play the role of victims in that temple of all vices. Gentle businessmen, passing through Barcelona; foreign tourists, among them some lady touched by perverted curiosity, the heroine of a novel by Hoyos y Vinent, wears the valuable jewel that will later be the object of a sensational robbery: some honest bureaucrat who has decided to break the monotony of the bureaucratic red tape. From time to time, groups of blond, tall, and well-built sailors burst in, amid laughter and almost inarticulate shouts, wearing uniforms on which the emblem of the British army now stands out, silhouetted by the swastika of present-day Germany. The blue innocence of their eyes is not enough to cloud their desires and wine.

And scattered around the room in an apparent disorder that is nothing more than a studied formation in which each one occupies his position. Peripatetics, pickpockets, gunmen, subjects of ambiguous backgrounds and undefinable ages. All living beings constitute the natural fauna of the establishment.

Whoever Owns the "Music Hall," "Flor de Otoño," Dances[101]

In a private room, the cabaret owner enjoys himself in the company of various clients within his close circle. A former pickpocket and the perfect connoisseur of Barcelona's delinquent ways, the owner of La Criolla likes to select his friendships among the sharpest characters in the Chinese Quarter. A comrade—a veteran Catalonian journalist—leads us to the chamber. Introductions, greetings, and then, the explosion produced by the uncorking of a bottle of champagne marks the resumption of the orgy that our entrance had to interrupt. A portable gramophone threshes out the enervating notes of a Moorish dance, and a boy, almost a teenager, begins to dance in the center of the room.

Flor de Otoño—the owner of La Criolla tells me—is one of those who gives the police the most work.

Gun Law and Sexual Inversion. "La Asturiana," "Trotski," Luz, and Sarah

Flor de Otoño continues his dance between effeminate contortions. Behind his plucked brows, facial makeup, and heart-shaped lips, this thirty-two-year-old metamorphoses to the extreme where the ambiguous subject appears precisely half of that. While the rest of the audience drinks and cheers on the dancer, my buddy told me all there is to know about Flor de Otoño. He is a very dangerous individual, a regular participant in the extremist ways and gunmen. He actively contributed to introducing anarchist propaganda in Atarazanas and participated in the movement started in those barracks in 1932, from where, as will be remembered, weapons and ammunition disappeared.

"The one with the glasses," my friend keeps telling me, "is Trotski, also a gunman, a member of the Sindicato Libre [Free Trade Union]." He was sentenced as a coconspirator in the assault on the Sarriá train. His appearance as a seminarian does not impede him from being the lover of the woman who sits next to him, Luz, who is said to be involved in espionage related to the Balearic Islands.

The Emergence and Diversions of Gender 43

The music has ended, and Flor de Otoño, on the floor, remains for a moment in a genuflecting attitude with the air of an oriental bayadere. While contemplating him there, I evoke the asexual figures of the adolescent Moorish boys who typically perform in the small cafés of Tangier and Tetouan. After, another individual, dressed in women's clothing, which complements well his equally effeminate gestures, sings a cuplé with Andalusian motifs in a high-pitched voice. It is La Asturiana, a well-known impressionist of the stars and celebrated in the music halls of the Chinese Quarter.

Sarah, a Hebrew girl with bulging lips, jet-black eyes, and iodized skin, sniffs cocaine without moving one of her arms from the neck of the owner of La Criolla, her lover.

In Full Bacchanal. "They Have Stolen a Wallet"

The wine, music, and toxins are rousing the attendees. Dancing is becoming widespread. Luz and Sarah, totally embedded in the respective chests of Trotski and the owner of La Criolla, shake in lubricious contortions. As there are no more women among the revelers, homosexual couples form, grotesquely moving their bodies to the rhythm of the dance. Suddenly, the room door opens, and a huge black man urgently calls the establishment's owner.

"Come quickly, boss."

Everyone is suspended for a moment, but they react quickly and begin to flee hastily. Loud voices resound in the main room of the music hall, terrible interjections. My friend says, "There's a ruckus. It is best that we leave." And holding me by one arm, he leads me out to the street. Already there, a police officer, known by the Barcelona journalist who has been my guide in my journey through the next suburb about to disappear, learns that a foreigner's wallet full of bills has been stolen. "Who was it?" I ask, full of curiosity. "I don't know," the agent replies. "Anyone! Here everyone is 'on the job.'" Any other would have been silent, but the foreigner began to yell loudly and utter threats, and it wouldn't have ended well if we weren't here.

And so it is, reader, Barcelona's Chinese Quarter. The crossroads of vice, hotbed of crimes, whose inhabitants will have to seek, if they manage to escape the action of the police, a new area for their punishable activity, by effect of the Ley de Vagos [y Maleantes, Law of Vagrants and Thugs].[102]

Explanatory Theory on the Unequal Social Acceptance between Male and Female Drag

Multiple theories explain the different acceptance of male and female drag. First, it is worth noting the eroticization of the female body dressed in pants, thanks to which the legs and hips become more visible. This effect used to produce, as Retana noted, great excitement among the heterosexual male audience, even though female transformistas also received negative criticism, such as the following that appeared as a result of a performance by Dora la Gitana in Cáceres in 1909:

> Between the nudes and mimicry that scandalize so . . . and the beautiful Dora's suit, when she shone . . . her silhouettes with the high-waisted suit, I suppose that the most modest person will prefer the nudity of now to the prurient movements of Dora in a well-fitted men's suit of very fine fabric.[103]

Second, it would be important to indicate to what extent, and given the historical invisibility of lesbianism, female drag has not been linked to "abnormal" sexuality. This was the case with male transformistas, who became suspected of homosexuality almost immediately.

The Decline of the Café Cantante and the Birth of Flamenco Opera

The decline of the cafés cantantes can be explained, in part, as a consequence of the birth of what the multifaceted Álvaro Retana calls the "frivolous genre" and the success of "modern"—non-Spanish—music that arrives in Spain, according to the author, in 1910 with the opening of the Trianon Palace in Madrid. These new music styles will see their greatest development after the First World War (1914–1918) since the neutrality of Spain in the conflict led to the arrival of a good number of foreign artists, especially from France. This new type of "foreign" show began to experience its own decline after 1926, partly because of the aging of a first generation of artists who could not find successors and partly, according to Retana, because of the "dictatorship of the Charleston," which comes into fashion in Spain via Josephine Baker.[104] These shows took place in spaces such as the Salón de Actualidades (4 Calle Alcalá), the Japonés (16 Calle Alcalá), the Bleue and the Rouge (near the Iglesia de las Calatravas), the Romea (on Calle Carretas), the Paris Salon (Calle Montera),[105] the Paris Théâtre (Calle Cedaceros), the Ideal Rosales (24 Calle Pintor Rosales), or La Parisiana (Avenida Reyes Católicos). According to the historian Servando Rocha, La Parisiana, opened in 1907 and owned by the Sociedad Franco-Española de Grandes Hoteles y Viajes en España y Portugal, was an early instance of attractions with bars and restaurants that offered jazz concerts, cuplé singers, and vedettes.[106] Destroyed during the Spanish Civil War due to its proximity to the Moncloa front, it presented variety shows in which transformistas and other flamenco artists shared the bill, as evidenced by an advertisement that appeared in the newspaper *El imparcial* on July 4, 1911:

> PARISIANA: Tomorrow, Wednesday, this aristocratic theater will celebrate the opening function of the season. The notable Borrull sisters, the eminent guitarist Adela Cubas, the genteel cuplé singer Silvia Silvanys, the famous "impersonator of the stars" Foliers, the beautiful comedic soprano Carlota Paisano, the great dancer La Argentinita, and the famous and first soprano Julita Mesa will take part. The extraordinarily applauded Gitano cuadro, a great success of Príncipe Alfonso, will also be onstage. "Mirando a la Alhambra." A sensational program of new films from the production company Pathé Frères will complete the lineup.[107]

Aside from a new type of dance and music, a new type of drug is also offered in these spaces, in addition to alcohol. According to the research conducted by the historian Juan Carlos Usó, the consumption of euphoric drugs such as cocaine—outside of a therapeutic framework—appeared in Spain during the First World War. Mainly in large cities such as Madrid, Barcelona, and San Sebastián, this shift occurred in places like the American bar Maxim's in Madrid during a moment when cafés cantantes were starting to decline:

> The moment was a great boom for French prostitutes [*cocottes*] who came to Spain during the war. Here, they did well. They were much finer and more worldly than the Spaniards and much less beastly. Cocaine was brought to Spain by the French, and they used it to get good clients intoxicated. The Spanish ones were so dumb that they started taking cocaine themselves, which was stupid and ruined their business.[108]

In addition to the rivalry among the spaces in which "modern music" is performed, a flamenco successor emerges from the cafés cantante: the *ópera flamenca* [flamenco opera]. This type of show, created by the producer Vedrines in 1924, allows flamenco to develop within larger spaces (primarily theaters and bullrings) where shows are produced that blend the lighter styles of flamenco singing—such as the fandango—with other forms of Spanish popular song. This format is extremely successful among the national audience, despite the complaints of great connoisseurs of cante jondo, who denounce "the dictatorship of the fandango and the fandanguillo" and take refuge in singing and playing music, especially after the Civil War in 1939, in the sizable restaurants of *ventas* [inns near urban entry points] and *colmaos* [urban taverns] set up beside highways on the outskirts of large cities.[109] As noted by the historian Escribano, public establishments had to close by midnight after the war. Los Gabrieles and Villarrosa, which were staples of Madrid's nightlife in the 1910s and 1920s, respectively, become mere meeting points where subsequent flamenco parties emerge and take place "that began timidly and ended with the size and flavor that their environment required, at the inns on France's and Barcelona's highways—shortly before reaching San Fernando de Henares—or in Dehesa de la Villa Park or Ciudad Lineal, to name a couple of the best-known spots on Madrid's periphery."[110]

The limited access to these spaces outside the city walls and the exclusion of the most serious, solemn, or somber songs—such as the soleá or the *seguiriya*—in flamenco opera shows will later become dialectical motors of the History of flamenco, which will end by abandoning said model to try to reengage a flamenco judged less "commercial" and more "pure." In this way, a new stage, known as "neoclassicism" or *neojondismo*, opened between 1950 and 1980, marked by events such as the publication of the *Antología del cante flamenco* in 1954 by Hispavox; the release of the book *Flamencología* in 1955 by Anselmo González Climent; the creation of the Concurso Nacional de Arte Flamenco de Córdoba in 1956 and the Cátedra de Flamencología y de Jerez de la Frontera in 1958; and, finally, the publication in1963 of the book *Mundo y formas del cante flamenco* by singer Antonio Mairena and Ricardo Molina, a work in which the authors reinforce the already existing hierarchy, modeled after the body-soul dualism, between dance and music. Within this hierarchy, singing is considered spiritually and artistically superior to dance, which as a bodily practice makes it immediately inferior. There is also a connection between singing and the world of men, which implies a reinforcement of a form of gender distribution that further contributes to the feminization of dance.[111] Despite all of this, the neojondismo movement defends the need to create its own exclusive space for flamenco in which it can develop independently without mixing with other styles, a fact that, at least theoretically, assists in the creation of the tablaos.

The Creation of the Tablao and the Invention of Traditional Flamenco Dancing (1954)

A State-Sponsored and Nationalist Use of Flamenco

Despite the details mentioned earlier, the influence of neojondismo on the creation of tablaos in the 1950s seems uncertain. Another version of history reveals that the birth of this type of space was less related to an aesthetic need of the flamenco community than to a commercial and economic perspective. The Ministry of Information and Tourism, which was created in 1951 and brought together the areas of communication and entertainment (the press, cinema, theater, and radio),[112] along with the Madrid hotel magnate Alfonso Camorra and his family, in effect conceived of "the basic lines by which a flamenco tablao should be channeled: tourists and personalities, singing, dancing, guitar, grub, and shots. The Ministry offered financing for the tablaos to promote exquisite local products to their foreign clientele."[113]

In the 1950s, what became known as the *segundo franquismo* [second Francoism] was inaugurated in Spain, characterized by the abandonment of economic autarky after 1951 and even more so after the rise to power of a government of technocrats from the Opus Dei in 1957. Until that moment, Spain had run the risk of bankruptcy due to enormous inflation, the depletion of foreign currencies—which made it difficult to pay for imports of important resources like oil—and an intense economic recession. In 1959, with the Economic Stabilization Plan the balance of payments stabilized, and the government promoted a progressive economic liberalization, both internally and externally.

Within this framework, tourism emerged as one of the key elements that enabled the "Spanish economic miracle," which statistics can verify, demonstrating an increase from six million tourists in 1960 to thirty-four million in 1973.[114] Among the different activities offered to international tourists, flamenco became a *must*. After the opening in 1954 of Zambra, the first tablao in Madrid, this type of venue, focused on foreign clients, multiplied. After the opening of Zambra (closed in January 1975), the following locales opened in Madrid: El Corral de la Morería in 1956 (which still exists) and El Duende, run by Pastora Imperio and her son-in-law, "Gitanillo de Triana," in 1958; Torres Bermejas (which still exists) and Las Cuevas de Nemesio in 1960; Las Brujas (closed in 1982) and Arco de Cuchilleros (currently called La Taberna de Mr. Pinkleton) in 1961; Los Canasteros in 1963, run by Manolo Caracol (closed in 1972); Las Cuevas de Nerja and Villarrosa (which still exists) in 1964; and finally, Café de Chinitas (which still exists) in 1969. During the 1970s, El Corral de la Pacheca opened in 1971 and Los Cabales in 1972.[115]

However, the tablaos are only some of the artistic spaces that are part of the strategy developed by the regime to attract foreign tourists and obtain a certain external legitimacy. In the field of arts and culture and especially during the period in which Professor Joaquín Ruiz Giménez was minister of education (1951–1956), as dance historian Ana Elvira Esteban notes, a whole series of events are organized, such as the Primera Bienal Hispanoamericana de Arte in Madrid (1951); the Festival Internacional de Santander, the Primer Festival de Músicas y Danzas Españolas de Granada, the Semana Mundial de la Publicidad, and the Thirty-Fifth Congreso Eucarístico Internacional en Barcelona (1952); the Semana Internacional del Cine de San Sebastián and the Primer Congreso de Arte Abstracto de Santander (1953); and the Festival de Teatro Clásico de Mérida (1954).[116]

In dance, between 1960 and 1969, the Festivales de España were set up, in which flamenco dance does not appear as an independent genre but as part of mixed programs of "Spanish ballets," such as Luisillo y su Teatro de Danza Española, Ballet Español de Antonio, Ballet Español de Alberto Portillo, Ballet Español de Pilar López, Ballet Español de María Rosa, Lucero Tena, Ballet Gitano de Luisa Ortega y Arturo Pavón, Ballet Español de Rafael de Córdova, Antonio Gades y Su Espectáculo de Arte Español, Susan y José, Baile Español Ronda de España, Antoñita Moreno, La Singla y Su Conjunto Español, and Mariemma Ballet de España.[117]

To analyze just one example of this type of dance troupe, in the case of Mariemma Ballet de España, which performed at Festivales de España every year between 1962 and 1969, we see that all the shows begin with the piece "Aragón" and end with the "Zapateado" by Sarasate.[118] Flamenco mixes with other dances and musical styles between these two bookending dances. Here is the program for one of Mariemma's shows from 1962:

"Aragón" (popular)
"Chiclana y Huelva": *tarantas*, alegrías, *farruca*, soleares, *cantiñas*
"Clásico y gitano" (M. Ravel / Mariemma)
"Danzas fantásticas" (J. Turina / Mariemma): "Exaltación," "Sueño," "Orgía"
"Danzas folklóricas": from the countryside, *sardana*, *valenciana*, Navarran *jota*, *verdiales*
El amor brujo (M. Falla / Mariemma)
Fandango-flamencos de Santa María: Flamenco variations, zapateado, *seguirillas*, boleros, and *corraleras*
Homenaje a Lope de Vega: *zarabanda, villano, marizápalos, canaria*
Paso clásico español. Bailes de escuela bolera (choreographic arrangements by Mariemma): panaderos, "La Maja y el Torero," malagueña, bolero
"Polo Gitano" (T. Bretón / Mariemma)
"Zapateado" (P. Sarasate)[119]

We see that flamenco appears in this program at two different moments: at the beginning, after the Aragonese jota, and in the middle, perhaps after an intermission. What is interesting is not so much the number of flamenco dances within the entire program—which is relatively balanced among the regional dances, Bolero School dances,[120] and the choreographies from classical Spanish or *danza estilizada* (a stylized mixture of flamenco, bolero, and regional dances)—as the discursive thread that unifies them: the idea of a people, the Spanish, who dance in a different way depending on the region they belong to but who constitute an indivisible unit, which does not fail to remind us of the idea of Spain as a *unidad de destino en lo universal* [unity of destiny in all things universal][121] promoted during the Franco regime and an aspect of Falangist idiosyncrasy.[122] To what extent is it possible to assert that these Spanish ballets translated onstage an aesthetic thought of Falangist origin? What idea of Spain does Spanish dance reveal? Is it trivial in our country to link together dances from different places, considered mere "regions," under the common denominator of Spanishness? And finally, is it possible to continue dancing Spanish dances without referring to this idea of Spain, or is it necessary—and perhaps urgent—to deconstruct this discourse about Spanishness? Where and how should this task begin? From the body and movement? From the structure of the spectacle and its dramaturgy? From the discourse and the depoliticization or the repoliticization of aesthetic categories?

The *Cuadro* and *Acts* in the Tablao

The structure of Spanish ballet shows differed significantly from that of the tablaos, in which flamenco was, in most cases, the only musical and choreographic style presented. This aspect also differentiated it from the cafés cantantes, in which, as we have seen, the flamenco repertoire was combined with other musical and choreographic styles. This "jondo exclusivity" of the tablao is produced, in part, thanks to the fact that, in the 1950s, the repertoire of danceable flamenco songs had expanded greatly compared to those performed at the end of the nineteenth century and beginning of the twentieth. Around 1905, Faíco (1850–1938), in collaboration with the guitarist Ramón Montoya (1880–1949), created the choreography for the farruca and, a little later, for the garrotín; Encarnación López, "La Argentinita" (1895–1945), staged her *caña* choreography with guitarist Manolo de Huelva for a short film recorded in 1935;[123] in 1941, Carmen Amaya (1918–1963) authored the first choreography of the *taranto*, with disputed authorship against Rosario (1918–2000), the artistic partner of Antonio Ruiz Soler; in 1942, Vicente Escudero (1888–1980) created the first seguiriya choreography;[124] and in 1952, Antonio Ruiz Soler (1921–1996) created the *martinete* dance for the Edgar Neville film *Duende y misterio del flamenco*.[125]

The show was divided into two parts: the *cuadro* and the *acts*.

> When the cuadro finishes, many of the tourists leave, thinking that the show is over or feeling that they have had all of the noise that they can stand for one night. If one has been sitting in a far corner, this is the time to move up closer to see the real show about to begin. In some clubs the attractions consist of the guitarists from the cuadro plus a new singer and dancer(s), but in the other clubs there will be a number of well-known performers and recording artists. Part of the fun is not knowing what or who to expect.[126]

As this text from 1977 shows us, and not unrelated to the differentiation of male and female roles, the tablao shows take place in two parts that not only constitute two acts of the same program but imply two artistic and economic levels along with two different types of audiences. The first part of the show, the *cuadro*, consisted of a suite of flamenco dances and songs, usually light or festive—such as the fandango and rumba—performed by a group of dancers and two or three musicians. This first part had a fundamentally touristy objective, an *amateur* audience for whom the flamenco show was part of a set of activities in Madrid. Meanwhile, the second part, in which the most renowned solo dancers and singers appeared, was directed toward the aficionados, that is, to the great flamenco connoisseurs.

This type of programming, which generally speaking offers a first show for *amateur* spectators and a second, more professional one for knowledgeable audiences, also establishes two economic regimes that exacerbate the wage gap between men and women that had existed in the flamenco world since its commercialization in the cafés cantantes in the mid-nineteenth century. A good example of this is one provided by Juan Rondón Rodríguez in his biography of the singer Rafael Pareja de Triana,[127] in which he gives some figures recalling that the salary difference between men and women was not only due to the allocation of stage roles but also because many of the singers were also owners of the cafés cantantes where the shows took place. The author tells us about the salaries [in pesetas / in USD for 2021] of the singers Don Antonio Chacón (30 pesetas / $145), Juan Breva (around 25 pesetas / $121), and Rafael Pareja (18 pesetas / $87), as well as the guitarist Maestro Pérez (17 pesetas / $82). He also compares them with those of the famous dancer Juana, "La Macarrona," who earned between ten and twelve pesetas ($48–$58).[128]

Returning to flamenco in the era of the tablaos, Eduardo Murillo Saborido estimates Rosa Durán's salary at the tablao Zambra in 1955 at eighty-two pesetas a day ($35).[129] In his article "Los jornaleros del flamenco" (Flamenco's day laborers), Antonio Burgos compares the situation of a young, beautiful, and unknown dancer who works between eleven at night and three in the morning, and whose salary is eight hundred pesetas ($100), with that of Merche Esmeralda, a renowned dancer of the time, whose daily shift was shorter (she had to only dance two numbers) and earned four thousand pesetas ($496).[130] Paco Sevilla, referencing the salaries of tablao dancers, gives a figure that used to oscillate between seven and twenty dollars for a four-hour workday.[131] These figures could explain the so-called feminization of work in the cuadro: given the low wages, the work of the cuadro could not constitute primary economic activity; the man, as "head of the family," had to work in other areas.[132]

Paco Sevilla also asserts that low wages result in not only the feminization of work but also a tendency toward amateurism since students who accept precarious economic conditions as a necessary step to begin their artistic careers often occupy jobs within the tablao.

Erotic Judgment and Artistic Judgment

A central element of the analysis carried out up to this point is the question of the spectator's gaze on dancing bodies. We can read how some of these eyes landed on the dancing bodies through the newspaper texts they produced, which, given the nature of their writings, could hardly fall into the category of "dance criticism":

> There are two dancers in the tablao, five women, and two guitarists. Like everywhere else, they have red or white plastic flowers in their hair, long earrings of something more than a half moon, curls and ringlets in their hair for those who do not leave it loose.[133]

As if it were a (pictorial) painting, the perception of the bailaora in the cuadro is *pliable*, with her body being perceived first as a living image constructed by clothing, accessories, hairstyle, and makeup. Additionally, Paco Sevilla attests to the existence of different roles or characters by the different bailaoras within the cuadro:

> The house cuadro begins its show between eleven and half-past eleven at night. This group typically has eight girls, one of whom will specialize in rumba dancing (lots of rumba but little dancing), another who will mostly sing, one or two Gitanas who may not dance but add a bit of color, and perhaps an older lady who controls everything and specializes in clapping. There will also be two or three guitarists, two singers, and maybe a dancer.[134]

The reason for the gender division between man-music and woman-dance would seem to reflect a conception of the woman's body as a sensual object offered to the gaze of the heterosexual male spectator, which would imply, as Cruces Roldán maintains, a hypercorporeality of women or an overexposure of their bodies by way of the dance.[135] This hypercorporeality of women leads to a conception of the aesthetic experience as an experience of pleasure and a confusion between aesthetic pleasure and erotic pleasure. In the case of dance, the body turns out to be a central element given its exposure to the gaze of the spectator, which complicates the dissociation between the aesthetic pleasure aroused by what the body *does* (as an artistic act) and an erotic pleasure aroused by the vision of what the body *is*.

Analyzing the newspaper texts, we see that the critics have no problem going back and forth between aesthetic judgment and erotic judgment. However, what they emphasize at first is indeed the physical beauty of the bailaora, only to later move on to speaking about her artistic quality as a performer.[136] Regarding men, however, the writers bracket the physical aspect of their bodies, blocking the possibility of an erotic judgment. As we will see later, following the parameters of the heterosexual male gaze, men do not appear to have bodies, even when they use them to dance.

> When we arrive, "La Muñeca" is dancing, a resolute woman who dances exhaustingly. . . . "La Muñeca" is not without suffering, that specific way of launching into flamenco. Indeed, she has the face of a doll, but a somewhat tragic and old doll at that.[137]
>
> Today we will talk about Las Brujas. There gathers the most beautiful group of women who have ever been seen together in the same "tablao." There we have the sculpture that is Encarnita Peña, referred to jokingly as "La Contrahecha," who, with Encarnita Llácer, another national monument, forms the two pillars of beauty wherever you are, being the most robust beauties and at the same time good dancers, who would make Ingres dream, even that delicate flower with a fine stem that is Mary España, one of the liveliest promises of the moment who fills the stage with grace. I do not remember all the names of this ever-so-perfect group, each in her own way, with her own beat and expertise. And then, apart from the "solos" of those already mentioned, the pure and classical dance of Matilde España, with her calm dancing, without a trace of acrobatics, that is reminiscent of a bailaora of the old temperament and essence of the *escuela sevillana* [Sevillian style of dance]. Another of the prominent figures is Tere Lorca, this beautiful dancer, all fire, all mischief, and an unusual beauty. And finally, Tatiana, an "out of the ordinary" woman, whose dance unsettles the viewer as he indulges in the passion with which Tatiana dances—the harmony of her waving body, the play of her arms like the jets of a fountain, the expression in her eyes, and the phenomenal temptation of her

mouth. Tatiana is a monument to which we must pay homage; she is a force of personality who goes beyond choreographies and training.[138]

Curiously, Francisco Diéguez, owner of Las Brujas, admits in his "biographical" book about the creation of this venue that Neville's pornification of bailaoras "had a great influence on the future of the business."[139] Neville continues:

> María Vargas has a calm and dark beauty, and she sings admirably, very Gitano, without forcing herself. Diego Pantoja and Dolores, "La Pescailla," are two very fine dancers. As if that were not enough, Caracol situates them between many beautiful girls and a super beauty called Carmen Montiel, who is not related to Caracol or me, unfortunately, but who is a pageant girl and, as the Gitanos say, enough to make you drool.[140]

Other sources, such as the work of Francisco Diéguez on the tablao Las Brujas, confirm that most tablao owners favored hiring bailaoras at a low artistic level who were very beautiful, which was already an existing practice at the time of the cafés cantantes, as we have previously seen.[141] Thus, the musicologist Eduardo Murillo Saborido, in an interview with "La Uchi," a bailaora in the 1960s and 1970s at Las Cuevas de Nemesio, Las Brujas, Torres Bermejas, Cuevas de Nerja, Corral de la Morería, and El Duende, states:

> I started in the tablao Las Cuevas de Nemesio. My friends and I would go to the owners and ask if they needed someone. They took me on right away. Even if you danced badly, if you were young and cute, they would hire you right away. I was just another bailaora, very ordinary. But you know, when there is a beautiful woman in a tablao . . .[142]

As a counterpoint to Edgar Neville's male point of view, which we have been analyzing here, I would like to pause at an article from the *ABC* newspaper on October 1, 1972, where we find a description of the bailaoras from the tablao Los Cabales, directed by a dancer of Mexican origin, Luisillo (1928–2007), written by journalist Pilar Trenas on the very night of the space's opening:

Three female dancers, three guitarists, two bailaores, and two singers appear. Paquita is the first to dance. She has class and elegance. The extraordinary movement of her hands dominates her dance. She is followed by Mary Luz, who sings and dances with ease and grace. Luisillo, standing in the front row, watches them. He accompanies them with clapping and head movements; he is very close to launching and dancing with them on this opening night. Rocío, all soul and thunder, with her flurry of ruffles, swept the tables near the stage.... Then it was the men's turn. They laid bare the maestro's teachings.

The journalist does not talk about the beauty of the bailaoras or the men but, subtly differently, describes the talents of both—all of them always dancing under the watchful eye of the "patriarch" Luisillo. She describes the talent of the women as related to the personality traits that color their gestures (class, elegance, poise, grace, soul, majesty), while the men come onstage to demonstrate "the value of the maestro's teachings," that is, a certain mastery in movement, a technique acquired through learning. When the women dance, what they do is reveal their most intimate being, while what men do is demonstrate their abilities.

The Paradoxes of the "Feminization" of Dance in the Tablaos

Regarding the presence of men as the minority onstage, bailaora Ana María, whose testimony Pulpón collected, states:

> Men had it and have it less complicated than women. It has always been less. Well, now they are, now things are very difficult, but the number of men has always been fewer than women. And then I have seen crises in general, like I have seen fat people dancing.... That's to say, it has always been much easier. Women have always been more of a showcase than men because, of course, whether you like it or not, there were ten female and two male dancers in a cuadro. The rest were guitarists and singers. And in comparison, there was much more competition among women than men. That was always more demand for men. Always. Because they were scarce.[143]

Given the difference in supply and demand for male dancers, they are better paid. It is the comparative advantage of what we could call, complementing the notion of "hypercorporeality" of women proposed by Cruces Roldán, the "hypocorporeality" of men. This hypocorporeality could be considered a bracketing, in the guise of phenomenological epoché, of the male body and would be one of the original causes of the distribution of roles between men-music and women-dance. It is much easier for men to occupy the role of musicians since their bodies are not the immediate object of the gaze, although, let us not forget, other men are watching them.

In the case of singers, the body *is there*, but it can be considered a mere support for the voice, and the aesthetic judgment will be cast on this immaterial element without having to pay attention to the flesh. The voice and sung text *occult* the singer's body, covered with enough veils (melodic, rhythmic, textual) so that the question of its eroticization can appear. In the case of guitarists, we find ourselves in the same situation, with an additional intermediary between the body and the spectator's gaze. Behind the materiality of the guitar, the body hides and protects itself from a gaze that, looking at it, as philosopher René Descartes asserts, *touches it from a distance*.[144] If that were the case, if we could consider the gaze a form of teletouch (*teletacto*), what areas of the dancer's body do we touch when we are looking at it, and in what way do we touch them? Scratching, rubbing, pressing, pounding, squeezing, smoothing, scraping, scrubbing, caressing, feeling, kneading, massaging, embracing, crushing, hitting, pinching, biting, sucking, wetting, holding, releasing, licking, masturbating, smelling, savoring, avoiding, kissing, cradling, swinging, carrying, weighing ... ?[145]

In her article "Dancing as a Man: An Orthopedics of the National Body," Victoria Mateos traces the genealogy of this hypocorporeity—which she does not name as such—from a certain number of primary sources collected by the historian Navarro García and shows how, in the reception of the fandango during the nineteenth century, writers (men) describe women's dancing in much more detail, giving it a much more important role than men's, despite writing about a couple's dance.[146]

Consequently, the lack of beauty in the male body (as opposed to the case of women) not only does not constitute a *handicap* but rather facilitates the perception of the artistic act. We see it clearly in Neville's description of the singer Terremoto:

> El Terremoto's dancing is stunning precisely because he does not have a typical dancer's slender figure or anything that physically helps him as he gets going. His dancing has that extraordinary

beauty and that fabulous and authentic duende that grabs us by the throat.[147]

The beauty of the female body enhances the artistic presentation, while that of the male's body is distracting or uncomfortable. An ugly body on men seems to somehow block the possibility of its eroticization, erases the body's corporeality, and allows the *typical* spectator to concentrate on the aesthetic quality of the performance. This block is not only a distraction strategy but also constitutes an operation of a metaphysical order that reintroduces the body-spirit dualism where dance, by its very nature, had destroyed it, making its ideality an immanent trace of matter to the body and its movement.[148] When spectators see a woman dance, they mix the aesthetic judgment and the erotic judgment, but always differentiate the latter, linked to the materiality of the body, and the former, linked to the spirit or soul of the artist.

When it comes to a man, the spectator remains in the "clouds of ideas" despite the materiality of the body before them. The manly style of dancing seems to be perceived *through the man's body*, but not *in the body*. Needless to say, if this distribution of male-female perceptive roles has occurred in this way, it has not done so due to a de jure impossibility of its happening otherwise but rather due to the social and political reality that prevented the public expression of desires—and forms of a gaze associated with them—that were not that of the heterosexual man.

Curiously, as we will see later, the consideration of the male body as erotic capital varied notably in the following decades, as Francisco Diéguez points out when recalling the era of Las Brujas: "Aesthetics, that is, beauty or great personality, nowadays is critical for a *bailaor* [male flamenco dancer]. If he is a dancing genius but does not have the accompanying figure, then he should focus on teaching, much as the days of Enrique, 'El Cojo,' have gone down in history."[149] Likewise, it is necessary to clarify that the status of women as a "desiring subject" has not followed an unequivocal line of progress, but instead has suffered, throughout history and within each of its contexts, various fluctuations. An example that marks a clear contrast with this type of holy, prudish, or self-blaming spectator during the Franco regime is the case of Mariano Camprubí, a bolero dancer from the Teatro Real in Madrid, who in 1834 asked the head of the Paris Opera sewing department to put the covering of a girdle in his breeches to *accentuate his package* and emphasize his manliness. According to Camprubí, this would spice things up for the female dancers in

Spain, who, he said, only looked at men below the waist.[150] A photograph from 1862 provides strong evidence for this anecdote, which shows desiring women who welcomed the attention in the middle of the nineteenth century.

The Double Normativity of Gender in Flamenco Dance

The hypercorporeality of women and the hypocorporeality of men constitute the obverse and reverse of the same phenomenon. Not only is the behavior of women who expose their bodies onstage regulated, but so is that of men. A minority of male dancers had to adhere to a very precise model of masculinity through their attire, postures, and movement, perhaps with the aim of making the heterosexual spectator feel comfortably mirrored, as D. E. Pohren reveals:[151]

> The male dancer, on the other hand, has a better idea of how to be masculine. He performs well his strong, intricate footwork, his body is rigid and straight, his fingers snap fire, he tosses his head like a stallion, his facial expressions are fierce . . . and yet, it usually just doesn't come off. Most male Spanish dancers (and dancers in general) are quite unmanly, and generally no amount of high caliber acting can alter the fact. This condition is passable in the Spanish Ballet, but leaves much to be desired in the *Baile* flamenco.
>
> These impressions are aggravated if you see much flamenco dancing in theaters and night clubs, as many of the dancers who are hired for such places are classical Spanish ballet dancers who also dance a little flamenco. . . . The scarcity of good, manly *bailaores*, I believe, is due to the fact that the *Baile* demands *bailaores* with a certain rare personality; a man who can exhibit his emotions and passions and body unconditionally, and yet remain uneffeminate. Most manly *bailaores* dance coldly, relying on their technique to transmit what they wish to communicate. They are afraid, or unable, to reveal their inner passions, to let themselves go, because it is just not in their physiological makeup. Others, of effeminate nature, have the ability to appear completely masculine when they dance. It can be said that the outstanding male dancers of the *baile grande* are of two types; those who are truly masculine and who are able to "let themselves go," and those who are definitely effeminate, but who possess the ability to transform themselves into *machos*

(real men) when they dance. Both types are rare, with a resultant lack of truly moving male dancers.[152]

Beyond the condensate of heteronormative thought contained in these text fragments taken from Pohren's *The Art of Flamenco*, the excerpt points to an expressive block in male bailaores that is important to analyze in detail. The inability to express their emotions and passions and the difficulty in showing their body do not come from the male psychological nature but from the fear of appearing effeminate and seeing themselves occupying the place of the woman as an object of the masculine gaze, which objectifies and reads the body as a susceptible sensual object of *belonging* to him symbolically through the sexual act.

These fears and this expressive block favor an artistic situation in which there is a lack of male bailaores, and they "lack something" since what is necessary for the development of their own expressiveness is, in reality, prohibited. "Femininity" would be, at the same time, the necessary condition for the development of artistic expressiveness and, if it were abused, a shameful condition for men. Inoculating with the exact dose of femininity makes the bailaor's body an alchemical body, always between the possibility of miraculous success and the danger of social punishment.

The analysis of certain paradigmatic cases will show us how this alchemy of gesture works by accumulating a series of elements that, taken together, make the artist's performance intolerable in terms of gender.[153] One thing is not to walk down the center of the path of gender norms, another is to stray toward the edges, and the other is to run across the field.

I would like to focus, first of all, on the famous *soleá por bulerías* danced as a duet by two heterosexual bailaores, El Güito and Mario Maya, in 1974 at the tablao Café de Chinitas.[154] Despite presenting a couple of men onstage who dance at times completely glued to one another, they seem not to have caused any intense adverse reactions by the audience. This result is partly explained by the visual contact between the performers, which impedes a homoerotic reading of their relationship, but also because they wear traditional short jackets and dance, utterly respecting the movement codes of flamenco masculinity. We are facing two "real men," following Pohren's terminology, who dance close together but without real contact between them.

A second example could be Miguel Vargas Jiménez, "Bambino" (1940–1999), a homosexual singer who first worked in the cuadro of the tablao El Duende and continued as an act at Los Canasteros, Las Cuevas de Nerja, and Torres Bermejas. Even though his homosexuality is an open secret and he often goes onstage dressed in shiny jackets, the singer's gestures could be considered more dramatic, broad, or exaggerated than effeminate, and his performances do not seem to cross the perceptive borders that might make homophobic viewers uncomfortable.[155]

These boundaries are constantly being crossed, for example, by Antonio Ruiz Soler (1921–1996), "El Bailarín," whose physical beauty and, above all, his virtuosity with jumps, turns, and footwork seem to have constituted a form of aesthetic compensation that allowed him not only to survive over the years but to do so occupying the exceptional place of genius, a myth probably also fueled by his multiple tours of the Americas, which kept him away from Spain between 1937 and 1949.

In his *martinete* choreography for the Edgar Neville film *Duende y misterio del flamenco*, from 1952, for example, we see Antonio dressed in bullfighter pants and a polka-dot shirt.[156] The dancer accompanies his marking steps, which follow the percussive rhythm of the seguiriya tirelessly, with a pendulous movement of the hips, small upward blows of the head, snaps, and circular movements with the hands and open fingers. The dryness of the rhythm marked with his feet against the background of the singer's voice, who sings a cappella, is thus nuanced with this series of ornamentation, which makes a restrained *palo* [rhythmic-melodic style within flamenco genre], topped off with falls to the ground and windmill turns—a piece of gold.

One final case in this increasingly risky alchemy would be that of dancers whose effeminate character is not balanced by other elements, either because the performers are not virtuous enough or because they are too effeminate to somehow compensate for their *plumas* (effeminacies). This is the case, among others, of two flamenco and copla singers and dancers: Miguel de Molina (1908–1993), who, after being tortured by the police, went into exile in Argentina in 1942 until his death, and Pedrito Rico (1932–1988), who was arrested numerous times and also went to Argentina until the arrival of Spain's democracy. In both cases, they are artists who do not hide their homosexuality (Pedrito Rico maintained a more or less public relationship with Miguel de Mairena before he transitioned and became Carmen de Mairena), who dressed in shiny, abundantly ornamented jackets and wore makeup, and whose soft gestures with equally ornamented undulations of the hands, shoulders, and hips are, from the point of view of canonical flamenco masculinity, effeminate.

Beyond this casuistry, we have to ask what happens to women whose codes of expression could be considered, in this predemocratic era, as "masculine," such as Fernando Jiménez Peña (1923–2006), "Fernanda de Utrera";[157] her sister Bernarda Jiménez Peña (1927–2009), "Bernarda de Utrera";[158] or Francisca Méndez Garrido (1934–2004), "La Paquera de Jerez." The Utrera sisters, thanks in part to the support of singer Antonio Mairena and to having won the Concurso Nacional de Cante de Córdoba in 1968, worked in, among others, tablaos in Madrid: Zambra, El Corral de la Morería, Torres Bermejas, and Las Brujas. As for La Paquera de Jerez, who had released her first album in 1953, released her second in 1957 and began working that same year at El Corral de la Morería and later at Torres Bermejas, Las Brujas, and Los Canasteros.

In all three cases, they are single women who were highly successful during and after the dictatorship and whose voices, despite their stylistic, meaningful subtleties, were considered masculine because of their intensity, seriousness, and stance.[159] Among them, however, La Paquera is the one who develops an aesthetic that, beyond her voice, calls into question the feminine gender codes of the time. The first comes from the gestures that accompany her singing: beyond the grimaces and the visible tension in her open hands, typical in the execution of cante jondo, La Paquera accompanies her singing—especially when she sings bulerías standing up—with numerous powerful gestures including jumping, beating her chest with her hands, and headbutting into the air to finish with the melody.[160] In addition to the masculinity of her voice and gestures, La Paquera sings a *zambra* in her 1957 album *Soleá de mis pesares*, whose lyrics, written by Antonio Gallardo and Nicolás Sánchez, speak of a lover who, despite having the same name as a flamenco song—Soleá—has the human characteristics of a woman:

> I have in my senses
> The smell of your hair
> And in my mouth, I feel
> The taste of your mouth
> And the anger and jealousy
> Are killing me
> And I dream of you
> And kiss your clothes
> Why, without telling me
> Not even a goodbye, sister,
> Did your blindness leave

On another path
If I never told you to
Get away from me
Soleá of my sorrows, soleá,
Long live luxury and wealth
You and I are not equals
And you can have your money
Because I'll win with passion
And even if you count by the thousands
Your diamonds from the sultan
I prefer my regrets
And my seas of sorrows
Oh, soleá, soleá of my sorrows.
You and I are not equals
And you can have your money
Because I'll win with passion
And even if you count by the thousands
Your diamonds from the sultan
I prefer my regrets
And my seas of sorrows
Oh, soleá, soleá of my sorrows

What effect did these female singers with masculine voices and gestures, who sometimes evoke homosexual relationships in their songs, produce in Spain as a Catholic nation-state? Was suspicion possible? Could it be said that masculinity is a positive value in flamenco that not only applies to men but also, just as naturally, to women? Could we claim that the acceptance and enormous success of these "masculine" women in Spanish society were due to a certain historical invisibility of homosexual women who, contrary to men, did not appear as potentially criminal subjects neither in the Law of Vagrants and Thugs of 1954[161] nor the Ley de Peligrosidad y Rehabilitación Social [Law on Social Danger and Rehabilitation] of 1970?[162] Why were effeminate male artists quickly suspected of homosexuality and masculine female artists were not? Or were they suspected but given greater permissibility? What disconnect is there between gender expression and sexuality here? What actionable power is in the invisibility of lesbians? I am thinking, for example, of another *cantaora* (female flamenco singer) from this period, María Barrús Martínez, "La Niña de

Antequera" (1920–1972), who Pedro G. Romero also confirms was a lesbian and in whose repertoire appears, among conventional zambra lyrics about heartbreak, a song titled, "Ay mi perro!," with lyrics by M. Gordillo and Pepe del Valle, which says:[163]

> In Coto Doñana they have killed,
> They killed my dog.
> He was following
> A doe through the green Labdanum trees.
> Around the contours of Andalusia,
> There wasn't another dog like my dog.
> Oh, how nice it was when he jumped
> After the hares through the rosemary.
> Oh, how happy he was when he returned.
> How carefully he brought them to me.
> He was the key to my farmhouse
> And the sentinel of the cattle.
> No wolf dared come near
> The lambs on the shore.
> He was the bravest of the brave
> And no other had more nobility.
> You had to see him when he played
> With my children in the meadow.
> There will never be another dog like my dog!
> At the fountain of Stone Cross,
> Thyme and rosemary,
> And in the shade of a gray oak
> I buried my dog.
> My joys have ended.
> Oh, what a shame, my Lucero.
> He consoled the sorrow
> And suffering of my life.
> Oh, how happy he was when he returned
> Hunting in those mountains.

Does this song constitute an anecdote or an animalistic gem in which a cantaora with short, curly hair, dressed as an Amazonian flamenca with a shirt buttoned up to the neck, a jacket, a closed skirt, and high boots, professes her love for her beloved Lucero? Is there anything more queer than describing the relationship one has with an animal companion with this feeling of a copla that extols the beauty of the dog and its moral virtues?

The Spectacle as Promise

After the show, the spectators could propose to some artists to "continue partying" with singing and dancing in a reserved space in the tablao. The artists usually accepted this proposal since it allowed them to obtain a bonus. Thus, the show, already satisfying in and of itself, contained the promise of extra satisfaction after it was over. Pulpón collects in her dissertation the testimonies of a group of bailaoras who worked in the Sevillian tablaos between 1950 and 1980.[164] According to these testimonies, the interaction between the artists and the spectators after the show grew in an environment that did not transgress "moral limits" and in which there was no confusion between the role of artists and that of sex workers, despite a series of elements that suggest the contrary. Although the oral and written sources do not allow us to confirm, evidently, that all the dancers were prostitutes, what seems clear is that prostitution in the tablaos is an element that we cannot avoid mentioning, as have authors such as Washabaugh,[165] Hayes,[166] and Wright,[167] and as other testimonies that I have been able to collect confirm, such as that of my teacher José Racero, a bailaor from Triana in Los Cabales during the 1970s who verifies that prostitution even existed in dance companies, "especially during foreign tours."[168] The guitarist and former cuadro leader of El Corral de la Morería, Antonio, "El Muñeco," also confessed to us in an interview:

> The parties of before are not like they are now. The old parties occurred when the tablao was over. Well, there were people who liked flamenco or whoremongers who went there—not with our girls, all right? People were confused. They went to the Molino Rojo or they went to two or three places that were there and went to the tablaos . . . because they knew something about flamenco. It's not like they were stupid. But they did nothing there. . . . Or they went alone [to] the one with the refrigerators or the one with the bellows, who had a bus company there in Santa María de la Cabeza.[169]

Francisco Diéguez, the owner of Las Brujas and brother of the owner of the Molino Rojo cabaret (16 Tribulete Street), also takes this slightly protectionist stance, defending "his" bailaoras from any comment that might confuse them with prostitutes:

> I suppose it's clear that the gatherings, small private parties held over twenty-odd years in Las Brujas, were society parties that shaped those years, taking place almost daily and for a very long time. The manager, Mr. Salcedo, whom I will talk about later, responding to a client's request, led him to the main party room, as it was called. The elegant gentleman presented him with such an offer: "Look, I want you to bring me several of the ladies that I have seen perform and, of course, he who wishes can sleep with my wife. In exchange, I will sleep with one of the artists, the one I like the most." Verbatim, Mr. Salcedo . . . replied, "Listen, sir. In Spain, we are not such bastards that we allow you all to sleep with our women and even less that we offer them to others. And as for the artists, you are mistaken, because the only woman who could be compared to them is your mother. So, please, get out of here immediately. I'll walk you to the street."[170]

Not only the owners, but also the mothers of the artists themselves, acted as protectors of "their" bailaoras, watching over the sanctity of their daughters in that "intermediate" status between the innocence of childhood and the "transfer of property" to the husband in marriage:

> The artists were accompanied by their mothers at that time, and taking into account that these artists began working from a very young age. They looked like their older sisters, but in those days . . . those mothers were apparently older ladies, fat, with their bodies already disfigured without repair, and almost all of them dressed in black. In short, they were like a sect.[171]

The bailaoras looked at each other but did not touch each other. Of course, you could ask for greater proximity to them and a chat. Beyond the exchange of paid sexual services, bailaoras were often forced to "share," that is, to have a drink with the clients after the show, in such a way that the exposure of the women's bodies continued offstage and after the show.[172] The bailaora Trini España states, perhaps without much critical awareness, the following in a testimony collected by Pulpón:

You had to pay yourself and then you had to buy street clothes . . . you couldn't go to a tablao dressed as if you had to go clean an office. You had to go all dressed up, with your cute dresses, makeup, high-heeled shoes. . . . In other words, you had to go looking good.[173]

This obligation to socialize with clients is not specific to tablaos. It also existed in the cafés cantantes, music halls, and certain nightclubs where Spanish ballet shows took place. Álvaro Retana describes it as follows:

Artists in the lineup who received minuscule wages . . . were "tirelessly hunting in the foyer" for a clueless man who would invite them for a drink so they could receive the house commission and leave at the end of the show with a bonus.[174]

We conclude, then, that as a continuation of the cafés cantantes, the presence of prostitutes in the tablaos was not just a fantasy but a reality that ended up forming part of the collective imagination, as demonstrated by an anecdote related to the opening of the tablao Los Canasteros, owned by singer Manolo Caracol.[175] In an interview, journalist José Antonio Blázquez tells how the Madrid City Council denied Caracol permission to open his tablao because the street location of the establishment—Barbieri Street, in the heart of the Chueca neighborhood—was frequented by prostitutes. The residents who lived on the street, "therefore," did not want them to open a tablao there. It goes without saying that the focus was on prostitution. Blázquez also tells how Caracol managed to talk to Franco after a show held at the Palacio de La Granja in Segovia and how he sent a letter of recommendation to the city council that finally allowed him to open his tablao.[176]

Male Prostitution in the Tablao

According to the authors of *Chaperos*, between 1950 and 1970, homosexual male prostitution in Spain followed an "outdoor" model and occurred mainly on the street. However, I have managed to find, in a book from 1976, proof of the existence of homosexual prostitutes in the tablaos, who also mingled with clients: "[The transformista Mr. Artur and his friend go to the tablao] Los Canasteros, where they mingle with well-known bullfighters from the Margot de Salamanca cabaret, such as 'Juan de Palma,' 'Jumillano,' 'los Corpas.'"[177] Like the bailaoras, the transformistas of the time were forced to have a drink with clients:

It is the time, now past for him, not for all gays, in which in order to perform, he has to alternate: the salary must be justified, and it is necessary to give a good handful of money to the manager every night by making the clients drink. . . . And the site of Tula—the other name of Mr. Artur—was not the downtown theater, not even a cabaret, but rather a private room in a cabaret. There he went, one day, with seven or eight bullfighters, another day with a group of wealthy South American students or some soccer players, and together, when the Spanish revelry was in full swing, they would strip Modesto naked and bathe him in champagne.

Prostitution, prohibited in 1935 during the Second Republic, was decriminalized again by the Franco regime in 1941. However, on March 3, 1956, an executive order was issued that forced the closure of brothels and made prostitutes "migrate" to other nightlife spaces:[178] "Prostitution remained in a situation of absolute clandestinity, meaning for many prostitutes recycling old careers as waitresses, among other professions, since that way they could be present in places mostly frequented by men without raising too much suspicion, thus conforming to the appearance of new forms of practicing prostitution from the creation, for example, of the so-called American bars."[179]

Later, Decree 16/1970, from August 4, known as the Law on Social Danger and Rehabilitation, led to the treatment of many prostitutes as criminals. It was not until 1995 (LO [constitutional law] 10/1995 of December 23), twenty years after the death of the dictator, when a modification of the Criminal Code abolished all laws against prostitution, except those that concern minors or people with cognitive disabilities.[180]

The interaction between these laws against prostitution and the daily improvement of this practice seems uncertain. However, it indicates the need to interpret this "historical silence" less as a sign of its nonexistence than as the logical consequence of a practice that is both sneakily and morally rejected by Spanish society, which makes access to reliable sources challenging since many of those involved in the first person categorically deny the existence of these practices in order to preserve their personal narrative. An exceptional case is that of Lola Flores (1923–1995), a tremendous artist who recounted this issue in detail in an interview for the television program *El coraje de vivir*:

> My mother, as always, accompanied me, but when we arrived in Valladolid, my father called us to say that my sister Carmen was

severely sick. My mother felt forced to leave me alone for the first time. She had two worries: my sister and that something could happen to me. I calmed her. I brought her to the station, and she gave me plenty of advice again. But fate had planned what my mother feared, and one night, in a boardinghouse in Valladolid, I made love for the first time in my life with Niño Ricardo. Simple as that. But inside, I already thought I could accept some of the advances that my admirers made toward me daily, but not invitations to take me to the movies or out to dinner. . . . I was totally determined that my parents and my brothers would not suffer any more calamities, and although artistically I was well received, I did not get the financial compensation in the contracts that I thought I deserved. The thing with Niño Ricardo did not happen again, but when I returned to Madrid, I got an invitation. . . . The man was madly in love with me . . . until one day he said to me: "Do you need money?" And I told him: "Yes, fifty thousand pesetas [$52,721]." He left me alone in the restaurant for a moment, left, and returned with the money and said: "Here, it's yours. Let's go." . . . He arranged a date with me at the Hotel Nacional, and I went there to pay the contracted debt with my body. When I got home and took the fifty thousand pesetas to my parents, I thought I was giving them back the money for which they refinanced the bar in Jerez so that I could be an artist. I told them: "Don't ever ask me where I got this from." . . . Their eyes filled with tears.[181]

The authors of *Chaperos* account for this epistemological difficulty; however, they have managed to compile a compendium of data that allows them to conclude that in Spain, "sex work is tolerated enough to make it a destination for sex tourism (both gay and straight). The entire Mediterranean coast is a potent sex tourism zone, and part of the Spanish economy depends upon the trilogy: sex, tourism, and drugs (including easy and cheap access to alcohol)."[182]

Effectively, the consumption of euphoric drugs, such as cocaine, ceased to be exclusive to foreign cabarets in the 1920s and became part of the flamenco universe, about which Antonio, "El Muñeco" recounts:

I've seen barbarities. . . . I've been there with them, but up to a certain point. Got it? You have to be in it, otherwise you don't work. . . . But I've seen things from leaders of the government. I've been there . . . Because I'm lucky to have worked with La Polaca, with Rocío Jurado.[183]

Besides cocaine use, it is important to note the presence of other drugs, such as LSD, especially during the 1960s and 1970s, whose psychedelic experiences gave rise to a musical genre known as "progressive and underground music" or even "lysergic music."[184] According to historian Juan Carlos Usó, this drug reaches Spain via the United States military installations at Morón de la Frontera (Seville), Rota (Cádiz), Torrejón de Ardoz (Madrid), and Zaragoza, thanks to the agreement signed between Spain and the United States in 1953.[185] Following Usó, the first traces of LSD use in flamenco appeared in the music of the flamenco rock group Smash (1968–1973) and also the flamenco rock band Triana (1974–1983), which released its album *Triana* with two songs that evoke a lysergic experience: "Abre la puerta" and "En el lago" (lyrics by Andrés N., "El Alemán"). Decades later, the drama of heroin will appear in flamenco in various musical compositions, such as a bulería from 2007 performed by "El Torta" that says:

In the neighborhood, I met
A bad companion.
She was called heroin.
I can't get away from her
And now I don't know what to do
And I don't know where to go
And I have to steal
To be able to get her.
Without you, I sing to the moon again
Without you, I hear the night again.
And if they see me get high
Let no one blame me
I'm high
Hooked
They usually say when they see me
They don't know that you've left me
And that I want to die.
I'm always lying in the street
In the bars and on the corners.
I'd trade life for death
For fucking heroin

I cannot live!
Because I lead a bad life.
I cannot live!
Because the drug controls me.
Between unconscious and a party
And that's how my life goes.
And my heart is stronger
And my chest is a treasure trove
And I thank you, God!
That you have taken me away from heroin
My goodness,
My goodness,
My goodness
How bad is the night,
The street,
And life.

Gone is the therapeutic nature and generator of new forms of knowledge of LSD, captured by Triana on "Abre la puerta": "I wanted to go up to heaven to see / And go down to hell to understand / What reason it is / That prevents us from seeing / Inside of you / Inside of you / Inside of me." And "En el lago": "Yesterday afternoon I went to the lake / With the intention of meeting / Something new / We met there / And everything began to emerge / Like a dream / I seem to remember that at night / The white bird took flight / In our hearts / In search of a shooting star."

The Other Promise

The regime of the promise in the tablao concerned not only the spectators-consumers but also the artists since it constituted a kind of showcase for unknown dancers, singers, and guitarists who could be "discovered" by the programmers or by other, more renowned artists who were often present in the tablao. This was the case for singers like Camarón de la Isla, Enrique Morente, and Rocío Jurado and dancers like Mario Maya, el Güito, Matilde Coral, and even Antonio Gades, about whom Blanca del Rey tells how the dancer from Alicante was hired to perform at the 1964 New York World's Fair, a true springboard in the artist's career, after having been discovered in El Corral de la Morería, where its founder, Manuel del Rey, gave him his artistic surname of Gades.[186]

This promise of success, all the more deeply rooted as it involved artists from modest backgrounds who saw an opportunity to change their living conditions, is nurtured in artists from an early age, to which life stories from artists of the time attest. Blanca del Rey, for example, began dancing at the age of twelve in the tablao El Zoco, in Córdoba, after winning several dance competitions from the time she was six. Then she traveled to Madrid at age fourteen, where she began dancing in Las Cuevas de Nemesio and quickly moved on to El Corral de la Morería, whose owner, Manuel del Rey, she would later marry.

> I could not perform beyond midnight because of the Ley del Menor [Child Protection Law]. I also needed a special permit signed by my parents and to be accompanied by my mother. Plus, the censor would arrive, and since we wore a lot back then, I had my blouse tied here (to the sternum) and couldn't put it on. And I used to wear that in Córdoba, but only until midnight. In El Zoco de Córdoba, I used to dance until midnight because I was twelve years old, and here it's the same, until midnight.[187]

In this testimony, we see how the artist, driven by a promise of success that was not wholly fruitless, dodged the difficulties resulting from her premature age to be able to work. In the same way, the Vallecano guitarist Antonio, "El Muñeco" confesses that he had to "camouflage" himself with a suit and frilled shirt to appear more adult than he was.[188] Like Blanca del Rey and El Muñeco, Francisca Sadornil Ruiz, "La Tati" (Madrid, 1945), began dancing at the age of twelve, first in the tablao Zambra, then in El Duende "at fourteen or fifteen years old," and finally, in Torres Bermejas, where she would perform between 1960 and 1965.

> Every year Zambra went to the Theater of Nations in Paris (the small cuadro and some artists from the big cuadro), and they looked for substitutes for that month or those two months. La Quica found out and said, "Let Tati go. Let them test her out. See if they take her! . . ." And indeed: I debuted there. I earned 75 pesetas. Then they raised me to 125. I was there for about a year. And it was a very serious thing. They let me lead the cuadro because I sang a little, and they immediately saw that I was very sharp. . . . Of course, everyone said: "Tati sits so well!" Clearly! The thing is, even if I sat onstage that well, my feet didn't reach the floor because I was very small. . . .

And shortly after, a guitarist and a singer called me for El Patio Andaluz, what was then Alcalá 20; it was the starting block for Alcázar, of the Alcázar Theater, the starting block for Alcázar, which was a cabaret, and a tablao that was El Patio Andaluz. Since I was younger, I worked in the afternoon. I also danced classical Spanish at that time: I danced "Triana"; "Orgía," by Turina; "Sacromonte"; "El zapateado" by Sarasate. . . . In the afternoon, I did a show in the cabaret in the main hall. At night I was in the tablao, and if the police came, I would hide because then the legal age was twenty-one, but they didn't let you work until you were eighteen. I didn't have an ID. . . . Then there were exams . . . on Calle Fuencarral. There was a jury. And it was the ID for FENS [Front of National-Syndicalist Students] and JONS [Councils of National-Syndicalist Offensive]—an ID card for everything: the theater, circus, variety shows. I was part of the variety shows because there wasn't an ID for bailaoras . . . , and the union was in Santo Domingo. Sure we had a union! The Sindicato Vertical [Vertical Trade Union]. . . . I was there until Torres Bermejas opened. . . . Torres Bermejas was already called La Taberna Gitana, and it was like a kind of cabaret: the women worked. . . . They made Torres Bermejas with that decoration because, before, the tavern was like an inn. When the owner of Hotel Regente took it over, they made Torres Bermejas. . . . I didn't want to leave because I earned a lot of money in El Patio Andaluz, but I left in 1961 because, in 1963, I was already there [at Torres Bemejas], which was when Carmen Amaya died. . . . But I immediately began to work in great ballets and theaters. At seventeen, I already went on my first tour.[189]

The guitarist El Muñeco remembers the following anecdote:

At that time I still couldn't work. What happened is that I was camouflaged. The thing is that at that time, I was lanky, and we used to wear a suit with frilled shirts—that's stopped now—which made it look like I was older.

Like Blanca del Rey's story, La Tati constructs hers narratively, following a line of progressive success due in part to the natural talent of the artists. Her success was also, however, a consequence of a set of circumstantial factors that generated successive opportunities for job improvement from the earliest age in a context in which the Ley del Contrato de Trabajo (LCT) [Labor Contract Law] of 1944 prevented minors under fourteen years of age from working, especially when it was related to a nocturnal activity:

> Regarding night work, the LCT of 1944 already prohibited this work for minors under sixteen years old, understanding night as the period from eight in the evening to six in the morning. The Spanish regulation did not specify what type of work; it simply prohibited all night work. In 1960, the prohibition was extended to eighteen-year-olds, covering from eight in the evening to seven in the morning.[190]

After 1976, the new Ley de Relaciones Laborales [Labor Relations Law] established the legal age at sixteen years, although participation in public shows was considered an exception as long as the legal guardians provided authorization and it "did not pose a danger to physical health or to their professional and human development." This narrow legal gap, and despite the nighttime nature of the work, which remains prohibited for minors between ten at night and six in the morning (article 6.2 of the Estatuto de los Trabajadores [Workers' Statute]), allowed the continuation of this practice once democracy arrived in Spain. One of the most publicized cases was that of bailaor Israel Galván, whose parents were also dancers.

Exceptional Spectators

In contrast to what happened in the cafés cantantes, where, as Navarro García argues, the spectators were mainly peasants and Spanish merchants who traveled to the big cities to do business and who took advantage of these occasions to quench their thirst both for flamenco and for other "masculine whims," in the tablaos the typical spectators were mainly foreign tourists with a higher purchasing power than the locals.[191] Francisco Diéguez, owner of Las Brujas, in addition to the regular presence of the kings emeriti, provides in his biographical book photographs and anecdotes with luxury spectators, such as the president of Argentina, the Duchess of Alba, and artists such as Ava Gardner, Charlton Heston, Cantinflas, Massiel, and Julio Iglesias.

Among the different tablaos, El Corral de la Morería always occupied a privileged place, which resulted in numerous visits by foreign celebrities starting in the 1970s, such as Bill Clinton (governor of Arkansas at that time), President Ronald Reagan,[192] and artists like Roger Moore,[193] Jack Lemmon, Jean Cocteau, and Rudolf Nureyev,[194] who is said to have ended up taking the stage at the request of the Mexican bailaora Lucero Tena to dance with her. Some of these celebrities were photographed and continue to hang in the lobby of the tablao today.

A decade before the arrival of these stars, El Corral de la Morería was already part of the activities proposed by the governors of the time when diplomatic visits were organized in Madrid, such as the reception of the Italian ambassador to Spain in 1962, after which the attendees dined at the prestigious tablao, or the visit in 1965 of Brigadier General França Borges, president of the Lisbon Municipal Chamber.[195]

These official visits to the tablao must be considered not only a political instrumentalization of the tablao but also, above all, a sign of patrimonialization: the tablao becomes a sort of national monument and is integrated into the program of activities offered to visitors, which included, for example—as was the case in the visit of Ambassador Pellegrino Chici—a visit to El Escorial monastery, the Valley of the Fallen, and the Prado Museum.

This patrimonialization of El Corral de la Morería in the 1960s–1970s is also visible in two television appearances of *NO-DO* (*Noticiarios y documentales* [Newscasts and documentaries]) and contrasts with the anonymous appearance of another tablao, Torres Bermejas, in the 1960s.[196] Torres Bermejas is presented as "a locale from Madrid with its evocative feeling of the Alhambra" in the context of an international flamenco dance competition that the voice-over calls "the UN of flamenco" and without any relation to the urban landscape from the city of Madrid. Regarding the appearances of El Corral de la Morería, in the first broadcast, from 1959, we see a kind of *fin de fiesta* ["end of the party" that closes flamenco shows] in which a young bailaora moves her skirt, in the middle of a group of men who cheer her on, as a finale to a series of images that have previously shown us Madrid at night: the Plaza de la Villa, the Royal Palace, typical restaurants in the Plaza Mayor (probably Luis Candelas's Las Cuevas), Gran Vía, Plaza de Callao, illuminated advertisements, large cinemas, more restaurants, and in a last section to which this sort of choreographic *bukkake* belongs, a dance section.[197] We see a Spanish dance troupe performing a jota, revue shows, an Orientalist dancer, a shot of a woman's legs, acrobats, and Russian dances. Flamenco is, then, the golden brooch that closes or finishes off the series of images, the end of the festival in a broad sense, and the gesture that, paradoxically, has the last word.

In the second television appearance, from 1974, the tablao also appears as a closing, but this time with a series of images about the touristic points of interest in Madrid.[198] In the sequence, much longer than the one from 1959, after having seen the bailaoras in the group, the male audience, a solo singer performing *rumbas*, and a bailaora-attraction, Lucero Tena—dancing to alegrías in a white bata de cola—the voice-over of the documentary recites the following text:

> With the final clapping by Lucero Tena, Madrid is silent; with the rumor of the last applause, the capital of flamenco fades away; with the last lights, the capital of Spain sleeps. That's how it remains, until the next day, in its silence.
>
> In this way, Madrid is presented as a city-show that offers countless activities during the day (museums, soccer matches, bullfights, etc.) and whose final number takes place on the floorboards of El Corral de la Morería.

The treatment given to flamenco in the *Diccionario turístico de España* (1972) is quite different, where it also appears as a grand finale for the documentary, associated with the letter Z for *zapateado*, despite that no proper zapateado is seen or heard throughout the image sequence.[199] Instead, we see an interesting overlapping of images with the musical background of the flamenco-style bolero *Historia de un amor* (Carlos Eleta Almarán, 1955) performed by Lola Flores, who also appears in the images performing at her tablao in Marbella with another bailaora and singer. Here the sound of the rumba blends shots of the artists, sunsets over the sea, planes landing, highways . . . necklines, and asses covered by bikini bottoms: pornification of flamenco as an audiovisual logic (again) and a scatological narrative positioning as a closing at the end of all the images. What does flamenco have that inspires there to be nothing behind it? Is flamenco in itself—due to its aesthetics, energy, or structure—a closure? What makes it a necessary closing element but an impossible inaugural and one more uncomfortable component in the middle of a series of other links? Can the bailaor give birth as well as finish off?

Flamenco Drag between 1936 and 1960

The Spanish Civil War (1936–1939) and the establishment of the Franco dictatorship produced a paradigm shift in transformismo that implied less a total disappearance of the phenomenon than a step away from the scene to the private sphere: drag ceases to be, thus, an artistic phenomenon that can be presented publicly and becomes hidden or semi-hidden entertainment. As the dancer José Luis Vega stated, "Let there be fire, but don't let anyone see it."[200] The author of *El látigo y la pluma* explains how certain transformistas who worked in the artistic milieu during the Republic, such as Pirouletz—a comedian who appeared onstage dressed as a female flamenco dancer—and El Chache, had to abandon their profession after Franco's triumph. Others, like Mirco, were able to continue working singing the same repertoire but substituting women's clothing for men's.[201] The author also gives numerous examples of male drag outside the scene, such as Manuel Granda Terrón, "La Pirula," who had drag picnics with his friends by the river in Villalba. La Pirula also performed as a transformista singer at the tablao El Patio Andaluz, probably beginning in the 1960s, since the first tablao, Zambra, opened in Madrid in 1954.

In the case of female drag, it would be necessary to speak of a certain continuity between the stage and the private sphere, where, according to Olmeda, other artists dressed up and reproduced androgynous attitudes to evoke actresses like Marlene Dietrich and Greta Garbo.[202] In this last area, it is necessary to highlight the paradigmatic case of Carmen Amaya (1918–1963), who, despite having received some negative criticism on her return to Spain in 1947 after eleven years of touring America and Europe, continued to dance to alegrías in pants without much issue, even becoming a role model for subsequent bailaoras who also danced in pants.[203] One of her first artistic descendants—similar to how Salud Rodríguez was the progeny of La Cuenca—was Fernanda Romero, who, dressed in a short dress and with finger cymbals, recorded her "Ritual del taranto" for the show *Oración de la tierra*, by Alfonso Jiménez Romero and Francisco García Velázquez, in 1969.[204] In the game of filiations, it is not trivial that the rhythmic-song form danced by Romero is a taranto since the first choreography made for this musical style—although the authorship is disputed with Rosario, the artistic partner of Antonio Ruiz Soler—was authored by Amaya.

TWO

Transitions and New Identities (1975–2008)

A Polemic Chronology

After the death of dictator Franco on November 20, 1975, a democratic transformation began in Spain that had as foundational events the first democratic elections on June 15, 1977, and the referendum to vote on the Magna Carta on December 6, 1978. Despite the importance of these events, which frame the Transition between 1975 and 1978, Hispanist Teresa M. Vilarós argued that this era should be divided into two periods:

> The first, more or less between the years 1973 and 1982, would frame the period of transition itself and takes into account, above all, three key dates: December 23, 1973, the day of the attack against Carrero Blanco [Spanish military and politician]; November 20, 1975, the date of Francisco Franco's death; and finally, February 23, 1981, when the failed military coup by Lieutenant Colonel Antonio Tejero strengthens a democracy in Spain that had, up until that moment, not been fully affirmed by the national psychology....
> The second period, considered one of democratic reinforcement, falls in the decade from 1982, the year of the electoral victory by the socialist government, to 1993, when the Maastricht Treaty was signed, and the European and global map of the internationalist policy followed by the socialist government of Felipe González is consolidated.[1]

Following the chronology proposed by Vilarós, the Transition would end around 1993 with the signing of the Maastricht Treaty, which also coincides with the final years of the socialist government of Felipe González, who will be succeeded as president by the conservative José María Aznar

77

in 1996. It is the moment—always according to Vilarós—in which Spain "definitively joins the circuit of late capitalism,"[2] with substantial implications on the transformation of the culture, as Calvo Borobia argues:

> The consolidation of democracy propelled the modernization of Spanish society. . . . During the 1980s, the Spanish became wealthier, totally pro-European, and self-confident when participating in normalized and democratic politics. . . . In addition, a process of generational replacement caused notable transformations in their values system. . . . For example, in 1970, almost 45 percent of the population claimed to belong to the group of "practicing Catholics"; in 1982, this figure dropped to 25 percent.[3]

Delaying the Transition until 1993, the moment contemporary flamenco dance began to emerge, can be seen doubly contested from the LGTBIQ perspective. Indeed, from the legislative point of view, it is possible that for this group, the Transition did not arrive at the same time as for the rest of the Spaniards, given that the Law on Social Danger and Rehabilitation— applied to homosexual men, *travestis* (cross-dressers), and transsexuals (with prison sentences and treatments to "cure" them)—was not partially repealed until December 26, 1979.[4] This partial repeal occurred four years after the dictator's death and after the first LGBT protests were organized in Spain, first in Barcelona in 1977 and later in Madrid and Seville in 1978.[5]

Despite this partial repeal, the law will not be entirely eliminated until 1995, which could further delay the chronology proposed by Vilarós and allow us to state that, at least for LGTBIQ people—and perhaps, therefore, for the rest—the Transition did not arrive in Spain until at least twenty years after Franco's death.

On the other hand, paradoxically, the LGTBIQ perspective would also allow us to argue that the Transition could have started before the dictator died, around the 1960s, when we found the first traces of gay bars and cabarets in Spain, often embellished with drag shows.

The Gender Transition in Flamenco

Theatrical Drag after 1960

Starting in the 1950s, the opening of Spain to international tourism favored the creation of a more or less underground gay scene both in the big Spanish cities and in some tourist centers on the Mediterranean coast. In September 1962, Tony's—the first Spanish gay bar—opened its doors in Pasaje Begoña in Torremolinos (Málaga).[6] This city would become an international destination for gay tourism despite a certain number of raids, such as the one on June 1971, after which fourteen people were arrested.[7]

The first case to which we have references is that of Margarita, a flamenco dancer who appears in the documentary *Lejos de los árboles*, by Jacinto Esteva, filmed between 1963 and 1971. Margarita dances at the Copacabana lounge in Barcelona, when the venue still lacked a stage, dressed in a miniskirt made of newspaper that also covers her arms and adorns her head in the shape of a bow.[8] The travesti dancer—or *travestí* (emphasizing the final rather than the penultimate syllable), as they were called at that time—moves forward, dancing between the tables, and at one point lets the spectators set fire to his clothing. Margarita then begins to spin around while the paper burns and ends the dance on the ground doing a backbend.

The case of Alfonso Gamero Cruces, "La Esmeralda de Sevilla" (Seville, 1935–?), allows us to see the theatrical strategy followed by these artists, which we could call "inclusive exclusion." First of all, these "fairy (*mariquita*) shows" will take place outside the theater circuit and touristy areas of the tablaos, in underground venues like the Venta de la Esmeralda, located on the outskirts of Seville, or in downtown venues, especially after the death of the dictator and into the 1990s.[9] In Madrid, we find places like La Boîte del Pintor, Club Always (8 Hileras Street), Centauros (10 Santa Bárbara Street), Dimas (3 San Dimas Street), Sacha's (1 Plaza de Chueca), Micheleta (20 Costanilla de los Ángeles), Gay Club (48 Paseo del Prado), Top Less, Nueva Romana, and York Club. In Barcelona, Barcelona de Noche, Whisky Twist, and La Taberna de Apolo. In Alicante, Sala Liverpool.

Second, this kind of quasi-zoological spectacularization of the travesti, now explicitly perceived as homosexual, is going to take place in a type of self-humiliating and comical show aimed at a heterosexual audience that attends these places to laugh with and at the fairies, confirming their abnormal character and the legitimacy of heteronormative codes. The show, visible in the film *"La Esmeralda"*, by Joaquín Arbide (1970), mixes fairy jokes, songs, folkloric dances such as sevillanas, and what Antonio Burgos calls in his *Guía secreta de Sevilla* "comic passages" (*pasajes cómicos*), which were stage numbers with a funny edge similar to those shown in the cafés cantantes between 1850 and 1920.[10]

The shows are introduced by the figure of the "entertainer," embodied by artists like Mr. Artur, Paco España, Pavlovsky, Bello Paco, Marquesa, and Mimí Pompón:

[They are] the essential character in a gay show. They are in charge of maintaining the *buffo* or sophisticated tone, mysterious or shameless, depending on whether the show is of one style or another. There are two clearly differentiated types of shows: one in which *transformistas* predominate, who are actors who dress as women onstage and who, most often, scrupulously imitate famous female characters, actresses, or singers; and another in which primarily *travestís* act, who are ladies in every way, in their private life, in their clothing, in their customs, except in possession of primary male sexual characteristics; in the jargon: "who have tits and a package." If the first type of show tilts towards buffoonery and the grotesque (almost always due to commercial and administrative impositions), the example of the *travestís* follows a "chic" route, of great "quality," of highly sophisticated and international spectacle.[11]

Although some artists sing their own songs, such as Paco España ("La tomate," "Guerra pa mi cuerpo")[12] and Mr. Artur ("Paca la fría"),[13] most of the performances are imitations of folk singers such as Rocío Jurado, Lola Flores, Guillermina Mota, Concha Piquer, and Sara Montiel. These imitations, according to the authors of *Celtiberia gay*, achieve unanimous success among different types of audiences, although for different reasons:

In fact, the audience, the entire audience, fully absorbs it, and the lefty with the beard says, "You don't know how important what you do is"; the intellectual says, "This connects with Solana, Valle, and the Goya from the engravings"; and the common man has fun and laughs a lot: "This is bitchin'. I like it more than Concha Piquer."[14]

The success of these shows is such that, despite the underground character of many of the halls where they are held, they are attended by "exceptional spectators": the police chief of the police station on Calle de la Luna in Madrid, the journalist Amilibia with his wife Ketty Kaufmann, and artists such as Susana Estrada, Sara Montiel, Analía Gadé, Marisol, Antonio Gades, and Lola Flores.[15] The latter, despite having been known as an artist who explicitly supported and stood up for homosexuals, in 1977 was involved in a scandal as a spectator of Paco España's show *Madrid, pecado mortal*.[16] After seeing the imitation that the travesti did of her, which Flores considered "burlesque and offensive," she insulted the artists, the manager, and the creators of the show and stood in front of the Muñoz Seca Theater box office to convince the passersby not to buy tickets for the show. The owner of the theater, Andrés Magdaleno, denounced Flores, who was sentenced to pay a fine of 255 pesetas [$15.86], according to one of the sources,[17] and 3,000 pesetas [$186.79] and fifteen days in prison, according to another source.[18]

Among all these artists, absent from the pages of the History of flamenco, at least four of them should be presented in more detail, especially on their relationship to the flamenco world: Mr. Artur, Paco España, and Carmen de Mairena as stage artists, and Ocaña as a "street artist."

Mr. Artur

Modesto Mangas Mateos (Salamanca, 1923–1999) was known as Madame Artur, Mr. Artur, and "La Tula." The name of this artist, first a feminine name and later masculine, could be a reference to the Parisian venue Madame Artur, located on rue des Martyrs in the eighteenth district of the French capital, which was the first travesti cabaret opened in the city in 1946, and whose name, in turn, refers to the song of the same name by Paul Kock written in 1850 and performed by Yvette Guilbert. Mr. Artur was an eminent figure in the drag community during the Transition and, thanks to interviews archived online by the trans activist and politician Carla Antonelli, we know that he spent three months in the Modelo Prison in Madrid during the dictatorship, was enormously successful primarily in Barcelona, and recited flamenco poems such as this one:[19] "When I was seventeen years old . . . / I was the son of 'La Mejorana'; / La Mejorana, / the one with the burgundy hair / and the hat with a turned-up brim / she only has one love / who is of the Gitano race." Rosario Monje, "La Mejorana" (Cádiz, 1862—Madrid, 1922), to whom Mr. Artur refers in this poem, was a flamenco dancer and singer, a leading figure in the El Burrero and Silverio cafés in Seville. Her artistic career lasted only three years, ending once she married the bullfighter couturier Víctor Rojas. From this marriage were born the guitarist Víctor Rojas and the famous artist Pastora Imperio, a symbol of the escuela sevillana of flamenco dance but also, like so many other figures of the early twentieth century, a variety artist capable of dancing in different stylistic registers, like singing and performing monologues in a somewhat comedic fashion.

Paco España

Francisco Morero García (Las Palmas de Gran Canaria, 1951–2012) was one of the most successful travestis after the dictator's death and had a longer artistic career, lasting until the 2000s. He performed in Barcelona and Madrid on stages such as Barcelona de Noche, the Alfil Theater, the Muñoz Seca, the Gay Club hall, and the Lido, with different shows: "Madrid, pecado mortal, Pecar . . . en Madrid" (a piece by Antonio D. Olano and Juan Pardo, directed by José Francisco Tamarit and in trans artist Yeda Brown's company), "Libérate" (choreographed by Jorge Agüer), "Guerra pa mi cuerpo," "El triángulo de las tetudas," and "El show de Paco España."

He also carried out international tours with well-known flamenco artists such as Los Chichos, with whom he worked in Venezuela,[20] and participated in various films, such as *Haz la loca . . . no la guerra* (1976), by José Truchado; *El transexual* (1977), by José Jara; *Los placeres ocultos* (1977), by Eloy de la Iglesia; *Un hombre llamado flor de otoño* (1978), by Pedro Olea;[21] *Gay Club* (1981), by Ramón Fernández; and *La Carmen* (1976), by Julio Diamante, with a soundtrack by guitarist Manolo Sanlúcar, images of the tablao Las Brujas (now Sauna Paraíso), and the involvement of flamenco artists like bailaora Sara Lezana, bailaor and maestro Enrique el Cojo, bailaor Rafael de Córdova—who appears only as an actor—and singers Agujetas and Enrique Morente.

Carmen de Mairena

Despite the gradual disappearance of these drag cabarets starting in the 1980s, some continue to exist, such as El Cangrejo in Barcelona, a venue where Miguel Brau Gou, "Carmen de Mairena" (Barcelona, 1933), used to perform, noting he felt proud to work there because Carmen Amaya had also done it before her.[22] Miguel debuted in 1956 as a variety artist in Barcelona in places like the Ambos Mundos lounge, Café Nuevo, Copacabana, Bodega Apolo, and Ciros. Due to his relationship with the copla singer and bailaor Pedrito Rico, he went to prison several times, where he suffered physical abuse that forced him to take an artistic hiatus at a particular moment in his life. After his recovery, he returned to work in places like Whisky Twist, Patio Andaluz, Macarena de Flamenco, Gambrinus, and Barcelona de Noche.[23] Starting in the 1970s, she began her gender transition and changed her name to Carmen de Mairena, performing imitations of Sara Montiel, Marujita Días, and other artists without achieving much success. At the beginning of the 2000s, her television appearances transformed her into a media personality.

Ocaña: Cross-Dressing in the Streets in the 1970s

José Pérez Ocaña (Cantillana, 1947–1983) was a visual artist who would most likely fall under the category of performance artist today. As recounted in *Ocaña, la memoria del sol*, a 2009 documentary directed by Juan J. Moreno, his life was suddenly interrupted apparently due to the burns caused by dressing as the sun for Carnival festivities in his town since the dress, made of papier-mâché, was decorated with lighted flares that ended up setting it on fire. Unlike Margarita, the travesti from the Copacabana in Barcelona who emerged unscathed from the self-inflicted fire and kept dancing, Ocaña could not continue her fiery performance and stopped dancing in 1983. This story was narrated two years later by Carlos Cano in his song "Romance a Ocaña":

> She was a crazy, sexually free woman for wanting beer
> The mouth, the brown eyes
> And how beautifully she excited us
> And how pretty, singing on her balcony.
> She watered the roses, watered the carnations
> And between each copla, she dreamed of him.
> It was joy from Las Ramblas,
> Darling won our hearts over. It was the revolution.
> Virgin with a hair combo and shawl
> Feather of a whirlwind fan
> Oh! Virgin like Carmen de Lirio.
> Oh! She left, she left dressed as the day.
> Oh! She left, she left dressed as the sun.
> Oh! She left, the gossips said.

What fire would light her up?
The fire of her heart![24]

Ocaña was one of the few travestis who sang not only coplas, or Spanish songs, but also cante jondo. In addition to this, the fundamental difference for other artists of her time—which translates into a constant hesitancy on the part of the artist to consider herself a cross-dresser or not—resides in the fact that Ocaña was not a variety artist, nor did she work in cabarets and nightclubs, but in other contexts: exhibitions for art galleries and street performances for filming, among others.

Ocaña cross-dresses to provoke, revealing a conflict in terms of gender that cabarets diluted: she knows that the street is not the place to dress as a flamenco dancer, and she knows that doing so disturbs the space of the ordinary and time of everyday life. She walks along Las Ramblas in Barcelona and lifts her skirt to show her sex; she records herself in a cemetery singing a *polo* to the disappeared body of Federico García Lorca;[25] she recreates the procession of the Ascension of the Virgin on August 15 in the Rabal district of Barcelona; and, dressed as a woman and from a balcony, she sings a heartfelt *saeta* to one of her "dolls," a papier-mâché Virgin.[26]

Outside the cinematographic framework, we find various records of her *actuaciones* [performances] in the street, such as the one starring Ocaña in the Libertarian Days (*Jornadas Libertarias*), organized by the Confederación Nacional del Trabajo in Barcelona's Parc Güell in 1977. In it, we see the artist dressed in a polka-dot dress; she wears a necklace and hoop earrings, and her long hair is adorned with flowers. She sings the lyrics of a fandango that say, "People can be seen enjoying themselves," and then says aloud:

> Summer has passed, and now autumn is here, and everything is green-leafed. I want to stay naked like the autumn trees; clothes are useless to me! If I came into the world without clothes because repression has put these four dirty rags on me, I don't want the clothes. I give them to my audience, and here they are, gentlemen. I'm naked.

Ocaña raises her wiry arms and flaps from the outside in and from the inside out while stomping out a kind of double *remate* [phrase closer] two times. She gives two punches with her facial muscles contracted and falls to her knees with her right arm raised. Like the perishing flame of a candle about to be extinguished, the back of her neck dislocated, Ocaña lets the spotlights illuminate her face stained with sweat and makeup, recalling those flesh-colored virgins she referred to at the beginning of her monologue: the prostitutes of Las Ramblas. This little dance has no search for *soniquete* [groove] since the footwork is used as a direct, expressive tool without any stylization. The *patá* or *pataíta* [step sequence] in bulerías becomes a tantrum, and the dance becomes literal. It is what it expresses: a blow.

Ocaña introduces stripping as a symbol of liberation from imposed social codes: clothing, which until then could have been interpreted as a means of identity transformation and semantic displacement of the folkloric, is now shown from the perspective of its social weight. The costume turns into clothing, and the clothing "weighs down." The metaphor of nudity as a primitive stage, prior to the introduction of the social codes typical of the human sphere, as well as that of stripping naked as a liberation from these and regression to that previous happy stage, are somehow crushed by Ocaña because what remains after the act of stripping is the rage and collapse, not liberation.

Nudity, as Giorgio Agamben argues, is "a denudation and a baring, never as a form and a stable possession,"[27] and, therefore, a process that never ends: we always have the impression of not having shed all our layers, real or symbolic, and for this reason Ocaña's performance does not have a happy ending, nor does it allow us to access that hypothetical primordial state where there would be no coercive social codes. Nudity does not exist, per se, but is ontologically and epistemologically indebted to clothing; it is, therefore, impossible to conceive of the existence of one without the other. The only thing that nudity achieves, much like denudation, according to the Italian philosopher, is to "unveil" or reveal the existence of the clothing, of that series of sociocultural codes which "dress us," hiding our individual being at the same time that they grant a collective existence and constitute themselves as a kind of second skin.

But in what terms does Ocaña formulate his own artistic work?[28] We will attend two interviews, one on television and the other on the radio, conducted in 1982 and 1983, respectively. The first, conducted by Terenci Moix (in Catalan; Ocaña responds in Spanish) for his program *Terenci a la fresca*, and the second, by Jesús Quintero for his program *El loco de la colina*, in which we perceive a certain tendency on the part of the host to psychologize the artist by asking him insistently about his life, the suffering and exclusion he experienced due to his sexual tendencies, confused with his effeminate gender identity, which, in turn, leads him to identify himself with domestic activities such as sewing or ironing.

Ocaña says of himself, "I am cross-dressed down to my soul (*yo tengo travestido hasta el alma*). . . . I have no privacy: everything is on the street." The soul is something (a theatrical device?) capable of being cross-dressed: it is not an extracorporeal entity, but something that occurs out there, something that is exposed and that perhaps only exists by being exposed. It is not an essence, but a performance, something we do, an artistic production. Conversely, if the psychic ("soul" as *psyché*) is a theater, all theater—as a space for exhibition and visibility—is a psychic space in which the dynamics of the unconscious activity and a game free of associations intervene in a way that allows the artist from Cantillana to identify the Virgin with the figure of the mother; this one with María, a prostitute from Las Ramblas, and this one, in turn, with himself.

"I imitate myself," Ocaña also tells us: "I dress up as myself." One's relationship with oneself is not one of identity but of imitation. The model or ideal we seek to embody does not precede us and is not someone other than ourselves. Ocaña is not himself when he cross-dresses or imitates a song star or embodies an alter ego, but rather, by imitating himself, in a certain sense, he becomes himself.

What is Ocaña's artistic and human intention with these actions? The artist answers us: "I think that with what I do, I give a lot of joy to the world." Ocaña feels like a "messenger from the gods" whose mission is to fill with color a gray, violent, and depressed society in which he felt he was living. But if the artist tells us that "crying is like laughing" and that he is "someone serious," not "a cow from the fair," what is joy for Ocaña? It is not the ironic humor of the drag shows of his time or that which, as in the logic of Spinozist passions, would oppose sadness: joy is the antonym of hatred, of the lack of love and fear. It is the openness of spirit that allows us to remain attentive to the beauty of the world ("to the flowers, to the birds," he tells us); it is the openness that allows us to remain curious toward others beyond the "touches or caresses"—as Ortega y Gassett said—that their entry into our lives may produce.

Enrique, the Cripped Travesti

In all honesty, we have to say that Ocaña was not the only flamenco travesti who went out into a public space dressed as a woman "to see what was happening." Without placing it at the moment it happened, Sevillian bailaor and maestro Enrique, "El Cojo" (1912–1985), about whom we will talk in more detail at the end of this book, tells something in an interview with José Luis Ortiz Nuevo that, more than an anecdote, could be considered a flamenco *happening*: free, fleeting, and unnoticed by most passersby.

> A curious thing happened to me once. It was Holy Innocents' Day, and they didn't know what trick to play. So, I say to Illanes: "You want a good prank?" And he says, "What are we going to do?" I say, "I'm going to dress as a woman." . . . I put on makeup, got dressed, and stood next to the fireplace, looking at a catalog of Illanes's sculptures. Then the whole Town Hall was there, and everyone gasped. People came in and out and said, "Who is that?" "It's Princess Olga." I don't remember which country they said she was from. Belgium? No. From Norway, they said. And one came out and said, "But there aren't any princesses in Norway right now." "Well, she is a Norwegian princess. The only thing is she doesn't speak a lick of Spanish."
>
> I took out my cigarette, and all the men started offering me their lighters so I could light it. They came to greet me, and I gave them my hand, held it out to them, and they kissed it. The only thing I messed up was eating; I was starving.
>
> And there was a lady named Salud Beca next to the fireplace with her bag, and I tugged on her bag so she could meet me because I really wanted to laugh. And she said, "What a strange lady! Please stop pulling on my bag." And, then, Quique Hidalgo says, "Of course, one close look at the princess, and it's the spitting image of Enrique el Cojo."[29]

The context that makes El Cojo's action interesting lies in the fact that it occurred in the studio of a sculptor, Antonio Illanes (1901–1976), who specialized in religious imagery. His studio in Seville, through which the crème de la crème of Seville and some foreigners passed, became a costumbrist set in which Enrique, dressed as a woman, distractedly looked through a catalog of virgins and Christs. At the same time, representatives of the city council—we assume Francoists—walked around him, mistaking him for a foreign princess.

Beyond the unquestionable sense of humor of the time, we wonder about the politics of such an action, not only because it was carried out on Holy Innocents' Day, during which this kind of thing is supposed "to be allowed," but also the fact that no one seemed to notice. It seems that at least part of the subversive character of drag resides in its disclosure as a farce, fiction, or hoax and that those people who had greeted Enrique, who had given him a light, and who had kissed his hand realized that the "foreign princess" was a man. Is it for this reason that in Ventura Pons's *Retrato intermitente*, when Ocaña walks down Las Ramblas dressed as a woman and, greeting passersby, suddenly lifts his dress to show his butt and penis? In this short circuit between truth and disguise seems to reside the great provocation of the travesti, since he assumes that the heterosexual men who had previously treated him as a woman can realize that he was actually a man and find themselves—perhaps because they felt a certain desire toward him—in the shameful position of a faggot (*maricón*).

Trans Flamenco Women

Thanks to the recent work of Raúl Solís Galván (2019) and Valeria Vegas (2019), we have begun to have access to the testimony of trans folk artists, often confused with drag queens (*travestis*) or gays at a stage in our history in which the gender identity, gender expression, and sexual identity were intermingled in the collective imagination, not only of hetero- and cisgender people but also in that of the LGBTQ+ collective.

One of these artists is María José Navarro (Seville, 1953), whose stage name is "La Otra Pantoja." She worked in the travesti group Esmeralda de Sevilla with other artists, such as Candela, Triana, Lola de Sevilla, Orquidia, and Mayi.[30]

As for "La Petróleo" (Cádiz, 1944) and "La Salvaora" (Cádiz, 1951), the agent Manuel Portela hired them in the 1970s and proposed that they form a flamenco group made up exclusively of trans women (*mujeres transexuales*) and accompanied musically by two Gitano guitarists.[31] Under the name of Las Folclóricas Gaditanas, this group achieved enormous success, earning 5,000 pesetas ($394.50) a night at a time when the guaranteed monthly income (*salario mínimo interprofesional*) was 13,200 pesetas ($1,041.48). In 1986, they signed a contract to work in Miami, where they stayed for over two years, earning 12,000 pesetas ($946.80) a night.[32]

Soraya González (Seville, 1951), "La del Puente de Triana," began as an artist of Esmeralda's cuadro and ended up working at the famous Gay Club in Madrid, where she earned about two thousand pesetas, "ten times more than in Seville."[33] Other cases include that of Manolita Saborido (Arcos de la Frontera, 1943), who, after winning a singing contest promoted by the brothel performing "La morena de la copla," by Manolo Escobar, was hired by Paco España and became a leading lady in Barcelona with the stage name "Bella Helen,"[34] or that of Enloquecida Josette (La Solana, 1952), who imitated Lola Flores and worked in venues around Madrid such as Centauros, Sacha's, Gay Club, and Minotauro.[35]

Tamara (Benalmádena, 1960–1995) was ethnically Gitana and, according to Cristian de Samil, in addition to imitating Lolita and Isabel Pantoja, could have been an excellent bailaora had it not been for her trans identity, which prevented her from having a place in the little dancing world that also could have been hers.[36] Tamara herself worked in Madrid in the Dimas and Centauros lounges and alternated artistic work with prostitution until she died in 1995 due to complications from AIDS.[37]

Drag (Travestismo) in Flamenco Companies Starting in 1990

Beyond "purely gay" shows, in the world of theater we can begin to name examples of travestismo, both men and women, from 1990 to 2000. In the case of women, the use of masculine clothing (pants, vest, shirt) is fundamentally linked to the interpretation of the *farruca*. This dance became an emblem of flamenco masculinity in the 1960s.[38] Sara Baras seems to have been the first bailaora to reappropriate this dance and its "masculine aesthetic":

ABC: You perform a farruca, a traditionally masculine dance, and wear pants.
SARA BARAS: I was very excited to dance it again. I did it six or seven years ago for the first time, and I didn't expect it to cause such a reaction. I perfectly remember putting it together almost in secret, with two guitarists, and I didn't even tell my mother, who later cried when she saw it. It is a dance that makes me feel fulfilled, in which I feel very comfortable.
ABC: Gades has been the person who has danced the farruca the best.
SARA BARAS: He's been the great maestro. The first day I danced the farruca after his death, I dedicated it to him in silence. And I have included some of his steps in my dance. At first, they didn't come out quite right, but now they come out perfectly. Gades has taught the newer generations a lot, as a dancer, choreographer, and person. Spanish dance is going to miss him a lot. For me, every minute I shared with him and all the corrections and advice he gave me were very useful.[39]

Based on these statements from 2004, we could understand Sara Baras's cross-dressing as a tribute to the figure of Antonio Gades,[40] a tribute that does not intend to reconstruct or reproduce his farruca identically but instead tries to create a link between the past and the present following a logic of recognition and gratitude. After Baras, other bailaoras will dance the farruca fully or partially dressed like men, sometimes mixing "feminine" garments, such as a skirt, and other "masculine" items, such as a shirt or vest. However, for the other bailaoras (Mercedes Ruiz,[41] María Pagés,[42] Concha Jareño[43]), the farruca does not constitute a tribute to a specific figure in the History of flamenco dance. It is a kind of game with the codes of flamenco masculinity in which signs, gestures, or garments commonly used in men's dancing are literally incorporated (rectilinear lines of movement, long sequences of footwork, pirouettes, and falls to the ground).[44]

In the case of men, some feminine accessories started to be used, such as the bata de cola, one of the first cases being that of Joaquín Cortés in his 1996 show *Pasión gitana,* in which a contemporary dancer with a naked torso appears dancing with a sort of bata de cola and trouser combo. In 2014, at the Festival Flamenco de Jerez de la Frontera, Manuel Liñán danced a *caracoles* choreography wearing a bata de cola and shawl as a guest dancer in the production *Los invitados* by Belén Maya. He repeated this choreography in *Nómada,* a show he put on with his company that same year. Despite not being the first time that a flamenco dancer appeared onstage in a bata de cola or semi-cross-dressed, the media impact had on the flamenco world was so big that the following year, in 2015, he appeared as the poster image for the same festival with the bata de cola and shawl. In 2016, Manuel Liñán once again took out the bata de cola in a new show by his company, *Reversible,* and in the Certamen Coreográfico de Danza Española de Madrid, Emilio Ochando's company won first prize for group choreography with the piece "Timevo," danced by a group of four male dancers wearing a bata de cola.[45]

A second case of male drag (*travestismo masculino*) in the flamenco theatrical sphere occurs in the context of narrative ballets in which male dancers play female characters. One of these cases is found in 1992 with the character of Carmen's double, played by Juan Hidalgo in a loose version of Mérimée-Bizet's *Carmen* performed by the Ballet de Rafael Aguilar. This double of Carmen, who appears in the show around the sixtieth minute,[46] performs a duet with the real Carmen, proposing not so much an impersonation by the travesti as a game of mirrors: on a large table located in the center of the scene that serves as a tablao, Carmen executes practically the same gestures that the cross-dresser does on the floor until he gets on the table to dance a duet in which the two Carmens perform contortions, sometimes simulating postures similar to those of intercourse, and without taking her eyes off Don José, who is sitting on one side of the table-tablao and watching them. At the end of this duet, Don José takes the *real* Carmen in his arms, and the other, who is at the same time her lover, her double, her shadow, and her reflection, disappears. In this way, Aguilar leaves doubts about the ontological status of the travesti in the air without undoing the ambiguity of a scene in which we do not know whether the choreographer wants us to see a Carmen who likes to sleep with cross-dressers, or with various men at the same time, or wants to show us a Don José who has doubts about his sexuality but ends up choosing the real Carmen and not the travesti.

Another case of men cross-dressing as female characters can be found in 1997 in the *Suite de La casa de Bernarda Alba*, directed by Lluís Pasqual.[47] In it all the characters, except one, are played by men dressed as women in mourning. The mother's character, Bernarda Alba, is also interpreted—in the same way as in Mats Ek's neoclassical creation from 1978—by a man, in this case, Antonio Canales.

Drag and Nostalgia in the 2010s

I have tried to show how transformistas from the late nineteenth and early twentieth centuries, as well as travestis from the 1960s–1970s, imitated well-known performers of their respective eras. It is curious to see that present-day travestis maintain a memory-based relationship with flamenco and folklore and, instead of imitating current artists—as they do in the pop music field—they continue to imitate deceased singers and copla singers, like Lola Flores or Rocío Jurado. This practice is visible in artists like Kika Lorace, whose version of "El partido de la amistad," filmed in the tablao Villarrosa, includes in its video clip version a well-known anecdote by the artist Lola Flores, in which she interrupted the flow of a performance that was being presented at the Florida Park lounge in Madrid when she realized that she had lost an earring "that had cost her a lot of money."[48]

Another case study of a flamenco artist who references the past is that of "Nacha la Macha," a travesti singer who references not only the phrases or anecdotes associated with Lola Flores and other artists but also their gestures. The video clip for the song "Eres cobarde," for example, starts with a sound file in which Lola Flores is heard introducing the artist as follows: "She alone is a very important voice, a temperament, young, pretty, and I won't say anything more."[49] In the video clip, we see posters of a Flores concert alongside others advertising Nacha la Macha, who will appear dancing in the middle of a field of poppies wearing a black bata de cola similar to the one worn by Lola in the film *Sevillanas* (1992), by Carlos Saura.[50]

In another song, "Como la copla no hay ná," the artist expresses her love for the copla and, dancing in a red bata de cola in Madrid's Puerta del Sol, cites the names of those artists who have made an impression on her: Lola Flores, Concha Piquer, Juanita Reina, Gracia Montes, Rocío Jurado, and Isabel Pantoja.[51] In the video clip of one last song, "Muérete," the character of other folk artists is not embodied but that of the Virgin Mary, taking up the aesthetics of Holy Week processions.[52] We see voguing Nazarenes and a Nacha la Macha dressed in black with a headscarf and decorative comb. Images of Córdoba's city center are superimposed on shots of the Teatro Flamenco de Madrid, in which a bare-chested flamenco singer sings a saeta. As in other video clips, folk elements, which refer to the religious world and bullfighting, are mixed with images of pop artists such as Alaska and Madonna.

What kind of woman do artists like Rocío Jurado or Lola Flores represent so that travestis continue to identify with them and not with other current singers? Is there something in the character they offer us onstage that transcends them and that their personality possesses in a "conceptual" way? If we focus on the case of these two significant figures, we immediately realize that, despite their commonalities, each of them offers us a completely different model of a woman: Rocío Jurado is a figural character whose presence is enhanced by makeup, teased hair, and dresses, which enlarge her figure with fabric wings that make her body superhuman. Jurado can move around the stage and decorate her songs with small dance steps. Yet, fundamentally, she appears in front of the audience like a divinity statue who raises her arms, letting her voice, excellent and infinite, braid itself like a honeysuckle around her figure. "The greatest" has weight, majesty, and firmness, like an Arcana card from the Tarot of Marseille to which we could pray.

As for Flores, she is characterized less by the weight of her figure than by her flamboyant character, by an overflow of energy that breaks all the norms and makes the "essence" of her art originate and remain between the singing, dancing, and spoken words. If Jurado was an exceptional singer who placed her body in service of her voice, Flores allows the emotion to rise inside of her until she is suffocated, making her gesture and voice burst out beyond her cry, and puts forward onstage a woman possessed, stuck, on the verge of drowning from her own emotion, but victorious in the end. It shows us someone who knows the strength of emotions and does not respect limits but feels alive through them, who feels that living means going in with open arms and wide eyes upon finding joy and sorrow.

After the performance, we could imagine Jurado returning to an alcove while Flores would be worn-out after a visionary ritual that has left her exhausted. In both cases, we can feel the power, excess presence, and resistance of the bodies of two women who "stand firm." Perhaps for this reason, they continue to be sources of inspiration with which many travestis identify because they provide them with a posture, gestures, looks, and a "way of being" with which life is easier.

The Aesthetic Transitions of Flamenco

> The specter of Franco and Francoism will mark the period of political transition as the space of the Lacanian Real, the ominous place where "something else is projected," something that is at the origin of the signifying chain but outside of the signified. The democratic Transition is seen, thus, as the moment of a psychic negotiation with a brutal and totalitarian patriarchal structure (Franco and Francoism) to which we had become addicted.[53]

As Vilarós indicates, the democratic Transition was driven both by a desire for change on the part of an important segment of the population and by a change in the libidinal economy on both sides of the stage. For a broad portion of the public, it produced a desire to move away from certain cultural referents associated with Francoism and, for artists, a desire to channel the desire for repressed freedom and the need to break with everything that had limited it. In the 1970s, flamenco music was transformed to respond to its own desire and that of its audience. The flamenco wailing (*queijo*) of some artists became a complaint, a political protest committed to social critique and the end of the dictatorship.

Musically, two phenomena develop in parallel. On the one hand, there is the enormous success of guitarists like Paco de Lucía and Manolo Sanlúcar in 1975, thanks to the release of the rumbas "Entre dos aguas" and "Caballo negro," which marked the entry of flamenco into the musical universe. On the other hand, there is the appearance of a certain number of socially committed singers, such as Manuel Gerena, José Menese, "El Cabrero," or Enrique Morente, who continue to sing traditional melodies but transform the lyrics of their songs to give them a political dimension.

In dance, the touristy tablaos go on to coexist with other theatrical ideas of narrative styles that use different types of expressive means to tell stories whose underlying idea is usually the social and political repression of a disadvantaged group.[54] This is the case, for example, of *Quejío* (1972), by La Cuadra de Sevilla—formed three years earlier—in which we see a bailaor tied up with ropes, using footwork to try to escape.[55] The symbolism of this impeded gesture as a sign of freedom "handcuffed" by the Franco regime seems to have been very clear, given that this gesture was taken up years later by Mario Maya in a piece created in 1976 on the historical marginalization of the Gitanos, "Camelamos naquerar." In it, Maya does not appear tied up by ropes symbolizing an invisible power but rather trapped in the arms of two men who hold him by his fists.

From Spanish Ballet to Flamenco Ballet

Apart from the expressive needs of the sociopolitical kind typical of this historical moment, another distinct artistic format, the *ballet flamenco* [flamenco ballet or dance company], would achieve enormous success and remain the predominant show model for many years after the Transition. The discontinuous continuity between the first Spanish ballets of the 1920s, those of the late 1940s and 1950s, and the flamenco ballet of the 1970s has the form of a certain familial ancestry, given the participation of Encarnación López, "La Argentinita," in this Spanish avant-garde movement. La Argentinita was also the older sister of Pilar López (1912–2008), whose Spanish ballet featured the presence, during the 1960s, of two famous dancers: Mario Maya, between 1956 and 1958, and Antonio Gades, from 1951 onward.

For two fundamental reasons, Antonio Gades (1936–2004) could be considered the most important representative of flamenco ballet. First, his appointment as the first director of the Ballet Nacional de España in 1978 allowed him to expand his theatrical style during the two years of his direction. During that time, he created a repertoire comprising not only pieces by other renowned choreographers from the world of Spanish dance—such as Mariemma, Antonio Ruiz Soler, Pilar López, and Rafael Aguilar—but also his own pieces, such as his version of *Bodas de sangre* from 1974.

Furthermore, Gades was the subject of enormous media coverage because of the trilogy of movies he filmed with Carlos Saura: *Bodas de sangre* in 1981, *Carmen* in 1983, and *El amor brujo* in 1986. This last piece also reminds us of that discontinuous continuity that I addressed already between flamenco ballet and the first Spanish ballets of the early twentieth century, given that this ballet film proposes a flamenco version of the homonymous ballet premiered on March 15, 1915, at the Teatro Lara in Madrid, created for Pastora Imperio and recreated ten years later by Antonia Mercé, "La Argentina," in Paris. The discontinuous continuity is also produced in narrative terms since the flamenco ballets systematically narrate heterosexual romantic love stories, seasoned with obstacles of different kinds and articulated around love triangles that tinge the environment with jealousy and deadly revenge. This theme of love and violence creates the artistic need to rehabilitate the choreographic form of the duo, much less important in flamenco than the solo, perhaps transforming the scopic impulse of the spectator—who observed the beauty of solo bodies with pleasure—into "voyeurism" of danced paired relationships in which passion, understood as an excess of energy and the fused touch of the performers, prevails.

Trio of Duets: *El Amor Brujo, Bodas de Sangre,* and *Carmen*

It is essential to bring to light here that the libretto for *El amor brujo*, although for a long time it was thought to have been written by Gregorio Martínez Sierra, was the work of his wife, Maria de la O Lejárraga García (1874–1974). This feminist writer, a librettist and playwright, conceived texts of fundamental interest for the feminist movement of her time, such as *Cartas a las mujeres de España* (1914), *Feminismo, feminidad, y españolismo* (1917), and the five lectures delivered in 1931 in the Ateneo de Madrid for the *La mujer ante la república* cycle: "Realidad,"[56] "Egoísmo" (in defense of the republic), "Religión," "Federación" (about autonomies), and "Libertad,"[57] the latter being the one that more precisely addressed the specific problems of women, in relation to both the situation experienced up until that moment and what the future should bring.

In addition to joining the PSOE [Socialist Workers' Party] that same year, she had participated in the founding of the Unión de Mujeres de España in 1917 and, in 1932, began programming for the Asociación Femenina de Cultura Cívica, of which she was one of the developers, generating the magazine *Cultura integral y femenina*. In 1933, she was elected as a congressional representative for Granada, and in 1936, she was elected as commercial attaché of the Spanish delegation in Berne. After her dismissal in 1937, she began a lengthy exile in France, Mexico, and Argentina, where she eventually died. It would be of great value to carry out a comparative study between Lejárraga's political texts and her dramatic texts—of a much more costumbrist style—to assess to what extent the stories narrated onstage by the author in some way manifest her concerns about the place of women in society and how so-called romantic love is part of a relational politics that makes women an affective subject of men and becomes something it is necessary to question. In *El amor brujo*, Lejárraga traces a love triangle between Candela, her deceased husband—who, jealous, pursues her from beyond (the Specter)—and Carmelo, Candela's new lover. To put an end to this phantasmagoric chase and dissipate the haunting, Carmelo uses another girl, Lucía, as bait so that she seduces and distracts the Specter when he reappears, thus buying time to give Candela the "love's perfect kiss" that will undo the haunting.

Let us return to the other two ballet films by Saura and Gades and focus on their plots. In *Bodas de sangre*, a tragedy written by Federico García Lorca in 1931 that premiered on March 8, 1933, at the Beatriz Theater in Madrid, the Bride escapes on her wedding day with Leonardo, her former lover. The consequent outcome is a knife duel between the groom and Leonardo, which Gades dramatized in a scene without music and in slow motion that allows us to see in detail the movements of the fight and the frightened faces of the two men, who end up collapsing.

Finally, *Carmen*'s plot is probably the best known of all. Carmen seduces Don José, a French corporal whose passion for Carmen leads him to abandon his former love, rebel against his superior, and join a group of smugglers. When Carmen decides to leave with another man, the bullfighter Escamillo, Don José, moved by a fit of jealousy, murders her.

Despite her fatal fate, as the researcher Fernández-Montesinos Gurruchaga argues, Carmen, after the invention of the literary character by Prosper Mérimée in 1845 and its operatic translation by George Bizet thirty years later, became the universal Spanish woman: a woman with black eyes, passionate, unpredictable, and dangerous. Beyond the novel and the operatic revivals, we must not forget the more than 150 films that, according to Varela Ortega,[58] have been produced based on this plot, as well as fifteen great ballets (classical, neoclassical, Spanish classical, and flamenco), created both in Spain and abroad: in 1949 by the Ballet de la Ópera de París, with choreography by Roland Petit, and in 1965 by the Ballet Nacional de Cuba, with choreography by Alberto Alonso (classical dance);[59] in 1976 the film *La Carmen*, by Julio Diamante, with bailaora Sara Lezana in the role of Carmen and the presence of, among others, singer Enrique Morente, bailaores Rafael de Córdova and Enrique el Cojo, and travesti artist Paco España; in 1983 the ballet film by Carlos Saura with Antonio Gades in the leading role (flamenco); in 1992 the neoclassical ballet by Mats Ek and the flamenco version by Rafael Aguilar; in 1999 the version by Salvador Távora (flamenco and theater dance); in 2001 by the Ballet Flamenco de Madrid, directed by Sara Lezana; in 2006 by Aída Gómez (stylized Spanish dance) and the Royal Ballet of London, choreographed by Francesca Zambello; in 2007 the flamenco version by Sara Baras; in 2014 *Yo, Carmen* by Compañía María Pagés (flamenco); in 2015 the neoclassical version by the Compañía Nacional de Danza de España, choreographed by Johan Inger, and *Carmen VS Carmen* from the Compañía Ibérica de Danza (Spanish dance); in 2017 a new neoclassical version by the Ballet de Víctor Ullate; in 2018 *Carmen(s)* by José Montalvo; and so on.

Perhaps Carmen is not just a character or a stereotype of a woman, but the name we could give to the politics of the gaze that I have tried to describe in the first chapter of this book. Carmen is an object of desire, and although she does not represent a passive or submissive woman, her freedom is penalized by murder. Carmen is the concept in which the logic of the scopic drive is summarized, which distributes roles and positions of power and penalizes the transgressions of an unwritten norm that, however, has the force of law. To what extent is the stylization of gender violence and murder onstage innocent? Can we live in a violence-free society when we systematically "kill" women onstage living their lives freely? What should we do with Carmen so there are no more women who, like her, are killed because of men's jealousy? Should we abandon the show to tell other stories? Should we perhaps modify the play's plot and "save" Carmen in the final scene? Should we conduct a cultural mediation exercise—before, during, or after the show—that would allow us to contextualize the work in its historical moment and would allow us to measure the distance between our current society and the one described by Mérimée? A reading complementary to the one I propose here is one by Iñaki Vázquez in his chapter "La memoria contra el silencio sistémico: La resistencia de la disidencia sexual y de género romaní contra el mutismo antigitano":[60]

> Carmen shows an image of a Gitana woman opposite a non-Gitana [*paya*] woman of the time. Does this projection respond to the reality of Gitana women in Seville at the beginning of the nineteenth century? Absolutely not. It responds to the non-Gitano neurotic obsession of asserting oneself by displaying Gitano alterity.

The author makes us see here, beyond the moralizing end of the work in terms of gender violence, how *Carmen* makes "the Gitana" a stereotype that serves to embody the negative of the ideal woman of the time, since "For the hetero-patriarchal system, in this historical context, women had to be pious, religious, sexually inexperienced, obedient to male dominance, and of course, cut off from the salaried world."[61] That is to say, the opposite of Carmen. From this point of view, indispensable in order to understand what is at stake in the configuration of one of the most important stereotypes associated with both flamenco and Spanish identity in general, the construction of Carmen as a conceptual character would only be one more instance within the historical repetition of a gesture that makes "the female Gitana" or "the male Gitano" the equivalent of the abject:

> It should not be overlooked that the image projected of the Gitana woman in this operatic work is so far from the one that is projected today, in which the anti-Gitano prejudice tells us that Gitana women are submissive, obedient, and sexually inexperienced. The question is obvious: Is it not that the prevailing values for women today are independence, supposed sexual freedom, and non-subordination to the partner, among others? Anyone who knows more than two Gitana women will realize that this projection does not respond to the diversity, complexity, and living conditions of the majority of Gitanas in this country.[62]

The Decline of the Tablao and the Birth of Contemporary Flamenco Dance

The tablao and flamenco ballet as performance models and ways of life continue to exist without essentially modifying their dynamics until the

2000s. However, perhaps because of the better economic conditions of this post-transitional moment, the model of flamenco ballet and big companies won out, and the tablaos began to be considered places "for tourists" and low quality.

According to Blanca del Rey (Córdoba, 1946)—bailaora, choreographer, and widow of the owner of the tablao El Corral de la Morería, which opened in 1957—this devaluation of the tablao became common in the 1990s due to the better conditions offered by companies. This resulted in a "diaspora" of the most qualified artists, whose positions in the tablaos started to be filled by regular artists, who, despite the semi-improvised structure of the shows, ended up falling into routine and boredom. Mario Maya provides an example of this nascent boredom in an interview given in 1970, collected by José María Velázquez-Gaztelu and reprinted by Navarro García in the volume mentioned earlier of his *Historia del baile flamenco*:

> The owner of the Torres Bermejas tablao, where I danced, didn't know much about flamenco—he was only successful in business—and on one occasion, I told him I was leaving. I was bored with always dancing the same thing and wasn't interested in continuing the routine.[63]

Unlike the tablao, flamenco ballet allows character work that entails a specific gesture—often approached through mime—and a different wardrobe. The performer's individuality, a fundamental aesthetic value of flamenco tablaos, is found here by acting abilities that allow the dancers, at least in theory, to go beyond themselves in artistic terms. Additionally, flamenco ballet permits the development of a greater diversity of choreographic forms, which in the tablao are limited to the form of the solo and, eventually, the duet (in the sevillanas, for example). In its balleticized version, flamenco can propose solos and duets—often performed by the protagonists—and group choreographies where individual identity is erased behind the collective "corps de ballet," which often translates into the joint execution of the same choreography. Flamenco ballet also proposes a different scenographic approach, not only related to the possibility of introducing scenery but also the entrances to and exits from the scenic space and the distribution of the dancers in the space, often recreating geometric shapes, such as circles, semicircles, diagonals, and straight lines, always honoring the spatial hierarchy that privileges the center with respect to the periphery and the frontal area of the stage in the background.

If in the tablao we only had one "set" (not considered as such),[64] a single character ("himself," not considered as such), the same spectacular structure (one dance after another, interspersed with singing and guitar solos), two choreographic forms (basically solo and duet), a single spatial arrangement (front: the musicians behind and the dancers in front), and two very limited possibilities of starting and ending the dance (entering the stage from the dressing rooms or getting up from the chair when one is already present onstage), the artistic options multiply with flamenco ballet, in spite of which this format will also become worn-out due to the repetition of the same stage formula. Faced with this situation of double boredom (of the tablaos and the flamenco ballets), a certain number of artists will start creating their own dance companies to create "more personal" projects after having gone through tablaos and the big companies, such as those led by Antonio Gades and Mario Maya, who created the Compañía Andaluza de Danza en Sevilla (renamed the Ballet Flamenco de Andalucía in 2004), in which four of the most influential contemporary flamenco artists crossed paths: Maya's daughter Belén Maya, Israel Galván, and two students of Matilde Coral, Isabel Bayón and Rafaela Carrasco.

In this context, María Pagés (Seville, 1963) created her own company in 1990 after passing through Antonio Gades's company and participating in Carlos Saura's films *Carmen, El amor brujo*, and, later, *Flamenco*. In 1992, Joaquín Cortés (Córdoba, 1969) created his first show, *Cibayí*, after dancing in the Ballet Nacional de España. In 1993, the company Increpación Danza was born in Barcelona, directed by Montse Sánchez and Ramón Baeza.

In 1996, Belén Maya (New York, 1966) presented *La diosa dentro de nosotros* after making her debut in Madrid's tablaos (Café de Chinitas, Zambra, and El Corral de la Pacheca) and dancing in the company of her father, Mario Maya. The same year, the company Arrieritos was born, composed of Tasha González, Elena Santonja, Patricia Torrero, Florencio Campo, Kelian Jiménez, and Teresa Nieto. They debuted in Madrid with the piece *Arrieritos somos*.

In 1998, Juan Carlos Lérida (Seville, 1971) created the company 2D1 in Barcelona. The same year, Israel Galván (Seville, 1973) presented the first show of his company at the Bienal de Flamenco de Sevilla, *¡Mira!/Los zapatos rojos*, after passing through, among others, the Compañía Andaluza de Danza. Also in 1998, Eva Yerbabuena (Frankfurt, 1970) created her own company after working in Rafael Aguilar's company and being in the corps de ballet of Javier Latorre's (Valencia, 1963) production *La fuerza del destino* and Manolete's (Granada, 1945) *El amor brujo*. In 2000, Andrés Marín (Seville, 1969) created his own company.

The path of contemporary flamenco dance continued to develop in the 2000s, producing an accumulation of individual projects conceived by dancers from large companies, in which they had worked as part of the "corps de ballet," as impassioned members of a larger body to which they no longer wanted to belong slipped into other terrains to germinate new identities: in 2005, Olga Pericet (1975), Daniel Doña (1977), and Marco Flores (1980) create their company Chanta La Mui ("Shut Up" in Caló). In 2006, Rocío Molina (Málaga, 1984) created her own company and first show, *El eterno retorno*, for the Festival Flamenco de Jerez de la Frontera after having danced in María Pagés's company. In 2009, the Festival Flamenco Empírico was born in Barcelona, curated by Juan Carlos Lérida. In 2010, Carlos Saura directed the film *Flamenco, flamenco*, a sequel to *Flamenco* (1995). In 2011, Olga Pericet created her own company with the show *Rosa, metal y ceniza*, after the dissolution of Chanta La Mui and her tenure in the companies of Rafael Amargo and Rafaela Carrasco.

This phenomenon of "dismemberment" from dancers who had formed part of the corps de ballets of large companies seems to be inseparable from a certain drive for differentiation typical of the establishment of a homogenizing middle class, in which individuals seek to distinguish themselves, as researcher Daniel Bernabé argues, through the "diversity market" (*mercado de la diversidad*).[65] This middle class settled definitively in Spain between the second term of José María Aznar (2000–2004) and the initial years of the government of José Luis Rodríguez Zapatero (2004–2008).[66]

Following Bernabé, the middle class "is not a class in and of itself in terms of its relationship with production, but rather a construction between culture and purchasing power [that] has spread to all strata of society, not in a material way, that is, by way of wealth, but through a perceived and aspirational form."[67] Could we consider contemporary flamenco dancing, from this perspective, not only as an artistic phenomenon that comes to generate aesthetic reforms or ruptures in so-called traditional flamenco, but also as a "middle-class art," simultaneously searching for individuality and, nevertheless, profoundly homogeneous? What do we artists lose when all our artistic work revolves around the desire—or the need—to be "original" or carry out "very personal" projects? Does the horizon of the collective not blur in some way? Did these artists abandon the uncritical mass of the corps de ballet to become carefree individualists? How is the happy medium between the two negotiated in the creative sphere?[68]

We would be making a grave mistake if we understood "contemporary flamenco dance" to be exclusively connected to a desire for individual differentiation on the part of the artists. In this search, which often seems like an escape, desires of various kinds are intermingled with psychological needs of a much deeper nature that are derived from the potential hostility of the work environment for people who do not meet the bodily, psychological, intellectual, or identity-based standards that constitute the "invisible score" respected and followed by all. For LGBTQ+ people with a high intellectual curiosity—with "heightened abilities" or not—or other differential identity traits, work in the tablao or large companies could become an absolute nightmare, which is why creating "solo" projects became both an artistic and a vital alternative.

The Erotic Capital of Bailaores

We will close this chapter by trying to account for one of the elements of that "invisible score" that seems to undergo various transformations with the advent of democracy: the erotic capital of bodies. In the film *Flamenco* (1995), directed by Carlos Saura, the dancer Joaquín Cortés (Córdoba, 1969) dances a "sexy" farruca. Against a background of amber light, the dancer appears bare-chested, dressed in black pants. The scene as a whole gives us the impression of a seductive relationship between the dancer—young, handsome, and slim—and the audience. Cortés enters the scene, takes off his jacket, and plays with it, making a semicircular movement similar to the one bullfighters make with their cape, finally letting it fall to the ground. The classic moment in the performance of this farruca, in which the dancer faces the audience slightly diagonally and with his feet together, slowly raising his arms in a sign of reverence or greeting, becomes here a moment of bodily display of the dancer who agrees to be observed, perhaps desired. However, this "turning into a display" by Cortés does not lead him to abandon an exhibition of his technical virtuosity. He will sprinkle the rest of his choreography with pirouettes and rapid footwork.

The conversion of the male body into an erotic object in such a clear way—which is not to say that it did not previously exist with other beautiful bodies, such as those of José Greco or Antonio Gades—could constitute an important step in terms of gender, since traditionally, according to the famous formula of John Berger, "*Men act* and *women appear*," which means that the activities to "offer oneself" were considered as typically feminine and that offering oneself as the object of the gaze could implicate one in the "chance of being feminized."[69]

Nevertheless, another reading of this gesture is possible by considering a change in the distribution of roles in the logic of the gaze and accepting that women can begin to occupy, publicly and accepted by all, the role of observers. In this case, progress in terms of gender would have to do not only with the possibility of men becoming the object of the gaze but with the possibility of women being the ones who look at, desire, and even objectify bodies.

One would have to wonder if the true progress concerning the erotic objectification of bodies has to do with the democratic access of all bodies (men, women, and others) to the field of the gaze or with the very abolition of that scopic logic that objectifies desirable bodies. At the same time that dancers begin to assert their right to be looked at erotically, some bailaoras denounce the violence of said gaze, "both from the musicians and from the spectators," to which they feel subjected. Belén Maya tells us:

> I get into an image of the bailaora they ask of me from the outside because I'm afraid of having another image that might not be very outwardly feminine. Right? So I try to be very feminine according to what they tell me from the outside, according to what the critics tell me or the flamenco tradition tells me. It doesn't have to be a person but rather the elite of the flamenco tradition. Suddenly I enter that little box that they tell me because I'm afraid of being another type of woman, so I have to be the woman that flamenco says I have to be: in my opinion, that is machismo.[70]

It is essential to emphasize that the implicit violence in the demand for bodily beauty or erotic capital, denounced here by Maya, not only implies "having a pretty face" and enhancing it through clothing, accessories, and makeup but also, and fundamentally, being thin. Although thinness seems to have been a constant feature of beauty for centuries, as the sociologist José Luis Moreno Pestaña argues, the 1980s and 1990s seem to have been decisive in the emphasis that thinness came to be an essential feature of "beautiful" bodies for both men and women.[71] The World Health Organization initiated the fight against obesity in 1990, and in 1997, the Body Mass Index was reduced to twenty-five points in order to broaden the range within which "overweight" people fall. We should perhaps add, in the case of flamenco, the imprint that the aesthetics of ballet must have had on the flamenco art form, given its markedly formalist nature, which reinforces the ideal of homogenous and stylized bodies capable of creating "beautiful figures." This is supported by Moreno Pestaña, based on various interviews with bailaoras that he has conducted:

> Aesthetic correctness in flamenco, therefore, includes thinness. Consequently, specific measures must accompany the remodeling of the body: it does not allow, in order to feel aesthetically presentable, the shortcut of expensive and quality clothing. . . . The bodily restriction is placed within the everyday landscape.[72]

One of the interviewees states that before the end of the eighties, bailaores "didn't dance with their torsos out unless it was a [specific] work; they didn't dance. Plus, there were chubby ones; there were thicker bailaoras. The problem of 'Oh, I'm chubby' was not an issue. Now they're all very worried. A chubby bailaora is entertaining, and there are some, but most of them are all flat, with extremely slim bodies. It's another dance. It produces another aesthetic."[73]

Faced with this logic of desire, a certain number of bailaoras, whom researcher Hayes calls *antiguapas* [anti-beauties], position themselves by developing different strategies to disrupt the spectator's gaze.[74] In the case of Pastora Galván, sister of Israel Galván, who co-choreographed the show *La francesa* (2007), it is about ridiculing the stereotype of Carmen.[75] Yet, in the case of Rocío Molina, according to the American researcher, it is about the launch of an unstructured gesture that had previously only been developed by men like Andrés Marín and the same Israel Galván.[76]

Finally, in the case of Belén Maya, and according to Hayes's point of view, the strategy has to do with developing a choreographic vocabulary and representing other ideas that depart from the imaginary traditionally associated with the flamenco universe.[77] We can verify this strategy by seeing the bulería she performed for the famous Saura film in 1995, built on five choreographic scenes. In the first scene, we see the musicians and dancers seated around a table listening to singing as a staging of "useflamenco"—following the expression of Cruces Roldán. In the second, Maya appears unfolklorized, dressed in a plain olive-green dress without flowers or polka-dot print, and her hair simply brushed with a bow, without combs or accessories. She dances to a ternary rhythm without singing or guitar, relying only on the rhythmic skeleton of the percussion, going through the scene from one end to the other and introducing new gestures executed with force and precision without breaking her facial expression. At one point, the bailaora looks like a fallen angel; then she rises, slaps the ground with her hands, rounds her chest forward, encircles the air with her arms, and caresses her cheeks with the backs of her hands.

After this solo outing, she returns to the table where the rest of the members of the "flamenco community" are seated and, after a new passage of singing, it is bailaor Joaquín Grilo who enters the scene to dance a fragment accompanied by singing and guitar with a large focus on footwork. When he finishes, Maya joins him to end the dancing together as if the bailaora's soliloquy had not existed: everything continues as usual. In this sense, Maya's bulería seems symptomatic of its time since the different scenes show the existing tension between the traditional, as a common code shared by all, and the newness, as an idiolect of a dancer who gets up from her chair in order to go explore an unknown space without the musical "company" of singing, guitars, and clapping. It is a dance that shows the solitary path of those who want to dance something else or in another way, similar to how the end of this scene—Maya's return to the table and her traditional duet with Grilo—seems to show us the return of a prodigal daughter who returns home by desire or necessity, putting aside her personal poetics and embracing once again the common language of those who continue to do "the same as always."

This dancing soliloquy by Maya, for which the camera makes a movement that extracts the group of singers, guitarists, and dancers as if they were not there, could be included in a History of bulerías dances through the various choreographies that show different interactions between the solo bailaora and the group of men (musicians or dancers).

We could start with a bulería danced and sung by Encarnación López, "La Argentinita," in 1935, in which the artist, after clapping with the musicians, leaves the scene and performs a dance full of comedic winks, as announced by the French text preceding the video.[78] La Argentinita appears dressed in a polka-dot dress with a small shawl covering her chest that she will play with by making a kind of whirlpool. It is not the only joke that she will make while dancing: before leaving the stage, she will mess up her bun while winking and making flower shapes with her hands at chest level with her mouth slightly open as if mocking the viewer.

In a short film from 1960, *Madrid de noche*, an anonymous bailaora appears on the stage of El Corral de la Morería surrounded by men who clap and rhythmically cheer her on. The bailaora moves with her hair loose from the beginning and moves her skirt front to back, accompanied by the gestures of the men surrounding her. These men also raise and lower their arms, making this dance a sort of "assisted solo." An abrupt change in speed marks the end of the bulería with a group *llamada* [call][79] accompanied by the singer's cry: the male choir and female soloist unite in this way to "finish together."

In a clip from the 1970s, we see Manuela Carrasco dancing in Los Canasteros, accompanied by the singing of Juan Villar.[80] In this bulería, Carrasco shows the forceful personality of a bailaora dressed in red and black who listens to the singing, making broad movements with her arms, lateral inclinations, and phrase closers that are invigorating enough to make the flower she is wearing fall from her hair, undoing her bow. We could say that we are jumping off this history of the purposefully undone bun by La Argentinita to Maya's Apollonian bun, passing through the loose and disheveled hair of the bailaora of El Corral de la Morería, and on to the fallen or tossed flower from Carrasco's head.

Even though there is a continuity between the serious nature of Carrasco's and Maya's bulerías, in terms of group construction, the latter is much closer to the bulería of 1935 by La Argentinita since in both cases, the bailaoras leave the group to perform their dance alone. A counterexample of Maya's loneliness and the teasing tremors of La Argentinita's hands is that of Eva Yerbabuena at the end of a bulería that includes the song lyrics to "Se nos rompió el amor" and constitutes the final number of her 2008 show, *Lluvia*.[81] If the tremor in La Argentinita's hands made us smile, Yerbabuena, dressed in a black velvet bata de cola and covered with a blood-red shawl that one of the singers throws over her shoulders, employs tremors that hurt us. The bailaora makes her hands tremble, leaning back with her arms open in a cross, her brow furrowed, her eyes closed and her mouth open, mournful of herself, dramatic in every sense of the term, but remains accompanied by the three singers following her until they disappear from the stage together.

Figures

Fig. 1. Café cantante El Burrero. (Photographer: E. Beauchy.)

Fig. 2. Trinidad Huertas, "La Cuenca." (Photographer: Antonio Esplugas.)

Fig. 3. Carmen Amaya. (Photographer unknown.)

Fig. 4. Esmeralda de Sevilla

Fig. 5. Ocaña. (Photographer: Nazario Luque Vera.)

Fig. 6. Enrique, "El Cojo"

Fig. 7. Belén Maya in *Romnia* (2016)

Fig. 8. Rocío Molina in *Caída del cielo* (2018). (Photographer: Javier Fergó.)

Fig. 9. Israel Galván in *El amor brujo* (2019). (Photographer: Javier Fergó.)

Fig. 10. Manuel Liñán's company in *¡Viva!* (2019). (Photographer: Paco Manzano.)

Fig. 11. José Galán and Lola López in *Sueños reales para cuerpos posibles* (2018). (Photographer: Florentino Yamuza.)

THREE

The Reactivation and Circulation of the *Tablao* in Times of Crisis (2008–2018)

The Economic Crisis of 2008

Being an Artist in Times of Crisis

In 2008, what at first was called a "deceleration" by President José Luis Rodríguez Zapatero revealed itself as a world economic crisis that would increase the unemployment rate, which had fluctuated between 7.95 percent and 11.96 percent between the years 2002 and 2007, until reaching 25.77 percent. After winning the general elections in 2011, the Partido Popular [People's Party], led by Mariano Rajoy, increased the tax rate for cultural industries, going from 10 percent to 21 percent,[1] which is going to cause a progressive disappearance of audiences from the performing arts, as demonstrated by the study carried out by Jaume Colomer.[2]

According to a second study conducted by Fátima Anillo for the Federación Estatal de Compañías y Empresas de Danza[3] on the state of the private sector of dance companies in Spain, income fell by 82 percent between 2009 and 2017, in such a way that the average appearance fee per show, which was around €12,049 ($16,748) in 2009, fell to €1,370 ($1,822) in 2013, recovering to €2,189 ($2,474) in 2017. The companies remained active, thanks to the private investment of the artists themselves as a response to a reduction of almost 50 percent in public subsidies as of 2013, but continued to struggle financially, going from ninety-two days of subsidized performances in 2013 to sixty in 2017 and experiencing a drop in the number of full-time workers, an increase—of 4.8 percent—in unstable contracts (interns, volunteers, under the table, etc.), and an average of only twenty-two performances per company per year.

The tablaos, which maintained their programming thanks to the presence of foreign tourists capable of paying the high prices for this type of show—between €35 ($47) and €60 ($81) on average—become, in addition to teaching, one of the only sectors in which flamenco artists can find work. This situation led to the renovation of this type of establishment and the show offered in them, given the presence of artists who used to work only in large companies. Jonatan Miró, dancer and artistic director of the tablao Villarrosa, expresses it as follows:

> Because of the crisis and the disappearance of the big companies and the big productions, not just dancers who worked in others' companies but also the big stars who had their own companies have returned to the tablao because now it's the only living we have for our day to day . . . there's no other way out.[4]

The Disappearance of Cuadros in the Tablaos

> Las Carboneras: that's not a tablao. It's a mini-tablao. It's a tablao because people sit down [to clap], but it's not a tablao. Before, the most "tablao" was El Corral . . . now, not even. Now they hire you for a week because the real tablaos, the ones with jaleos . . . the flamenco cuadros are over.[5]

As Francisca Sadornil, "La Tati," a bailaora from Madrid, declares nostalgically, a profound change took place in the tablaos starting in 2008 as a result of the elimination of the two-part show (the first scene, while dinner was served to liven things up, and the main acts after). This shift is due, in part, to the retirement of a whole generation of artists who had been part of the recurring cuadros in different tablaos and to the greater profitability of a new type of show in which only solo artists were presented, which allowed tablaos to offer two sets of the same performance on the same day, thus doubling the number of spectators. The shows, which used to start around ten o'clock at night and last until dawn, were put on much earlier, around seven or eight in the evening, to "do a double" around ten at night.

Given the imposition of this new regime of soloists, the recurring cuadros and the "indefinite" artists disappear, and the weekly model is imposed: all performers will have to rotate among the different tablaos for periods of one or two weeks, which causes greater mobility and job insecurity. Accordingly, as art scholar Teresa Marín García, citing Standing, points out, its characteristics include the discontinuous nature of work (temporary, seasonal, or infrequent), economic insecurity and instability (low wages that do not usually exceed €50–€60 per day, with some honorable exceptions), the lack of rights and protections at work (we understand that this only occurs in unregulated establishments), systematic insecurity (produced by flexibility in employment), and ongoing exclusion from the system and absence of identity (based on a secure job).[6] Some dancers who manage their own tablao consider this precarity the price to pay to avoid routine and boredom onstage. Melody Nicholls, "La Rubia de Vallecas," justifies it in this way:

> In any profession, if you do the same thing every day, you end up getting bored. Even with dancing or the guitar, which can be very different because it's a vocational profession, even doing that, one can end up getting bored. So yes, it can happen. You have to avoid it. And the day I don't feel like going onstage to dance anymore will be the day I stop all of this because I've seen shows where you realize the artists are there just out of routine, and the people feel it, and it's horrible . . . I think less so now because artists move a lot more than before, which implies more insecurity, of course, but in the end, it's better for everyone because nobody gets stuck.[7]

Carolina Fernández Oliva, co-owner with Nicholls of the flamenco tavern El Cortijo, explains how they change guest artists to nourish themselves artistically:

> One of the ways that we have here to escape is by constantly changing guitarists, singers, and guest dancers. It's a way to see what others are doing, stimulate yourself, and try not to get stuck because it's very easy. It's true. When you dance every day, it's very easy when you have so much time taking classes every day. It is very difficult to start studying alone. You have to love this very much, have too much love for it, because it's a crazy profession.[8]

Jonatan Miró, in his own way, criticizes the old tablao system, in which the same group of artists stayed fixed for years:

> I don't agree that artists should stay in the same place beyond a determined amount of time. I think the artists should constantly

be recycled because it's a living art in constant evolution, and one cannot stay in the same place. Actually, the tablaos that dragged on with the same cuadro were what they were, and we all know what they were ... maybe there are still some out there.[9]

Despite this concern about showing quality onstage, Isabel Guerrero, the producer for Casa Patas, recognizes that the spectators who go to the tablaos are often incapable of distinguishing a renowned artist from another newcomer. So the strategy behind the "rotation" of artists responds more to the artists' desire than to the audiences'. If we assimilate creative desire to sexual desire in a Freudian way, this new model would imply a certain criticism of "artistic monogamy" and would speak to us of open artistic couples who receive "at home" guests, who in some way introduce excitement—and also learning—of novelty. The dark side of this new model, as recognized by Tasha González, co-owner of Las Carboneras along with Ana Romero, is the selfishness that this implies on the part of the artists who own tablaos in the face of artists who lack permanent work and need to rotate from one tablao to another:

> When we opened the tablao, we were very clear that we had to move people because when you constantly change the people you work with, you enrich everyone. I am here all the time because I am a member (*socia*), and it's my workplace, but, selfishly, it's a formula we use to prevent people from getting stuck and to keep everything in constant movement and alive.[10]

This precarity is much more pronounced for the lesser-known bailaores, who do not have as many opportunities to be scheduled or even enter the tablao circuit since other better-known bailaores are causing a "generation gap." Tasha González, aware of this situation, tells us:

> High-level bailaores, as I call them, are clogging and blocking the others, but the venues selfishly prefer to call people who are above them, although there are always new people coming in. This is why we created the tablao contest when the crisis began: it was a way for us to meet new artists. And for new dancers, it's like a kind of showcase. People can show their work, and we can see them.[11]

Miró coincides with González in stating:

I'm aware that there is a generation that, not for nothing, in other circumstances, would not have worked in the tablaos. The tablao is wonderful, and it's the best school there is for dancers to develop and find themselves with their own personality. . . . And it's true that there's a generation that's clogging things up because the tablao has always been the school, the place where young people began and coexisted with more mature artists. . . . And the generation that comes after cannot enter.[12]

The flexibility of work in the tablaos, that is, the elimination of the recurring cuadro and the implementation of weekly contracts—justified as the response to an artistic need to avoid routine and boredom—benefits only those who have a permanent position in a tablao (dancer-producer and dancer-owner) and, in a less noticeable way, those artists whose symbolic capital allows them to compete in the job market.

Thus, in the dressing rooms, coexistence takes place between artists who occupy unequal positions: those who are regulars and who are artistically nourished by the changing presence of the guest artists; those who are not permanent but who, thanks to their professional recognition, manage to circulate between multiple tablaos in a fairly stable manner; and, finally, those who manage to get scheduled and must demonstrate their abilities so their time at the tablao is not anecdotal, generating future possibilities of being hired again. The latter examples correspond to what economist Gilles Saint-Paul called in the 1990s the distribution between the system's insiders (workers with a set position who are protected by it) and the outsiders (the precarious). The Politikon Collective describes the distribution as follows:

> The *insiders* struggle to defend their comparatively higher-protected position. However, they have little incentive to shift the balance in either direction or undertake burdensome income transfers to the other extreme. . . . The greater the gap between one group and the other, the more complicated it is to bridge it in order to build an alternative coalition to which insiders and business people implicitly agree to shift the flexibility to the outsiders.[13]

By eliminating the cuadro, all the dancers become soloists. Still, this symbolic promotion does not translate into a higher salary, as was the case in the past with the main acts. The tablaos will have solo dancers at the expense of integral members of the cuadro, which could be considered a kind of miniature corps de ballet. La Tati relates this change in the economic conditions of the tablao to us:

> The tablao paid very well then, compared to how life was. You earned four hundred pesetas, but you had enough to eat, pay for electricity, have a phone and a washing machine. The thing is that now . . . they don't even have enough to eat. Later, there were extra parties . . . with the marquis of Villaverde, with Franco. You went to La Granja, where there were parties in the country. So it wasn't just the tablao. . . . The money they pay now is ridiculous, with the euro. . . . The poor girls come here, study, buy a dress, and want to dance, and they dance just to pay for their food.[14]

This spectacular regime change produced a more dynamic artistic system but more precarious labor structure, making it possible to offer greater aesthetic quality in the tablaos but excluding the young generations who, in the past, went to the tablao as if it were school to "learn by working." It also allows us to see to what extent it can be inconvenient to tell the History in terms of absolute progress. Often, each advance causes a setback in other terms—or for other people. Something like this also happens in terms of gender, given that the disappearance of the cuadro also implied the disappearance of the gender regime that it entailed and that I have tried to describe in the first chapter of this book. If all artists are now soloists, a part of the show where a sample of pretty girls, hired regardless of their artistic talents, are brought onstage no longer exists, which simultaneously means fewer job opportunities for them since there are fewer jobs to fill.

One last consequence of this return to the tablaos is the qualitative change in artists' lives, which is no longer based on the model of traveling and touring with the company but rather much more sedentary, similar to that of the dancers of the Paris Opera, as described by Isabelle Launay:

> The dancer's life is organized according to the productivist mode, a life that is "a bit silly, in which one doesn't ask many questions," confides star soloist dancer Élisabeth Platel, a life with a frenetic rhythm: class in the morning, rehearsals of one or two ballets at noon, performance in the afternoon, often up to ten hours of work per day.[15]

The bailaora Claudia Cruz describes it as follows:

> All day we are connected through flamenco: I get up, and I'm already here in the studio to rehearse, then the tablao. And if you're not working, you go see a buddy . . . we are always connected with flamenco, at least here in Madrid. When I'm not in Madrid, I get to disconnect.[16]

Survival Strategies for Dancers in Times of Crisis

Staging of Broken Promises

The issue of job precarity for young artists, as well as the difficulty of accessing the job market, has been staged by at least two different pieces in the field of contemporary flamenco: *Viva la guerra*, directed by Alberto Cortés in 2014, and *No estoy aquí para entreteneros*, choreographed by Paola T. Sanchís in 2016. In the first piece, the *verdiales* [folk dance from Málaga] is the element used as a musical, choreographic, and costuming starting point to denounce a society that has not kept its promises. In the second piece, which uses a "purely" flamenco choreographic language, the bailaoras, dressed in leotards, invoke the myth of Sisyphus to account for the repetitive tediousness of their work situation and criticize the gap between the economic and personal investment on the part of the dancers, especially in terms of training, and the real benefits of said investment. Curiously, the two pieces share two dramaturgical moments: in the first shared scene, the performers recite their curriculum vitae, always overqualified, and confess: "They told me that if I did all of this, I would be successful. Now I have nothing." In this way, Cortés and Sanchís bring to light the rupture of an intergenerational pact between previous generations and current youth, as well as the dysfunction of the promise as a speech act that laid, following Hannah Arendt, a safety bridge between the present and the uncertain future.[17] This speech act made it possible to justify the students' effort, who thought they could obtain future compensation because it could translate into a good job with fair remuneration, something that no longer exists. The "bridge" does not provide security but leads into a void, like the Bridge to Nowhere on the island of Abu Dhabi, which generates frustration, feelings of inadequacy, and anger against those who have broken their word and against those who have set them up for a world that does not exist.

In the second scene, common to both shows and constituting the final scene, the artists break the fourth wall and invite the spectators to dance with them. This point of contact can be interpreted as a request for solidarity to make precarity a common cause and as a symbolic destruction of the relationship between stage and theater seats, which no longer constitutes a division of positions in economic terms. If the artists who work onstage are poorly paid, unpaid, or even have to pay to do their work, then the spectators, who traditionally were the ones who paid and did not get paid to be there, can take their place and dance without anyone having to pay them.

The Fin de Fiesta: Crypto-interview and Enthusiasm

The bulerías finale (*fiesta por bulerías*) or fin de fiesta seemingly plays an anecdotal role at the end of flamenco shows that the anthropologist Cruces Roldán describes as an "institutionalization of spontaneity in flamenco" since it proposes a kind of spontaneous encore that makes the "commercial" nature of the show more easily digestible for tourists, giving them the impression that they have attended a unique, unexpected, and in some sense, "more alive" experience.[18] However, this "fiesta" has a second secret function since it constitutes a protocol so that the dancers can make themselves known to the tablaos' producers, who can see them onstage to consider scheduling them in the future. Sometimes the dancers make use of the encouragement of friends or colleagues who are performing that day in the tablao to "dance their résumé in an abridged manner," and other times it is the programmers themselves who invite a dancer to attend the show to do their pataíta step at the end as a sort of crypto-interview. This party, thus, seems like a joke in which the apparent relaxation and spontaneity of the artists hide power relations and an unspeakable tension on the part of the candidates, who must offer themselves onstage as if nothing were at stake. Following an expression by the writer Remedios Zafra, they are "subjects involved in precarity and disguised with feigned enthusiasm used to increase their productivity in exchange for symbolic payments or postponed life expectancy."[19]

"Illegal" Tablaos

As a consequence of the crisis, many venues began to offer flamenco shows, with the resulting negative things: unregistered artists, lower salaries, and declining prices. If I sell a show with a drink for thirty-six euros, they sell a show with dinner for the same price, and that's something that, with the number of employees I have to pay, I can't afford. It's been very damaging to us. In Madrid, fifty or sixty venues illegally offer flamenco shows. Realize that if ten spectators go to each venue, there are six hundred people who used to go to the traditional and regulated tablaos that we no longer have.[20]

In addition to the crypto-interviews through bulerías, in which the dancers pretend to be celebrating, we should add the tablaos described by the owner of Café de Chinitas as "illegal" as a second survival strategy for dancers in times of crisis. These "fake," "second rate," or "underground" tablaos constitute less an unfair competition generated by the owners of theaters in large cities—such as Barcelona, Madrid, or Seville—than a way found by young artists to work, given the saturation of the official market of the tablaos and the blockage generated by the most recognized artists. It is important to note that these artists, aside from a lack of registration with the Social Security system, do the same work as the high-level artists of the "respectable" tablao circuit but get paid based on box-office sales of the number of attendees, without exceeding, in any case, fifty euros per night.

In the Absence of Tablaos . . . Dancing in the Street

Even though the return to the tablaos seems to have been the consequence of an economic crisis that dissolved most of the big companies in Spain and significantly reduced the possibilities of working abroad due to the global nature of the crisis, the flamenco artists themselves seem to have turned the tables and developed a sort of psychological survival strategy. They have created an aesthetic conviction according to which working in the tablao is preferable to the theater because one finds "more freedom" in it—since they do not have to follow a predetermined script, fixed choreographies, or the instructions of the director or choreographer in charge— and "more communication" with the audience—due to the physical proximity of the latter in a much smaller space than the theater. In this way, the tablao becomes, in the collective imagination of the dancers, a "much more alive" space than the theater, synonymous with freedom and authenticity of the aesthetic experience.

This "self-convincing" psychological mechanism also appears in a group of artists who, due to the economic crisis and the labor market saturation in the tablaos, find an alternative space on the street where they can stage their performances. For them, as for the tablao artists regarding the theater, the street will be "a freer, livelier, and more accessible place than the stage." One of our interviewees, Pedro, states that "the connection factor" does not exist on the street, and concerning artistic freedom, Ander argues:[21]

> It is also a much freer space. It allows you to be more creative because it is not governed so much by what is sold ("You have to sell to fill the seats"). There's an aspect of flamenco where you allow more things for yourself, including not having to be as stylized as you would showing a more manufactured flamenco. No, I see street flamenco as more authentic, a much more common expression, with its sevillanas, even though many flamenco purists or those who are very avant-garde with flamenco say that sevillanas are useless, that they are very boring. . . . But, since people like them and at the end, when one sings and dances to them, there are so many lyrics and things—well, one has a good time. . . . It's a very diverse and freer world with less ego.[22]

Regarding the reception of this type of proposal by street users turned spectators, Lidia states:

> You aren't in control on the street: people of all kinds pass by. . . . The reaction of people says a lot. If you are on the street and you do it poorly, people don't stop; if you are on the street and you do it well, people stop, or at least, if they don't stop, they wink at you, they make a gesture. . . . It's a wise audience, the wisest of all. Because the one who pays at a theater maybe pays not to get bored or maybe because they have nothing better to do, or maybe they come because someone bought them the ticket and forced them. Perhaps they aren't coming to see you.[23]

Despite the positive aspects of the street as a stage space, all the artists involved acknowledge that they did not start working on the street out of an aesthetic choice but out of an economic necessity. Pedro tells us:

> I started . . . about six years ago [in 2012] as an alternative to the tablao because the tablao was something very closed-minded and

The Reactivation and Circulation of the Tablao 117

pretty conditioned to the Gitano race and the Sacromonte area and a very specific area of the city because there was a small group of kids . . . who decided to do flamenco there, in a very rudimentary way, with a board, I don't know, like a tile, to dance on, and without any type of amplification either. Basically, guitar, voice, and some dance.[24]

As for Ander, she says:

I arrived here [in Seville] in 2017, and flamenco has been my foundation, my livelihood. . . . I didn't have to depend on a work permit to get some money, and I got in touch with some street artists who did flamenco, and I decided to start doing it with them, and I began singing. . . . We started to make groups, like street tablaos, with people who were in the same situation, the same folks from Seville too, Spaniards, of course: people from Madrid, people from here, from Seville; from Greece, French, Argentines, Chileans, people from all over the world who love flamenco and who are trying to survive here.[25]

Lidia remembers:

I started playing in the street with a Brazilian who played the guitar . . . he played all right; I'll leave it there. And his daughter, who was twelve years old at the time, so, of course, she was younger, she couldn't dance in the street, but she came to dance. So I would go with them because, if the police came, she would sit down to clap because, since she was with her father, they couldn't say anything to her either, and I was the one who would start dancing. I've performed in several [places]: I've done Retiro Park . . . , I've done the downtown area . . . on Calle Arenal. . . . The thing is, they're high-traffic areas, which is where you're supposed to make some money: twenty, thirty, or forty euros a day. . . . I played in the street out of necessity. I've always done it out of necessity.[26]

In opposition to artists who preferred to perform in tablaos rather than in theaters, street artists show not only the positive side of this type of work but also the negative aspects (competitiveness with other artists, police chases, lack of equipment for sound, etc.) and its economic need as a motivational engine to carry out this type of activity. It is perhaps a more conscious position in which the artists do not convince themselves through a romantic discourse about street art but try to compensate with what remains positive in terms of artistic and personal learning:

> It's a very brief type of show. It didn't follow the normal structure of an alegría with its fifteen minutes at all; it wasn't that at all. It was much shorter. And in 2015, it was a bit of an explosion because, at the same time, there could be four, five little flamenco groups in the street in different areas of Granada. There could be people in Plaza Nueva, people in the Cathedral; there could be people in the Paseo de los Tristes (exactly where the Mario Maya sculpture is). And there could be one or two groups in each of those spots. In other words, one group plays, and then another plays. . . . You could do it with a permit from the city council, and I started, basically, for money and because it caught my attention.[27]

Pedro calls the type of show they put on "microtablao." The beginning of it corresponds to what in the tablao would appear in the middle. There is no time for an introduction or a warm-up of the artists and the spectators. The show begins with its climax to attract the attention of those passing by.

> In 2015, we systematized the show a bit: there was a signal, two or three dancers got on the board, a bigger board, well crafted, made of linoleum, a better-crafted material. The two or three dancers, such as a boy and two girls or a boy and a girl, would do an acceleration (*subida*) in bulerías, and that attracted people. . . . Then Cristo, a Mexican guy, would introduce the group and what we would do. We generally did three things: tangos or soleá por bulerías or bulería directly. . . . Our group was different because we dressed as if we were going to work in a tablao, in a conventional, canonical way: shirt, vest, pants, very canonical . . . and the girls in flamenco dresses, all very canonical.[28]

The type of show described here by Pedro, despite taking place in an alternative space in which, as Ander stated, "There is more freedom," tries to respect as much as possible the codes of the tablao in what it has to do with the gender distribution of dances, dress codes, and so on. Likewise, it should be noted that, despite the effort made by these artists to develop a certain staging, the amount of money earned does not exceed ninety euros per artist on the best of days, as Pedro confesses.

The Street as Stage

We distinguish these "street tablaos" from other uses of public space, such as the "massive" use of space in flashmobs, especially in events with a large turnout, such as the Festival Flamenco de Madrid or the Bienal de Flamenco de Sevilla. In these large events, many more or less amateur dancers execute a choreography previously learned through videos published on the internet by a recognized dancer (Marco Flores, Pastora Galván, Farruquito, Eduardo Guerrero, José Galán, etc.).

Another use of public space is what we could describe as "activist." Flamenco becomes a tool for political denunciation in this space by putting on performances in situ or through *escraches* or similar actions. *Escraches* are a type of protest in which a group of activists breaks into the private or work environment of a person or a group of people against whom they are protesting. The term arose in Argentina in 1995, used by Hijos, the group fighting for human rights, to denounce the impunity of genocides due to the grace conceded by Carlos Menem. In Spain, the term began to be used in 2013, not unrelated to the 15M movement of 2011, by the members of PAH (Plataforma de Afectados por las Hipotecas). In flamenco, the group of artists Flo6x8 stands out, which defines itself as an "activist-artistic-situationist-performative-folkloric and very flamenco collective" and proposes actions in banks, in the Parliament of Andalusia, and more recently, at the location of the feminist strike on March 8, 2018, in the Alameda de Hércules neighborhood in Seville.[29]

One final use of public space is demonstrated by contemporary flamenco artists who will use the category "dance in nonconventional spaces," adapting fragments of stage pieces to dance them in the street. Despite the difference between this type of piece and the "street tablaos," the deep motivation seems to have been the same: the economic need to work and, in the case of contemporary flamenco artists, the possibility of producing themselves in the framework of a contemporary dance festival, proposing these street pieces as activities parallel to its primary staged programming.

We could not end this discussion of "unconventional" spaces without talking about the performance *Máquinas sagradas* (2019) by Juan Carlos Lérida. This piece is part of a larger project entitled *La liturgia de las horas*.

This analysis is not about a work from the street but work in a nonstage space, or what in choreological terms has been called a "site specific" or "in situ" performance. The specificity of Lérida's work compared to other contemporary works resides in the fact that flamenco constitutes the starting point here, and the "site" appears to "feed flamenco," to nourish it with new structures, textures, colors, smells, and sounds. Still, it is not seen *by itself* but in relation to the possible relationships it can maintain with the flamenco universe. The "site" here is not the place from which the artistic work is built but the container that, in addition to hosting it, gives it content. Flamenco is the perspective from which car number plates are looked at, chosen, and used, upon which Lérida stomps; wrenches that remind us of the blows of the hammer on the forge, which give singing in the martinete style its metallic flavor; rear-view mirrors turned into fans, and repair platforms turned into elevated tablaos. Juan Carlos Lérida shows us flamenco as a perceptive structure, as a way of looking at things that allows us not only to "find flamenco in ordinary bodies" but also to invent it.[30]

Another recent project by Juan Carlos Lérida that also explores flamenco in public spaces, this time in the street, is one entitled *Mundos paralelos: Una ruta flamenca por el Paral•lel*, performed in Barcelona in December 2019 with scientific direction by historian Montse Madridejos. The spectators are taken by the artists and researcher through the flamenco memory of Barcelona at the beginning of the century, exorcising through different types of danced rituals the ghosts of old venues where flamenco could be seen and heard in the context, very often, of variety shows such as those given at the Edén Concert (present-day parking lot of the Hotel Gaudí), the Bagdad, and the Cabaret de la Muerte (currently the Teatre Victoria).[31] Here it is not a matter of extracting flamenco from a space in its current daily use, as it was in *Máquinas sagradas*, in which Lérida wants to connect with workers from other "professional guilds," but of going through a present space with the gaze filtered through the absent flamenco, which existed and is no longer there, to reactivate it in new ways and thus make the past an "excuse for the present," a motor of creativity in the here and now.

A "street and flamenco" performance by the artist Pilar Albarracín (Seville, 1968) also allows us to reconsider the status of the spectator in this type of artistic intervention, in which the attending audience occupies neither the place of mere observer nor of "participating spectator" who is invited to propose this or that action onstage. In *Que me quiten lo bailao*, the proposal engulfs the spectator. This *performance*-outing, which I attended in Madrid in November 2018, began at the Atocha Station and ended at La Tabacalera. This place was hosting a retrospective exhibition of the artist. Albarracín walked around smiling, dressed in flamenco ware and accompanied by about fifty women dressed like her, three or four photographers, and about twenty people, including myself, who were following the procession.

The outing, which sometimes seemed like a pilgrimage, other times a protest without signs, and other times a bachelorette party, made me realize that there were people who did not look at us and others who did not have time to stop and look: mothers holding children by the hand and Deliveroo workers running out of a building to get back on their bikes. This experience made me reflect on the attention regimes in the street and the real privilege we have when we "have time" to stop to watch something that happens. The outing also allowed me to hear the comments made by people who were part of that flamenco fishbowl and people who were watching from outside. Some wondered about the authenticity of the costumes; others wondered if they were travestis, and they threw bunches of words into the air that attempted to categorize what they were seeing: women from Seville, women dressed as Gitanas, and so forth. I understood to what extent I would not have been able to experience this artistic action without having been part of its development and to what extent the street offers the possibility of establishing new regimes of attention that force both the artist and the spectator to renegotiate their relative positions, as long as the street does not become a "new theater" with a handful of plastic chairs serving as theater stalls in which the spectators look univocally toward a "stage" where the city's skyline fills in as the set.

Spaces That Speak of Time

Let us compare this skyline-set with the sets of some of Madrid's tablaos. The Corral de la Morería preserves its columns, its wooden tables and chairs, the white walls dotted with paintings, predominantly of bullfighting themes, and the background of the stage dominated by a traditional painting by Juan Bravo. It is the atmosphere of an old café cantante, like Candela or La Taberna de Mr. Pinkleton; we immerse ourselves in the preindustrial time of the so-called golden age of flamenco (1850–1920) without there being a split between the stage and the room, making the aesthetic experience encompass everything.

This nineteenth-century atmosphere contrasts with that of Torres Bermejas—whose name designates two towers of the Alhambra Palace in Granada—conceived, like Villarrosa, with an Andalusian aesthetic. These two tablaos offer us an orientalist framework that reinforces the idea of an art that comes from afar (in time and space) and that makes us enter a vestigial universe in which flamenco appears as an indication of the Muslim presence in the Iberian Peninsula between the years 711 and 1492. Flamenco, then, is presented as the remains of a culture that has already disappeared but is still brightening up and giving flavor to certain Spanish art forms. Silvia Cruz Lapeña, a journalist specializing in flamenco, describes Villarrosa as follows:

> This house opened in 1911, although it was in 1919 when it debuted the look it has today and with which it recalls the arches of the Alhambra. Many of the vibrantly painted tiles on the walls are the work of the same ceramicist who made the street signs in the center of Madrid: Antonio Ruiz de Luna. Because this tablao is from Madrid, it cannot be Andalusian. Everything in it looks like a set, but it's bohemian at the same time, the capital of nowhere. It has the appearance of a den built to hide a runaway.[32]

Café de Chinitas, the name of an old café cantante and a song by Federico García Lorca, displays a large room with walls upholstered in green velvet that contrasts with the long red curtains and where shawls of different designs and colors entirely cover the back of the stage. This set was created by the painter Mampaso and the decorator Pinto Coelho, with furniture, chairs, and mirrors from the nineteenth century, paintings by Vicente Viudes, and sculptures by Sanguino. Here the room reproduces a kind of class schism between the stage, which also seems to reproduce the ambiance of popular cafés cantantes, and the luxurious lounge, which imitates what could be the gathering hall of a bourgeois mansion. In this way, the spectator and the artist travel to the past but in different ships, occupying different roles and creating an insurmountable distance between them.

Between these two spaces, a small element also reminds us of the disciplinary regime to which the artists onstage are subjected: a clock hanging from the wall at the end of the left corner of the stage that allows the artists to calculate the time and control the duration of their musical and choreographic numbers to fill each of the performances sufficiently. This clock also exists in other tablaos, such as El Corral de la Morería, but in this case, it is only visible to the artists and not to the audience since it is placed on the hidden side of a wooden beam that holds up the ceiling of the tablao.

As for Casa Patas, it was conceived—following the expression of its artistic director, Isabel Guerrero—as a "small theater," since the restaurant and the tablao area are separated into two different spaces in such a way that the spectators have dinner before entering the show, where they can only drink, sitting at small tables facing an Italian-style stage. In this small theater, the lack of light gives it a nocturnal atmosphere, even though it is possible to recognize the black and white faces of dancers, singers, and guitarists who fill the walls in a sort of artistic pantheon in which the living mingle with the dead, forming a second faction of spectators who attend the double spectacle that involves watching not only the artists but also the tourists and fans who watch the show. Following the Husserlian expression, a double temporality that combines the "having-been-present" of deceased artists and the "almost-past" of living artists traverses this gallery of ghosts. The fact that the ancestors are represented in this way reminds us that flamenco is inscribed in a long history to which some of the living artists we see onstage will belong. The possibility of "making history" is announced from the walls along with the inevitable "being-toward-death," in Heideggerian terms, that this implies.

Opposing these ambiances, which permanently refer to different periods of the past and give the show a kind of Ouija aesthetic, the tablaos created from the 2000s will try to create a lighter aesthetic, stripped of all folkloric ornamentation. This lightness becomes minimalist elegance in the case of Las Tablas, directed by Spanish bailaora Antonia Moya and the Costa Rican bailaora Marisol Navarro. Presented as a "new stage space" and not as a "tablao flamenco," the predominant colors are black and a range of grays:

> So what we wanted to do here is, first, a very minimalist space. If you've noticed, it's all black and white, with minimal decoration (the only things we have right now are some photographs by Alberto Romo, also from an exhibition) . . . with which, since it hardly has any decoration, the main thing is not a flamenco decoration but what happens onstage. Then we enhanced the scene space of the set: it is a stage of twenty-five [square] meters. I would say that it is one of the largest tablaos in Madrid, and we have preferred that to having more space for chairs and tables, for example.[33]

Las Carboneras, managed by the Spanish bailaora Tasha González and by the Australian bailaora Ana Romero and presented as an "avant-garde tablao," displays on its walls images of two current bailaores—Olga Pericet and Marco Flores—as well as a copy of the cigar factory scene from the film *Carmen*, by Saura and Gades. The rest of the room's walls are gallery walls where visual artists and photographers display their work, often with a flamenco theme. The concept of tablao-gallery could already be found in the 1970s, for example, in the tablao Los Cabales, whose opening was presided over by paintings by Vicente Maeso (1919–1993), described as follows by Pilar Trenas in *ABC*:

> An exhibition of thirty oil paintings combining the most diverse themes. From a *Fin de Carnaval*, through the very Spanish theme of bullfighters and people from Madrid, to the portrait of María del Carmen Martínez-Bordiú de Bourbon [Franco's granddaughter].[34]

This same aesthetic predominates at Café Ziryab, directed by the German bailaora Anja Volldhart. The name of the tablao refers to Abú el Hasán Ali ibn Nafi, a poet, gastronomist, singer, and musician known as Ziryab (Iraq, 789—Córdoba, 857), famous in the flamenco world thanks to the eponymous album by guitarist Paco de Lucía. In this café, therefore, Orientalist references are mixed with a polished aesthetic and a copy of a photograph of El Burrero, a nineteenth-century café singer from Seville. Accordingly, temporality is distorted.

Cardamomo opened the door to the conversion of the tablao into a "flamenco museum" after its latest renovation: the entrance is through a corridor where flamenco music can be heard, and videos are seen on small screens. Images of flamenco shows and quotations from artists in Spanish and English embellish the black walls. In this way, the exoticism and authenticity of attending a flamenco show "in its own environment" are renounced. Yet the spectators' experience is guided pedagogically by giving them some clues about the three essential elements of flamenco: guitar, singing, and dancing. Three quotations about dancing appear by Antonio Gades (1936–2004), Farruco (1935–1997), and Pastora Imperio (1887–1979). The first says, "The great thing about flamenco is its control. It doesn't explode, but there's an enormous energy, sensuality, and eroticism that vibrates all the time." The second, in support, says, "Art is an expression of what one is. You cannot dance like another person because nobody feels the same." The final one argues, "Dancing, what dancing says, must be from the waist up." These three quotations, from an unknown source, frame the aesthetic experience before it begins, extending it "through the entrance hallway" as if an ablution of the spectator's imagination were necessary to be able to perceive what is about to happen later onstage and which, according to the quotations, will have to do with the well-known clichés about flamenco dancing.

A completely different route is that of the flamenco tavern El Cortijo, one of the few tablaos in Madrid located outside of the city center (in Vallecas) and one that responds to the will of its owners, the British bailaora Melody Nicholls and the Chilean bailaora Carolina Fernández Oliva, to offer flamenco at an affordable price for the residents of a working-class neighborhood. According to Fernández Oliva:

> The difference is that we are trying to create supporters, so we are in a neighborhood with a cheaper offer so the Spanish public can come, because if we don't do that, the Spaniards can't be constant people in a tablao, which is our objective.[35]

The place effectively mixes the atmosphere of a neighborhood restaurant and an associative space, offering a "community" framework that seems to want to promote coexistence between artists and spectators, a fact reinforced by the conversation that Melody Nicholls, "La Rubia de Vallecas," maintains with the audience both from the stage during the show and intermissions and after the show walking between tables.

Here we are dealing with a space that evokes a poetics of the present time in which the most important thing—perhaps the only thing—is to be together here and now. Do the other tablaos offer a kind of "immersive experience" to the spectators so that they live a sort of flamenco fantasy? What is left of all this when the frame disappears, and the open spaces replace it? Is something not lost in the darkness and seclusion that suits flamenco so well when performed in the middle of the street and in broad daylight? Is flamenco agoraphobic? Does flamenco only go out at night, like vampires? What does this art take advantage of from urban elements if it maintains the fixed structure of footwork on a portable board and the arrangement of musicians seated behind the dancers? What happens when the flamenco artists leave this little stage to explore the asphalt? Should flamenco give up polka dots and ruffles to blend into the landscape, like dressing in Zara? Is a kind of flamenco possible not only in the street and of the street but also for the streets of our twenty-first-century cities? A flamenco that not only recreates the fantasy of the deep intensity that it was but also explores other forms of memory and, above all, other nonmemorial uses of space given by those who cross it, inhabit it, and cocreate it every day?

The Street beyond the Stage?

The anthropologist Cruces Roldán proposed an interesting differentiation between flamenco "de uso" [flamenco for use] (the one performed in the community, between us and for us) and flamenco "de cambio" [flamenco for exchange] (the one performed for those who do not belong to our community and mediated by financial remuneration).[36] Despite its unquestionable methodological utility, this pair of categories oversimplifies the series of variables that intervene in the motivation of artists on- and offstage. Sometimes, we dance onstage *for ourselves* even though we are paid and *others* are watching, and other times *for others* even if we do not charge. Sometimes, in "de uso," we invite others to be part of our community who do not belong to it (through payment or not), as proven by the immense number of photographs, documentary videos, and recordings of juergas, family parties (weddings, baptisms, and communions), popular festivals (such as the fairs or the Zambomba de Jerez de la Frontera), and religious pilgrimages (such as the one in El Rocío). In some sense, one could state that "there is no dance if there is no one watching" and that what said gaze sometimes does, often understood by the traditional flamenco bibliography as a disturbing element of the aesthetic experience, is produce the conditions of possibility of itself. We dance so that they look at us or because they are looking at us—sometimes ourselves in the mirror—and, in the worst case, regardless of who is looking at us.

In flamenco, there are no group dances offstage, as is the case in folk styles. We continue in the face of a solo dance that requires, as Bourdieu argued in *The Bachelors' Ball*, a "performance,"[37] a self-spectacularization of the body itself in front of others who are watching us, clapping their hands, or cheering. There are also some duets, such as sevillanas, that dance halfway between flamenco and folklore, and mirrored improvisations— usually to rumba or bulerías—in which the performers imitate each other, alternately offering their own gestures or copying their partner in an interesting game in which sometimes the dancers "do the same thing" and other times do completely different things, but following the same beat. Except for sevillanas, in these duets, there do not seem to be very marked gender roles, although there is a more or less noticeable distribution of power (active/passive). Even in the case of sevillanas, except in the last verse of the second sevillana and in the final positions of the four verses, in which the "man" grabs the "woman" by the waist, the danced choreographic text (the steps) is the same: it is up to the interpreter to reinforce the "masculine" tonality (adding footwork in the introduction to each of the four verses, substituting the turns that end each of the sevillanas passages with pirouettes, which can even end kneeling in a gesture of courtship) or "feminine" (playing with a gaze and smiles, tilt of the bust forward in some markings that allow it, use of a smoother quality of movement, etc.).

The Gender Crisis

Chronology of a "Revolution"

As of 2008, Spain has experienced more than just an economic crisis. A second crisis, perhaps as global as the economic one, is most likely linked to and definitely more "enriching" than the first. This crisis has threatened the clauses of the gender binary contract and has produced in the flamenco sphere the emergence of a series of discourses and artistic practices that, as a common point, question those practices.

This outbreak takes place during a historical moment in Spain during which the repoliticization of society, due in part to the 15M movement, seems to reactivate "grassroots" LGTBIQ movements, which appeared to have suffered a sharp decline after the legalization in 2005 of same-sex marriage, as some researchers and activists, such as Ramón Martínez, underscore.[38]

In the flamenco world, issues of gender and sexuality began to appear insistently in the 2010s, progressively but rapidly, accumulating a series of events that I think are necessary to present in an interconnected way. In 2013, framed within the Bienal de Flamenco de Málaga, Marco Flores's company presented *Laberíntica*, a show directed by Juan Carlos Lérida, whose theme—which, according to them, deals with "relationships between men"—quite clearly evokes or suggests a narrative about different types of sexual-affective relationships between men. In 2014, at the Festival Flamenco de Jerez de la Frontera, Manuel Liñán danced a caracoles wearing a bata de cola and shawl as a guest dancer in a show by Belén

Maya, *Los invitados*, and also in another production, *Nómada*, with his own company. Although it was not the first time that a bailaor appeared onstage in a bata de cola or semi-cross-dressed (*semitravestido*), the media impact of this piece was so strong that, a year later, the image of the bailaor dressed in these women's accessories would become the image of the official poster of the same festival. In 2016, Emilio Ochando's company won the Certamen Coreográfico de Danza Española y Flamenco in Madrid with the piece "Tinevo," danced by a group of four dancers wearing batas de cola and using castanets. In 2019, on the Canal Sur television program Tierra de Talento, fourteen-year-old Javier Valero, from Jaén, danced again with a bata de cola and shawl, ensuring a kind of intergenerational permeability of this gender *fluidity*.[39] It is as if the use of the bata de cola, which initially was nothing more than the train of a wedding dress that artists of the nineteenth century incorporated onto the stage for "aesthetic whim," was normalized little by little after the approval of equal marriage in Spain in 2005.[40]

Beyond these initial *attempts*, 2017 is undoubtedly the decisive year for the definitive articulation between the world of LGTBIQ activism and the flamenco world, coinciding with the fortieth anniversary of the first LGTB demonstration in Spain, organized in Barcelona in 1977, whose objective was the repeal of the Law of Social Danger and Rehabilitation of 1970, which was partially annulled on December 26, 1979.

In February 2017, Egales—the same company that published this work—published my book *De puertas para adentro: Disidencia sexual y disconformidad de género en la tradición flamenca*, presented with significant media impact at the Festival Flamenco de Jerez de la Frontera and later at the National Library of Spain. Journalist Silvia Cruz Lapeña also published a series of interviews with artists concerned about machismo in the flamenco sector: bailaora Rocío Molina with her show *Caída del cielo*, singer Rosario Montoya, bailaora Belén Maya, and yours truly. In June, within the context of World Pride held in Madrid, Marta Cariño's gay entertainment company proposed to the tablao El Corral de la Morería the organization of a flamenco festival "with an LGBTIQ wink" to attract gay tourists from all over the world. Despite the negative response from the owners of the tablao, the project ended up being carried out thanks to Ernesto Novales de la Escalera, thus creating the Flamenco Diverso festival, in which they presented *Dos tocaoras* (by Antonia Jiménez and Marta Robles) and Miguel Poveda in the musical field; for dance, they presented *Afectos* (by Rocío Molina and La Tremendita), *Titanium* (by Compañía de Rojas y Rodríguez), and my work *Bailar en hombre*."

In February 2019, preceded by my lecture contained in this book, "Apuntes para una historia travesti del flamenco," Manuel Liñán presented his new creation, "¡Viva!," in Madrid, in which seven male dancers dressed as women appear. A month later, in the context of the Festival Flamenco de Jerez de la Frontera, Israel Galván, who had previously dressed as a woman to embody the character of *la puta de Babilonia* (the whore of Babylon) in his 2009 show, "*El final de este estado de cosas*," presented his version of *El amor brujo*, assuming the role of his female alter ego, Eduarda de los Reyes, which is apparently the name of his biological aunt.

This notorious use of travestismo in the mainstream flamenco circuit by two men, both winners of Spain's Premios Nacionales de Danza [national dance prizes], has not left the flamenco community indifferent. Beyond the threats and insults that these artists have received through social networks from chauvinist and homophobic spectators (a situation that, on the other hand, all LGTBIQ activists have faced), some flamenco artists have criticized the gratuity with which these two shows treat issues such as femininity and cross-dressing. Putting on a wig and skirt "like at a bachelor party" can be funny for cisgender men, but it can end up ridiculing women, often portrayed as hysterical to create a humorous atmosphere, lacking the immersive depth of the processes carried out by artists for whom drag is not an anecdote in their career but a constant in their performative project, and letting "theatrical details" pass that can be offensive. Why does Manuel Liñán present a bunch of "women" who emulate bailaoras from the tablaos-showcases of the 1960s and 1970s? What does it mean for the bailaoras who have struggled to disidentify themselves with this model to see it staged in a "whitewashed" way, without showing the dark side of that bodily objectification, linked to the obligation to dress and put on makeup in a certain way, to the obligation to dance in a certain way, to the obligation to socialize with spectators, et cetera? What is the price of showing a romantic image of objectified women during the Franco regime? Why does Israel Galván confine his female alter ego to dancing for almost the entire play while sitting in a chair? Did he need to dress as a woman to reduce the amplitude of the stage space to its minimum expression, to a kind of small "domestic space"? Did he need to put on a wig to mime, slow down, smooth out the dynamics of his gestures, and use shoulder rotations and movements in the wrist and fingers?

This "internal artistic criticism," far from being an exercise in self-boycott by the community, seems to be a sign of good health, to the extent that it speaks to us of an actively reflective community, capable of asking itself "deep" questions beyond the lightning-fast *ole* and the thunderclap of first impressions. The reception of the flamenco show, traditionally reduced to the spasmodic space of cheers and applause, begins to expand and create a space for debate in which there is no question of dragging anyone to the ground or granting anyone *la llave del baile* [prestigious flamenco dance award] in order to parade them out in grand style. It is about retracing the steps taken to question both the artistic work and our own perceptual structures (our expectations, prejudices, frustrated desires, surprising discoveries, and interpretative delusions) and, in turn, creating an enriching, potentially infinite dialogue for all.

An Intergenerational Revolution

The qualitative leap in terms of "LGBTIQ artistic activism" and the risk these artists took—most, although not all, born in the 1990s—is flagrant, allowing us to speak of a "revolution" simmering for many years that has suddenly come to a boil. Part of this burst of steam is Carlos Carvento, a dancer and performer from Córdoba who presented a piece entitled *Maricón de España* for his thesis project at the Conservatorio Superior de Danza María de Ávila in Madrid. In it, he reclaims the *movimiento amanerado* [mannered movement] that some of his classical dance teachers—in some instances, also homosexuals—had tried to forbid to him.

Effectively, LGTBIQ-F (flamenco) activism implies a search for greater freedoms not only in the theatrical space but also in all areas of life, artistic or otherwise. Therefore, educational initiatives such as my workshop "Género, sexualidad, y tradición: Hacia una práctica inconformista del flamenco"—taught in 2019 at the Centro Danza Canal de Madrid in collaboration with Injuve and the invaluable joint supervision of Carlos Carvento and Álvaro Romero—must multiply to encompass artistic work from a place of "care," both of the body itself and of the bodies with which time and space are shared. Such workshops teach us to put forward scenic, pedagogical, and critical experiences that welcome other possible bodies, other types of artists beyond the virtuoso and heroic dancer who engenders admiration in their audience and who only uses dance as an expressive resource.

Carlos Carvento (Córdoba, 1995) also collaborates with other Andalusian artists who seek to reappropriate their folklore and reclaim the aesthetics of the copla divas, even organizing theme parties such as Lolailo in Madrid. This party offers a safe space where this new generation of young people flows between carnations and shawls, glitter and chest hair, heels and a curvy aesthetic, plaid shirts and hoop earrings. "Something"—many things—is happening, and it seems happily unstoppable.

As for Álvaro Romero (El Puerto de Santa María, 1983), he seems to have taken a seismic leap with his *marica* [fag] techno-flamenco project *RomeroMartín*, which reclaims the capacity of cante jondo to talk about what it means to be a marica today without falling into the curse typical of nineteenth-century Romanticism, but without neglecting issues such as sex or drug use, and using lyrics from poems such as "Manifiesto (Hablo por mi diferencia)," by the Chilean Pedro Lemebel (1952–2015):

You don't know
What it is to bear this leprosy
People keep their distance
People understand and say:
He's a *marica* but he writes well
. . .
My manhood was about biting myself with jibes
Consuming rage to not kill everyone
My manhood is about accepting myself differently
Being a coward is much harder
I don't turn the other cheek
I put my ass on the line, man

Close in time and space to Romero is Niño de Elche (b. 1985), who inhabits a space of open experimentation that, like many other artists, tries not to get caught up with labels that limit his creative freedom and could be described, without being pejorative, as "ambiguous." This ambiguity, both aesthetic and political, does not, however, prevent him from practicing a vehemence that becomes provocative in many cases and causes notorious seismic movements on stages as flamenco as that of Madrid's Casa Patas, in which he sang wearing a T-shirt that read *loca del coño* [crazy bitch].[41]

The homage to verses by Federico García Lorca performed by Miguel Poveda (Badalona, 1973) feels distant from this prior example and includes, paradoxically, a fragment from the homophobic "Oda a Walt Whitman" [Ode to Walt Whitman]:

That's why I don't raise my voice, old Walt Whitman,
against the little boy who writes
the name of a girl on his pillow,

nor against the boy who dresses as a bride
in the darkness of the wardrobe,
nor against the solitary men in casinos
who drink prostitution's water with revulsion,
nor against the men with that green look in their eyes
who love other men and burn their lips in silence.
But yes, against you, urban *maricas*,
tumescent flesh and unclean thoughts.
Mothers of mud. Harpies. Sleepless enemies
of the love that bestows crowns of joy.[42]

We need to write at the speed of a changing time, not only to leave written testimony of what is happening, but above all to create a certain reflective trace that allows us to continue advancing in a process of identifying, erasing, and resetting all those structures—external or internal—whose rigidity made us fragile. A visual example of this work with structures is *La oscilante*, a project by dancer Pol Jiménez (Barcelona, 1995), directed and choreographed by Juan Carlos Lérida.

The piece begins in the dark with the sound of striking mechanical tools—a piece *under construction*. Almost immediately, we see Pol Jiménez appear in the bottom right corner, squatting. He rises, and we begin to glimpse the profile of a vertical structure in the center of the room, covered by a square of shadow and surrounded, as in medieval forts, by a moat of light. The dancer is in the moat. His arms swing again, and the sound of *Asturias*, by Albéniz, begins. Pol goes into the shadow tapestry, crosses it diagonally, and, little by little, we see more clearly the configuration of the central structure: a brick column that could evoke a sacred totem or a great souvenir of the Burj Khalifa in Dubai. It could also be one of those *fascinus populi Romani* (the sacred image of the phallus) venerated by the vestal virgins in ancient Rome, which seem to have given rise to the word *fascination*.[43] It could also be a scarecrow. The dancer watches it from a distance and trembles, making his castanets sound again.

The tremor engenders a progressive spasm of castanets, increasingly rhythmic and in time with Albéniz's music. What does it mean for a Spanish dancer from Catalonia to dance to this music in 2018? Who or what does the verticality of that brick effigy represent? The state or the state of affairs? About what? About dance? About Spanish dance? About *España*? About *Espanya* [Spain in Catalan]?

The sound of the castanets, now constant, flutters next to the dancer's body around the baked clay phallus. "Danza (de) la Molinera," from *El sombrero de tres picos*, sounds like a distorted *Benamor*. The sound of the castanets is like a smooth rain that mists up everything: continuous and glassy. As a spectator of a striptease that is too long, I wish that the dancer would stop hanging around the structure and do something with it. Pol Jiménez tries to exorcise it with the sound of castanets as if he were trying to make a dead man speak. He takes off his castanets and moves in the space with his arms raised, showing the innocence of his hands. *La vida breve*. Exactly: life is too short not to raise our hands, not to try to stop with our skin the winds that work against us. As with a house of cards, the dancer dislodges the brick that crowns the column, extends his leg, feigning a kick, and continues dancing. *Córdoba*, by Albéniz. One by one, the dancer extracts the bricks from the structure, leaving their gums invisible for all to see. The separated teeth now form a thin denture that divides the stage diagonally. Finally, the dancer gets on the pedestal of the structure. For a few seconds, he is the totem.

What *La oscilante* teaches us is that it is less a matter of tearing down the structures than of intervening in their seams, in their folds, disrupting what at first seemed indissolubly one in order to recognize its parts separately and try to imagine new ways of placing them in the space, to create space with them, and to place ourselves before them. This is perhaps the rite of deconstruction in progress: giving ourselves the opportunity to (dis)order our lives in new ways, to constantly agree on the dramaturgy that makes us feel more alive.

A Transcultural Revolution

Beyond the national mainstream flamenco context, it is necessary to mention the work of Anna Natt (1975), an American living in Berlin who created the piece "Herztätigkeit" in 2014, in which she pays homage to Sylvan Rubinstein (1914–2022), a Jewish flamenco dancer of Russian-Polish origin who began to cross-dress in Hamburg after the World War II, and honors the death of his sister Maria, with whom he had formed the stage duo Dolores & Imperio, which had great success in Europe during the 1930s.

It is also worth mentioning international artists such as Ryan Rockmore (New York, 1989) and Daniel Moura (Salvador de Bahía, 1975), who conduct interesting practice-based research on the use of the bata de cola and something that we could call "queer flamenco." The work of Diego Ranz (Paris, 1984) in his piece *Akatomboy* (2011), where he stages the body of a bailaor-musician who sings, plays percussion, and dances at the same time, as well as the work of Clément Duvert Albistur, a dancer from Saint-Jean de Luz who trained in Madrid and mixes the codes of flamenco and Spanish dance with the codes of burlesque, are also very interesting.

Not without connection to this drag and transcultural flamenco and speaking in the first person, I would like to name the artistic work that I have been doing in recent years on gender canons and the possible strategies of dissidence and negotiation, among which drag is only one way among many others that I cannot discuss in detail here for the sake of brevity. In *H2-Ohno* (2014), I pay homage to the Japanese dancer Kazuo Ohno (1906–2010), who dressed as Antonia Mercé, "La Argentina," a Spanish dancer whom he saw dancing in Tokyo in 1929, in his 1976 piece *Admiring La Argentina*.[44] In *Bailar en hombre* (2015), I use cross-dressing to contextualize a reconstructed/reinvented farruca based on a movement score extracted from the *Tratado de bailes* (1912) by the Sevillian maestro José Otero; this time, drag serves to account for the amalgamation of genres that existed, as I have wanted to show in this text, in the performing arts of the early twentieth century. In *Intimo interior meo* (2016), I use drag to draw a parallel between the Gitano ritual of the handkerchief and the anal examinations conducted on homosexual men in different countries of the world.[45] And in *Pensaor un filósofo en el tablao* (2018), I dance with a leotard made of red sequins to "La tomate," by Paco España, to pay homage—as I also wanted to do in this text—to those who at some point were not allowed to dance and to those who danced but whose names were erased from a History to which we belong and which, of course, also belongs to us.

Finally, on the national scene but directed by a guitarist of British origin, Jero Férec, we must mention his recent initiative Flamenco Queer, which offers a queer tablao platform in Barcelona together with bailaor Rubén Heras and guest artists—among them, a voguing dancer—in which they try to develop a "BSDM," that is, a *bonito soniquete de maricas* [beautiful groove by fags], using different strategies with costumes, text, music, and movement to *queer* the traditional aesthetic of the tablao. The singers in this proposal rotate in each of the versions of the show, and the first of them was Álvaro Romero, with whom Férec also worked on my piece "*Pensaor*."

Notably, this transnational revolution occurred at the historical moment that followed the declaration of flamenco as an Intangible Cultural Heritage by UNESCO in 2010. Far from wanting to highlight the "expansive" effect of flamenco in the international arena thanks to this event, I would like to emphasize the paradoxical or at least curious nature of how binary gender codes start to be an explicit object of negotiation by a large number of artists once they have become a sort of written norm that appears formulated as followed on the UNESCO website:

> Flamenco dancing, a dance of passion and seduction, also expresses a whole series of emotions ranging from sadness to joy. Its technique is complex, and the interpretation is different, depending on who performs it: if it is a man, he will dance it with great force, resorting above all to his feet; and if it is a woman, she will execute it with more sensual movements.[46]

It is not, however, the only *legislative development* of gender regulations in flamenco. The resolution from November 6, 2012, by the Dirección General de Bienes Culturales de la Junta de Andalucía, which begins the procedure to register the activity of ethnological interest, la Escuela Sevillana de Baile, in the *Catálogo General de Patrimonio Histórico Andaluz* [general catalog of Andalusian historical heritage] as an asset of cultural interest, cites the following unpublished text by the bailaora and maestra Matilde Coral (1935), entitled *Código de la escuela sevillana: La importancia de bailar como una mujer*, from the year 2011:

> Flamenco dancing, to be as God intended, is a four-way dialogue: the muse, the angel, the duende, and the bailaora. When the four of them talk to each other in silence, the spontaneous and irreparable manifestation of the "ole" arises as a witness to the miracle. This word derives from "Allah" and summarizes gratitude to God for allowing us to recreate ourselves in the inexhaustible prodigy of dance....
> The bailaora has to seduce: every gesture and every movement is a promise. May the movement of her arms be like a silent cry of freedom. Project them toward the heavens of the chosen ones, molding the most perfect sculpture without gouges or chisels.
> Be a woman at all times and even in an outburst; surrender body and soul to the vehemence of an impossible lover....
> Stick to your waist and let each turn become a swerve of hidden

and complicit sensuality. Broad and firm hips, as the wise poet al-Murabi wanted them.

Do not forget that the Sevillian School of dance is also an insinuation. That is why too explicit of a display within it spills into vulgarity.

Be feminine, voluptuously feminine. With a slightly haughty gaze, caressing hands, half-open mouth, dashing waist, and defiant bosom.

Discover the smoothness of your thighs, but in the eyes of the beholder, the discovery is fleeting like lightning.

In short, dance by giving yourself to yourself so entirely that the most irreducible free thinker has to say, "Blessed be God."

What "force of law" do these words have for artists? Was it necessary to write the norm to start breaking it? Was it necessary to make it explicit in order to make us aware of its existence and implications in our dancing? How important is the role of words in this "revolution," since they allow us to name that which our bodies have embodied by unconscious imitation and make it emerge "little by little" to de-indoctrinate our skin, our muscles, and our bones? If this revolution of gender in flamenco means going in search of a holistic body beyond the division of dances into womanly dancing ("from the waist up") and manly dancing ("from the waist down"), will we not also have to recognize the need to abandon dancing "from the shoulders down," the kind that demonizes intellectual work by considering the rest of the body as the only truth? Is it not also necessary, in order to continue giving flight to this revolution, to allow the hand to transfer its tapping of castanets and its clapping to the blank page or the computer keyboard? Are the reviled "notepad bailaoras" not also part of this revolution, who halted their movement in the middle of a class driven by the need to take notes, to write to understand, to understand in order to dance?

Furreteos: Toward a "Guiri" History of Flamenco

The cases mentioned earlier of non-Spanish flamenco artists, residents or not of Spain, who do not comply with certain gender norms involved in flamenco, would be included in a longer and broader history that we could call a "guiri History of flamenco." In this History would appear artists other than foreign artists who, inside or outside of Spain, develop a flamenco life by bending to the traditional canons or the "flamenco scene" in cities outside Spain. One example of this effort is the catalog from the *100 Years of Flamenco* exhibition in New York, curated by K. Meira Goldberg and Ninotchka Bennahum in 2013. To continue nuancing the Spanish-centrist history of flamenco, it would be necessary, above all, to give an account of those artists who, having passed through flamenco or crossed by it, develop artistic projects that do not try to conform to the traditional canons of flamenco fully, but instead create using flamenco as the starting point.

Thus, we would leave out flamenco artists born abroad, such as José Greco (Montorio nei Frentani, 1918–Lancaster, 2000),[47] Lucero Tena (Mexico City, 1938), Shoji Kojima, "El Gitano Japonés" (Tokushima, 1939), Ryo Matsumoto (Osaka, 1966), and even the high-profile weirdo "Pollito de California,"[48] many of whom changed their identity by leaving their countries of origin to move permanently to Spain guided by the prophetic voice of flamenco.

La Meri and the Ethnologization of Spanish Dance

We would mention, however, as a special case, Russell Meriwether Hughes (San Antonio, Texas, 1898–1988), whose artistic name was "La Meri" and whose treatment of flamenco and Spanish dance as an "ethnic dance" or a "world dance" allowed her to create an artistic and pedagogical project in which she and her students moved between dances of diverse origins and characteristics that had in common only the fact that they were not Western. La Meri completed her initiation trip to Spain in 1920. However, until 1940, she traveled through Central and South America, Europe, North Africa, Australia, New Zealand, Tasmania, India, Myanmar, Indonesia, the Philippines, China, Japan, Sri Lanka, and Hawaii. In 1940, she founded the School of Natya in New York with the famous modern dancer Ruth St. Denis (1879–1968), which was converted five years later into the Ethnologic Dance Center.

La Meri's artistic and pedagogical project led this Texas artist to carry out in-depth research on the different "world dances" that she studied and, although her descriptions of them are frequently tinged with cultural misunderstandings—which play an important role in the transcultural transmission of dances—and exoticism—with a profound impact on *gitanismo*[49] and the poetics of passion in flamenco—it is still true that La

Meri is an excellent reader of the body, posture, and movement and who in her treatises goes so far as to describe with enough sharpness and precision the "postural project" of flamenco and Spanish dance. The "Spanish body" does not respond to a specific appearance (dark hair, black eyes) but to a type of postural project.[50] Therefore, flamenco is not an art transmitted genetically but by contagion in the bodily habitus, in the internalization of the body's way of simply standing up and initiating movement—what Hubert Godard calls "pre-movement."[51] Foreigners can learn to dance Spanish dance only if Spanishness is a matter of posture and not a question of nature. Hence, La Meri stresses that her students learn about the history and context of the different dances and integrate their movement into a posturally worked body.

Despite the interest in this project and the specific importance that La Meri attaches to Spanish dance, which led her to publish in 1948 a complete treatise on this art entitled *Spanish Dancing*, it must be noted to what extent our dances end up being ethnologized and form part of a pan-cultural project in which the gestures of flamenco, jotas, and other regional Spanish dances coexist with those of the various dances of the Indian subcontinent, different types of African dances, Japanese dances, and so on, which leads to the Texas artist to publish in 1977 her major work *Total Education in Ethnic Dance*. As stated by Nancy Lee Ruyter in her article "La Meri and the World of Dance":[52]

> As popularly used, the term "ethnic dance" refers to dances from all over the world, excluding western theater and urban social forms. La Meri claimed to have introduced this term prior to the 1940s and she defined it as "all those indigenous dance arts that have grown from popular or typical dance expressions of a particular race." She wished to give ethnic dance as a theater art an identity and status comparable to that of ballet and modern dance. The term obviously has many problems—which she herself recognized—and has been more or less discarded in the United States today in favor of designations such as "world dance" or "cultural forms" (which are also problematic).

As Mahalia Lassibille argues, "ethnic" dances will be taken on as an object of study by anthropology and ethnology, excluding the field of aesthetics that will deal mainly with "Western" dances.[53] This alignment is not without practical consequences. It can be an excuse for suggesting the fickle status of Spain, from the aesthetic-cultural perspective, as an intermediate point between East and West, the discourses and categories of one or the other being applicable, alternatively, both in the field of research and in artistic production. What does it mean for flamenco to become one among other "world dances"?

Returning to our "guiri History of flamenco," we would also have to talk about contemporary artists who, after the aesthetic shock experienced from attending a flamenco show, did not decide to become flamenco artists but rather took advantage of the creative energy unleashed at that moment to imagine a new creation. Due to his importance in the history of dance in the twentieth century, it is impossible not to pause on Kazuo Ohno, who, like La Meri, was also fascinated when he saw Antonia Mercé, "La Argentina," dance.[54]

Antonia Mercé, "La Argentina" (Tokyo, 1929)

Antonia Mercé, "La Argentina" (1890–1936), was born in Buenos Aires while her parents, also artists, were on tour. At age ten, she began to train in classical dance with her father, Manuel Mercé, a dance teacher and choreographer at the Teatro Real [Royal Theater] in Madrid. Four years later, after her father's death, Mercé got ready to study Spanish folk dances with her mother, Josefa Mercé.[55] From this double education and the theatrical training that Mercé would accumulate as a dancer in cafés, music halls, and cinemas, she emerged as an artist with a hybrid profile who would enjoy enormous international success until the end of her life, suddenly interrupted by a heart attack on July 18, 1936, the day of the coup d'état perpetrated in Spain by a group of soldiers.

Among the multiple international tours carried out by Mercé, the one in 1929 will have enormous effects on the history of dance in the twentieth century. On this tour, in which Mercé dances accompanied by her pianist Carmencita Pérez, the artist travels by boat at the end of 1928 from San Francisco to Yokohama to appear afterward at the Imperial Theater in Tokyo in January 1929 and, later, in Shanghai, Hong Kong, Manila, and Saigon.[56] It is the recital in Tokyo, attended by an "exceptional spectator," that interests us. The recital included, according to the program from January 26, 27, and 28, 1929, the following choreographies authored by La Argentina: "Serenata" (Malats), "Danza V" (Enrique Granados), "La danza del fuego" (Manuel de Falla), "Danza de Gitana," from the ballet *Sonatina* (Ernesto Halffter Escriche), "Lagarterana" (J. Guerrero), and after an intermission, "Córdoba" (Isaac Albéniz), "Tango andaluz" (popular), "Bolero" (Iradier), "Seguidillas" (without music), and "La corrida" (Q. Valverde). As for the program from January 29 and 30, 1929, it was composed of "Andalucía sentimental" (Joaquín Turina), "Valenciana" (Enrique Granados), "La danza del fuego" (Manuel de Falla), "Danza andaluza" (M. Infante), "Cielo de Cuba" (popular), and after an intermission, "Córdoba" (Isaac Albéniz), "El garrotín" (popular), "Bolero," from the ballet *El fandango del candil* (G. Durán), and "La corrida" (Q. Valverde). The songs performed by the pianist Pérez between Mercé's dances were, in the first program, "Sevilla," by Isaac Albéniz; "El pelele," from the *Goyescas* suite, by Enrique Granados; and "Viva Navarra," a jota by J. Larregla. In the second program, Pérez performed "Seguidillas," by Isaac Albéniz; "Triana," from the *Iberia* suite by the same composer; and "El Vito," by M. Infante.[57]

It was, therefore, a program made up mainly of choreographies of what we would today call *danza española estilizada* and, to a much lesser extent, of folk dances ("Lagarterana" and "Seguidillas") and flamenco ("Tango andaluz" and "Garrotín"), which seems logical given that Mercé was accompanied musically only by a pianist and without singing or guitar, for example, in the case of flamenco.

Admiring La Argentina, by Kazuo Ohno (Tokyo, 1977)

The "exceptional spectator" who attended the recital by La Argentina at the Imperial Theater in Tokyo in 1929 was Kazuo Ohno (1906–2010), a young student at the Japan Athletic College who, after having seen Antonia Mercé dance, decided to make dancing his profession. In 1977, forty-eight years after experiencing this kind of aesthetic shock, Ohno visits the exhibition of his artist friend Natsuyuki Nakanishi and "recognizes" in one of the paintings, behind the colors and abstract lines, by way of a Proustian experience, Mercé's figure, which motivated him to create a piece in homage to said dancer.

In the first version of the homage, directed by Tatsumi Hijikata (1928–1986), Ohno takes up the structure of the recital from Mercé's show, which links dance numbers and musical numbers, and includes arias performed by the diva Maria Callas;[58] "Ave Maria" by Bach/Gounod, performed live by a pianist, in reference perhaps to the pianist who accompanied Mercé in 1929; and Argentina tangos, in reference to the native country that gave Mercé her stage name. Toshio Mizohata, director of the Dance Archives Network in Tokyo, confirms that, at the time of the creation of *Admiring*

La Argentina, Ohno had no sources to know the type of music performed at the Mercé recital and assumed, given her artistic name, that it would be some kind of Argentinian music, which is why he decided to use Argentine tangos for the second part of his tribute.[59]

Also, according to Mizohata, the piece, constructed in two parts with an interlude, recycles a fragment of the 1959 piece *Kinjiki*, considered the first butoh dance choreography, with which both Hijikata and Kazuo Ohno's son Yoshito Ohno would have made their debut. In an opening choreography, "Death and Birth," we see Ohno emerge from the theater stalls dressed as a woman and slowly take the stage to the musical background of the Toccata and Fugue (1703–1707) by Johanna Sebastian Bach. The second scene, titled "Daily Bread," was created from quotidian movements that Ohno performed at his job at a school where he was in charge of maintenance. The third scene, where the first part of the recital ends, is titled "Marriage of Heaven and Earth" and uses the aforementioned "Ave Maria" to execute a dance in which Ohno is seen motionless next to a grand piano in a crucifixion position, a posture that the dancer slowly and almost imperceptibly transforms until it is completely undone.

In the second part of the tribute, a live orchestra performs three tangos: the first as an overture and the next two danced by Ohno. In the final number, accompanied by a second aria performed by Callas, Ohno appears in a dress similar to the one Mercé wore in her "Cielo de Cuba" number.[60] The dancer lifts his skirt, walks, gets on his knees, raises his hands, and brings them to his face pretending to smell something and spread the scent by opening his arms. After this, he takes a bouquet of flowers offered by a spectator and holds his hat, which is about to fall off. The spectators applaud, and Ohno plays with his bouquet and disappears into the darkness as the music continues to play. He reappears hatless and waves. The spectators give him even more bouquets. Hijikata comes onstage and puts one of them on his head. A group of men and women with more bouquets appear on the stage and surround Ohno, who begins to intertwine his feet in a kind of floral paroxysm that transforms his greeting almost into a funeral scene. The curtain falls.[61]

In this second part of the tribute, Ohno takes up movements from Mercé, such as the *enveloppé sauté* and the gesture of playing the castanets, executing very pronounced *cambrés* that leave his head hanging back, thus transforming the omnipresent smile of La Argentina into a gesture of surprise, panic, or death in which the mouth remains open. The dancer's feet are positioned *en dedans*, in opposition to the classical aesthetics inherited by Mercé, and they stomp on the ground only a few times throughout the entire piece, as a kind of minimalist reduction of La Argentina's footwork that Ohno would have seen and heard forty-eight years earlier. The wrists are constantly broken inwards, as if the rotational movement of the hands typical of flamenco had stopped, and the movements merge without leaving a trace on the floor that is stepped on, without a bounce or accent, without leaving a sonic trace of its path. The aesthetic developed by Ohno is, therefore, both close to and far from that of Mercé. Ohno also shares the flexibility of La Argentina's spine and her grimacing smiles, as well as the eye movements and dialogue with imaginary beings with whom the performer seems to dance onstage. These elements constitute less a reinterpretation that Ohno would have made of Mercé than a true "citation" of La Argentina's gestures that Ohno would have conserved in her memory. However, the rest of the elements, especially the type of walk and the continuous gestural jog, seem to belong more to Ohno's aesthetic than Mercé's.

Three years after the premiere of *Admiring La Argentina*, on tour in France in 1980, Ohno received an album of photographs and some recordings from Mercé's heirs in which she played castanets to music from different composers.[62] Along with these recordings, taken by the French company Odéon in 1931, Ohno incorporated the music of *La corrida*, by Valverde, into his tribute, which allowed him to develop a new spectral poetics in which Mercé was no longer only evoked through her memory and her kinesthetic translation into a body that had become a medium. Her body was also made present onstage thanks to the sound of the castanets from the piece with which Mercé had ended her two recital programs in Tokyo in 1929.

In a video filmed by director Charles Picq at the Maison de la Danse de Lyon in 1986, we see Ohno dance his interpretation of *La corrida*: dressed in a skirt, wearing a beige Manila shawl, and with hair combed with red flowers, Ohno observes his hands in front of his face and allows himself to be guided by them through space.[63] With his index fingers, he imitates a bull's horns above, making micro-movements with his head, which the dancer moves from right to left while smiling. Ohno imitates the gesture of the veronica bullfighting pass, which Mercé also performed in her version, allowing the bull to pass in front of him with a semicircular movement of the arms. During a pause in the music, Ohno plunges an invisible sword into the also-invisible body of a bull, becoming the slain bull himself, which begins to die with the resumption of the music. The dancer puts his hands to his heart and falls to the ground with his mouth open; he gets down on all fours and back up again, smiling gently, to resume aerial gestures with his arms, walking across the stage with his head tilted upward, introducing small jumps with one of his legs *en passé*. In opposition to Mercé's *La corrida*, in which the dancer first imitated the entry of the bull into the bullring to quickly embody the character of the bullfighter, Ohno executives back-and-forth gestures between the man and animal, between the winner, who survives, and the loser, who dies. When the music ends, Ohno faces the spectators with his arms at the height of his head, showing the palms of his hands before putting his right hand to his heart, a gesture of gratitude with which his bullfight ends.

Mercé's *La corrida* by way of Ohno returns in this way to France during the Japanese dancer's second tour in 1981, where La Argentina had premiered it seventy-one years earlier. Ohno continued to dance it in his homage until 1994, making this creation his best-known work, which he occasionally accompanied with other pieces, such as "My Mother"[64] and "The Dead Sea."[65] La Argentina's gestures that motivated Ohno's professional and vital project in 1929 are still alive after Mercé's death in 1936, after having waited almost fifty years in the memory of the Japanese performer, which seems to have made Mercé less of a figure of inspiration than his artistic double. In this staged alchemy, drag seems to be less an aesthetic-political operation in terms of gender than a resource for invoking, both for the spectator and for Ohno, the absent female dancer.[66]

A "Floral" Theory of Gesture

As I analyze it in another place, *Admiring La Argentina* does not constitute the end of an era in the relationship of artistic fascination between two dancers.[67] Fascinated in turn by Kazuo Ohno and his piece on La Argentina, a series of contemporary artists have been creating new pieces in a kind of artistic chain reaction: the French artists Catherine Diverrès and Pauline Le Boulba in *O Senseï* (2012) and *Ôno-Sensation* (2019), restively; the American Trajal Harrell in *The Return of La Argentina* (2016), and myself in *H2-Ohno* (2014).[68]

The fascination that Mercé produced in Ohno is contained in the fascination that Ohno provokes in these contemporary artists, and something of their gestures—inevitably transformed—remains. We would have to propose here, then, a "floral" theory about the transmission of gestures in the presence of genetic (the gesture is transmitted through blood, from parents to children), lactating (the gesture is *suckled* directly from the familial breast), or educational (the gesture is transmitted unilaterally between teachers and students in contexts of pedagogical discipline) visions.

The floral theory of gesture takes into account the multiple possibilities that a gesture germinates in other bodies—through live viewing or audiovisual files of a creation—and ends up generating a new gesture: sometimes in distant places and bodies, sometimes in a completely unpredictable way, and always in a transformed way. Following the floral theory, the gesture is only transmitted by transformation. It is not copied identically from one body to another; it is not reincarnated as an invariable abstract form that would take bodily consistency. And perhaps the most faithful gesture to Antonia Mercé is precisely the one that seems to us furthest from her aesthetic idiosyncrasies, her stylization of movement, and her staged politics. Perhaps Mercé is much more present in those who invoke her through Ohno's body than in those who "faithfully" imitate her through photographs and videos.

> To speak about works is also to expose the nostalgic, even melancholic, layers that cover us. To remember the effects of a work on oneself is perhaps to try to combat nostalgic states and transform them into something else, into emancipatory and collective forces that we can share and transmit.[69]

As Le Boulba intelligently indicates, the process of self-analysis and explanation of what happens to us when we see a work is essential not only to show the reader how our gaze is constructed but also to show ourselves the dynamics of our own thoughts: the associations of ideas, focuses of attention and their correlative absences, overinterpretations, and delusions. Only in this way can the creative paralysis, both artistic and scientific, to which admiration can lead be resolved.

"Necesito, Pieza para Granada," by Dominique Bagouet (France, 1991)

Following this line of work, we will analyze one last case of a contemporary dancer's fascination and scopic affiliation resulting from the aesthetic shock produced by a flamenco show. This section is about Dominique Bagouet (1951–1992), a significant figure in the history of contemporary dance in France, and about the last piece he premiered while alive,

"Necesito, pieza para Granada," created in 1991, a year before the artist died from complications of AIDS.

In this creation, Bagouet returns to the memory of an aesthetic shock experienced in his childhood when he attended a flamenco show on Las Ramblas in Barcelona. This shock is not linked to the personality of a specific dancer but to the group of tablao workers, who are part of the imaginary that Bagouet associated with Spain. As noted by Chantal Aubry and cited by Isabelle Ginot:

> A trip to Spain, Barcelona, a cabaret on Las Ramblas. Such is the setting of what serves as a primitive scene in the mind of the choreographer, who was, then, three or four years old: "It was a flamenco show, with women, their skirts, the brilliant bailaor throwing his hat: this becomes a mental photograph, abundantly and preciously nourished by what came next. It seems I was out of my mind, standing on my chair, and could not fall asleep that night after the show. I clearly see that bailaor throwing his hat into the audience. In a family film recorded afterward, you see me, tiny, in a white shirt, imitating the Spanish bailaor."[70]

In an interview given on July 31, 1991, the choreographer states that he wanted to "tell through dance the little mythologies of my Spain, that of my friends as well, performers, dancers—our Spain, keeping ourselves a bit in the position of the tourist, but of the tourist in love," as if he did not intend to imitate the gesture of the bailaor, but rather "rarefy" his own.[71]

In this imaginary Spain invoked by Bagouet, the flamenco universe appears musically through a paso doble group dance and the "Nana de los Gitanos," sung by Lola Flores. Both in the paso doble and the lullaby, a certain rejection of communion between music and movement establishes a relationship between the two. When specific flamenco figures and gestures appear, they do so from a movement quality that is not typical of a flamenco body but a body that swims "like a tourist in love" in the deep waters of the flamenco universe, much in the way that the bullfighter's posture facing the bull becomes softer. Muscular tension appears and disappears without effect. The foot that strikes the floor does not strike but falls on it with the weight of a feather, and the rotations of the wrist do not serve to finish off a series of movements but appear as little curls in a never-ending strand of hair.

This was the progression of the aesthetic experience that Dominique

Bagouet lived in the tablao: Bagouet, hysterical after the show, unable to sleep at the age of four, touched by a dance that remained in his mind and body for years—like Mercé's gesture on Ohno's body—and which motivated the creation of "Necesito."

> The disheveledness, the contractions, the broken-down gestures, the self-congratulatory shouting are as grotesque on the crossdresser who tries to ridicule them as in the folkloric that shows off those attitudes. The show, Spanish to the core, is par excellence, a hysterical show. . . . All these facets of Gitano-ness are, without a doubt, what give a gay Spanish show its authentic spice, its local flavor, its idiosyncrasy. Everything else, as has already been said, is an imitation of French cabarets, with more pretenses and airs—in most cases—than particular results.[72]

This aesthetic hysteria, as the philosopher Gilles Deleuze emphasizes when describing the paintings by Irish-born British painter Francis Bacon, would have to do with a rather specific form of presence and a mode of transmission to spectators whose immediacy we could describe as "contagion." The kind of presence of the dancers, singers, and guitarists, imposing or even invasive, seems to provoke a sort of immediate reception (Bagouet as a child getting on the chair). Still following Deleuze, this excess of presence translates into a situation in which "there is therefore little difference between the hysteric [the bailaor], the 'hystericized' [the spectator], and the 'hystericizor' [flamenco]."[73]

The theory of a hysterical aesthetic in flamenco would account for the device that articulates, due to the excessive presence of the artists onstage, their hysterical bodies, the hystericized spectators (who yell and cheer), and the aesthetic experience as hystericizor, which is traversed by a rarefaction of the living present, in which, according to the philosopher, what is already there and what has not yet arrived coincide: "Everywhere there is a presence acting directly on the nervous system, which makes representation, whether in place or at a distance, impossible."[74]

If this description of the aesthetic experience in the tablao turns out to be adequate, we would have to ask ourselves about the new horizons of representations in terms of gender, given the historical origin of hysteria as a "female disease" now also embodied by men. What would be the effects of said hysteria on the dancers' bodies after the performance? How do we describe the changes experienced by these hystericized bodies day after day? What would be the side effects?[75]

Decolonizing "Spanish Dance"

In order to complete our guiri History, the door must also be opened to studies on the evolution of the Spanish colonial legacy in different parts of the world to begin investigating all of the changes in flamenco throughout the globe after decolonization. A group of researchers has done this—for example, in the colossal anthology *Transatlantic Malagueñas and Zapateados in Music, Song and Dance*,[76] focused primarily on the diasporas of the zapateado and malagueña in America—and various authors have worked on Filipino dances of Spanish origin, such as the *pandanggo sa ilaw* and the *pandanggo rinconada* (fandango), the *cariñosa*, or even the jota *manileña* (from Manila).[77] What gestural remains of "Spanishness" are left in those dances? What could we learn about them from the former metropolis? Are they also part of the catalog of "Spanish dance"? What historical, political, epistemological, and even artistic debts do we still have to settle with our former colonies? And, if there were any, what would they be, and how do we settle them? By naming and describing them through research? Perhaps by learning to dance them and incorporate them into our repertoire?

Another silenced History, but whose echoes have begun to sound for some time now, is that of blackness in flamenco, the presence of people from sub-Saharan Africa in the History of this art form and their critical influence in the contribution of rhythms and movement forms, especially the tango, which according to different sources seems to have been an African dance imported from Havana to the ports of Cádiz and Seville, where it acquired its flamenco flavor and was called "American tango." In his lecture "Triana y el arte flamenco," Rafael Infante Macías, in addition to reminding us that the definition of the word "tango" in the 1952 edition of the dictionary from the Real Academia Española (Spanish Royal Academy) is "the meeting of Negros to dance to the sound of a drum," quotes a text by the costumbrista writer Charles Davillier, who in 1861 attended a party at the Taberna del Tío Miñarro in the Sevillian neighborhood of Triana:

> It didn't take long for the time to come for the dances, and a young Gitana woman of copper complexion, frizzly hair, and jet-black eyes (*ojos de azabache*), as the Spanish would say, danced the American tango with extraordinary grace. The tango is a negro dance that has a very marked and strongly accented rhythm.[78]

Regarding blackness in flamenco, two foundational works should be highlighted: *Semillas de ébano: El elemento negro y afroamericano en el baile flamenco*, by José Luis Ortiz Nuevo (Portada, 1998), and *Sonidos Negros: On the Blackness of Flamenco*, by K. Meira Goldberg (Oxford University Press, 2019). Likewise, it is necessary to name the documentary *Gurumbé: Canciones de tu memoria negra* (2016), directed by Miguel Ángel Rosales and focused on the transatlantic slave trade in the port cities of Seville, Cádiz, and Lisbon and transit locations like the city of Zafra in Extremadura province. In this documentary, Black bailaora Yinka Esi Graves (London, 1983), who lives in Seville and is of Jamaican and Ghanaian descent, also appears. We see her dancing bulerías, reminding us, as stated by some of the researchers who appear in the documentary, that what we call flamenco today is a palimpsest in which different histories and memories overlap, including those of Black people.

Toward a "Cripped" History of Flamenco

The totemic use that José Galán makes of the bata de cola at the end of his show *Sueños reales para cuerpos posibles* (2018) warns us of the need to tell another History that, until now, we have not addressed. In this scene, sustained by the musical ecstasy of the "macho" (high-energy, final section) of a seguiriya, Galán lifts Lola López, a disabled bailaora, onto his shoulders, whom we see disappear from the stage like a sort of gigantic double body wrapped in a Manila shawl, dragging the shadow of the bata de cola that lengthens from the bailaor's waist.

Incorporating people with physical or intellectual disabilities in José Galán's career is not anecdotal but instead forms part of his Flamenco Inclusivo project, which he has been developing since 2010. In addition to the pedagogical aspect of this project, José Galán has developed other shows, like *En mis cabales* (2012), also directed by Juan Carlos Lérida, in which disabled and nondisabled artists participate.[79] In this show, he uses some of the "cripped" references from the History of flamenco to show that physical and intellectual disability has never been a reason for exclusion in the flamenco arts and that "all bodies" have a place in the flamenco world.

I use the term *cripped* (*tullido*) here because the artists themselves transform a potential insult into an artistic name, which would be unthinkable, at least in the flamenco world, were they sexist or homophobic insults. Could we imagine a singer called "Fulanito el Chupapollas de

Triana" [whatshisname cocksucker from Triana]? Or a bailaora who promoted herself onstage as María, "La Camionera" [the bull dyke]?

In any case, if we would like to connect with the list of cripped flamenco references, we would have to name at least two singers from Jerez: the seguiriya performer Mateo Lasera, "El Loco Mateo" [crazy Mateo], whose stage name seems to have been due to his extreme sensitivity and temperamental imbalances,[80] which did not prevent him, however, from naturally developing an artistic career in the cafés of his time, and Manuela Domínguez, "La Ciega de Jerez" [the blind one from Jerez], who developed an important career in Madrid, singing in places such as the Kursaal Magdalena, the Teatro Avenida, and Circo Price, and accompanying in 1929, to saetas and together with Chano de las Ventas, the projections of the film *Currito de la cruz* at the Cinema Europa in Madrid.[81] Is there anything more curious than a blind singer musically accompanying the screening of a *silent* film? What does this happening teach us about the interdependence between devices, humans, and nonhumans, and the complementarity of their different abilities?

As one of the few bibliographical sources that we have found on this figure points out, "A benefit tribute was paid to him at the Goya Theater, in Madrid's Puente de Vallecas district, consisting of a festival called Gran Velada Flamenca, which the program explained as follows: 'This evening is to raise funds for an operation that they have to perform on this singer, because of which she will regain her sight, as promised by the eminent Dr. Rovirosa.'"[82]

A similar case is that of José Salazar Molina Porrina de Badajoz (1924–1977). This Gitano from Badajoz hid his visual impairment with large sunglasses, which became a kind of "brand image." The magnificent fandango performer completed the look with snakeskin shoes, extravagantly patterned and colored suits, and a carnation on his lapel.[83] In addition to his clothing, an element in Porrina's songs deviates his aesthetic from the Spanish-speaking norm of flamenco: Porrina often sang in Portuguese. The proximity between Badajoz and the neighboring country produced transfusions, contagions, and artistic porosity, especially for Gitano artists whose families, often focused on buying and selling cattle, moved from one side of the border to another.[84] Thus, we listen to Porrina singing some cantiñas and tangos in Portuguese where Spanish slips into another language that is not Gitano, *becoming foreign.*

In dance, we have "El Mate sin Pies" [no-feet Mateo], Enrique, "El Jorobao" [the humpback], Joaquín, "El Feo" [the ugly one], the bailaora from Jerez Juana Valencia Rodríguez, "La Sordita" [the little deaf one] (nineteenth to twentieth centuries), Enrique, "El Cojo" [the limper], "Miracielos" [cross-eyes],[85] and currently, María Ángeles Narváez (Switzerland, 1975), "La Niña de los Cupones" [raffle ticket girl], who has fused flamenco with sign language in shows like *Sorda* (2012).

Baltasar Mathé, "El Mate sin Pies," was a dancer born at the end of the nineteenth century and died during the twentieth century who achieved great professional success, becoming part of the show *Cuadro*, which the Ballets Russes premiered at the Gayté Lyrique Theater in Paris in 1921. Regarding the success of this bailaor, amputated up to the knees on both legs, we would have to wonder to what extent it was not produced, at least in part, by the morbid pleasure linked to the zoologization of *strange* bodies, which could turn Sergei Diaghilev's famous company into a driving force of a balletization of the freak show.

As for "Miracielos,"

It was the stage name of José Castro, Sevillian by birth, and he owed such an original stage name to a physical defect that prevented him from lowering his head. He performed in cafés cantantes and theaters. And according to Vicente Escudero, he was the first to dance accompanied by guitars at the beginning of the nineteenth century. Antonio "de Bilbao" declared that Miracielos created the dance for the *rosas* palo, performing in 1864 at the Salón Oriente in Seville, together with other flamenco artists of the decade.[86]

Enrique, "El Cojo," Paradigm of Queerness

The bailaor Vicente Escudero (1888–1980) said about Enrique, "El Jorobao":

In the old days, when I was a boy, there was a dancer called Enrique, "El Jorobao" from Linares, who had two "humps," and how that "humpback" would move his arms! All the flamencos of that time used to say: "What does this humpbacked [*sic*] Gitano possess that when he moves his arms, he looks beautiful!" This comment shows the importance they gave to arm work at that time. Now, it's about seeing who makes a hole first in the tablao or onstage.[87]

Indeed, Antonio, "El de Bilbao" was a disciple of Miracielos and Enrique, "El Jorobao" and Vicente Escudero's teacher, who was an inspirational figure for subsequent dancers, such as Antonio Gades and Israel Galván, and indisputably linked to a "masculine" aesthetic, understanding masculinity as "austerity." It could be more than a coincidence that this austerity and the subsequent development of an "ugly" aesthetic by dancers like Andrés Marín had its origin in these cripped bodies (*cuerpos tullidos*), devoid of erotic capital. It could also be more than a coincidence that the famous "Los diez mandamientos del baile flamenco puro masculino," presented at El Trascacho in Barcelona in 1951, was written by Vicente Escudero "against" Antonio Ruiz Soler, probably one of the dancers with the greatest erotic capital—aside from talent—of the twentieth century. Escudero invited Antonio, "El Bailarín" to comply with the precepts of his decalogue and described his dancing as "effeminate," which led Antonio to sue him and call him an "old failure."[88] Curiously, a relational game is produced here in which dancers with beautiful bodies "exhibit themselves," creating a "more commercial" flamenco and considered more "effeminate," and dancers with bodies lacking normative beauty end up becoming champions of an aesthetic in which categories such as "austerity," "purity," and "masculinity" overlap.

Another of our dancers who does not correspond to the masculine regulations proposed by Vicente Escudero is Enrique, "El Cojo" (Cáceres, 1912–Seville, 1985). His body did not reach the beauty standards that Ruiz Soler exceeded, which did not prevent him from becoming an essential figure in the History of flamenco dance, mainly in the field of teaching, developing an aesthetic centered on the torso and in the characteristic arm movements of the so-called womanly dancing of the Sevillian School.

> All that after limping and getting fat and bald . . . all that, and the company artists laughed. They laughed because they thought it was an insult, and it was the other way around. They were lifting me up because the newspaper said: How is it possible that a short, limping, fat, bald man doesn't make a fool of himself dancing? And that was a status they didn't understand.[89]

Enrique, the teacher of my teacher José Racero, and therefore, in part, my "flamenco grandfather," whom I never had the opportunity to meet (but in whose gestures I recognize myself to the point that gives me the shivers), "limped" in the fullest sense. Here I present a fragment of an interview conducted by José Luis Ortiz Nuevo through which we understand how El Cojo lived his affective-sexual life and how this, despite being considered a "lie" in the face of the "truth" of heterosexual marriage, was the fire that ignited and kept his art alive:

> In Buenos Aires, a funny thing happened to me. There was a guy in Buenos Aires who stopped at a café where I used to go, at Café España. And that man wanted to treat me and everything, and then, well, I said: Is this man a police officer? And, of course, I accepted his invitations.
>
> And one day he says to me: "Why don't you come to my place? Why don't you come to an apartment I have?" Mind, I say: "Why would I want to go to the apartment?" And he goes: "Come on, because" and on and on, and I say: "All right, I'll go."
>
> Look, I went to the apartment, and since I had, and still have, this hearing aid in my ear, of course, the guy went to give me his hand so he could hug me—hug me, nothing else, and he heard this high-pitched sound, but he didn't know what the ringing was, and the ringing *beeeeeeee*, and he went: "But, how strange if there's no one here and if we're alone in the house . . ." And I say: "Well, I don't know what it could be." And every time he came in to hug me: *beeeeeeee*, and he didn't notice.
>
> Falling in love? I've fallen in love like a madman, like crazy, honestly. But I've been a very smart person, modesty aside, because I've never thought of myself like that. I didn't believe those things because, you know, there are people like that who begin to believe things and that everything's true.
>
> If I've been able to do one thing in life, I've done it like this: I stop and I say no. Look, many times I've had friends, close friends, and they've told me: "Enrique, you're going to regret it, you're going to regret it." . . . I don't regret it; those things can't weigh me down because, in that moment, if you know how life goes, it can't weigh you down. Because everything's a lie, a lie. But it's never weighed me down, and I've had plenty, and I've loved because I haven't been a beast. But within that . . . an obvious example is that now I wouldn't have a big woman; if I start to think otherwise, I still wouldn't have a big woman, and I've always kept my head in its place.
>
> One time, a person I was really close with was about to get married. And she comes to my house one day and tells me: "I'm going to tell you something." I say: "To me? Well, tell me. However bad it

is, I still want to hear it." She says: "I'm getting married." I say: "And is that bad? So that's the only truth that there is in life. The one that's the lie is mine." And she began to cry. So I say: "We're going to turn this around. You're going to cry? Why? If you're getting married and you have gifts and stories and all that . . ."

I was always very talented and very honest, very honest, very honest. All the ladies and gentlemen told me so, and they've loved me because of that. Look, when I entered Doña Dolores Ibarra's house, she would say: "Look, Enrique, the thing is, we see you differently." That's how it is. I've had things for sixteen years—not a sixteen-year-old, something lasting sixteen years. Which is fine, and it wasn't a story or anything.

Because I'm going to tell you one thing. If you don't have love, you can't be talented at something. That's a lie. So love gives you talent, right? It gives you life; it gives you everything. Later, it turns out it's all a lie. But who can take dancing away from you? Well, nobody. So you've lived and you can express the dance, express the song, express the poetry, whatever you want. Because if love gets you like it did me at twenty-four . . . I was always in love and showed it and lived it. Who wouldn't live it all over again?[90]

In the film *Carmen*, by Julio Diamante (1975), in which our beloved Paco España also appears, Enrique embodies the character of Carmen's uncle, played by bailaora Sara Lezana. One of the scenes recreates a dance class in which El Cojo interrupts his students during an exercise with the same message that we have been able to read in the previous interview: "Move! This is frigid! You need to have more heart to do this; if not, you can't dance flamenco!" Watching him dance soleá, bulerías, and later, alegrías, we can imagine what Enrique's "cripped loves" were like: cunning, excessive, and without paying too much attention to who was watching.

In another video of him that circulates on the internet, already advanced in age, we see Enrique dance to alegrías again, making exquisite use of his shoulders, arms, and hands, which fill the entire space of his choreography.[91] We wonder with whom he was in love at that moment, to whom he was dancing with that cripped passion that kept him, nevertheless, in motion. Although he performs a glimpse of a footwork section in the corresponding part of the dance, his alegrías begins with a device that replaces the usual rhythmic accelerations of the footwork: Enrique appears seated, sharing a table with the musicians (Curro Fernández Jarillo singing and José Luis Postigo on guitar) and with a wooden ruler he manually stamps a llamada.

In this *cripped* history of flamenco that we barely dare to outline here, it would be necessary to describe the different artistic strategies that each of the artists has invited to make their "weakness" a strength, supplanting the traditional methods of footwork, for example, by other percussive systems, such as Enrique's wooden ruler. Lola López, the bailaora who costars with José Galán in *Sueños reales para cuerpos posibles*, elaborates an alternative strategy for footwork in a sevillanas that she dances in a duet with him. She manages to lift the wheels of her chair and hit the ground with them, performing a four-beat *remate* [phrase closer] both audibly and visually. As for Antonia Santiago Amador, "La Chana" (Barcelona, 1946), she dances seated without sacrificing a single detail of her footwork and also brings in her arm movements, especially at the end of choreographies. This figure, who had an extensive artistic career, has been recovered by the flamenco world as a result of the documentary that Lucija Stojevic made about her in 2016, which allowed her to return to the stage and shows us that it is possible to conceive a flamenco in which we can see all kinds of dancers and at whatever age.

However, conceiving it as an intellectual theory and noting certain "well accepted" examples within the flamenco family does not mean that this is a reality and a constant in the History of flamenco on the stage. How many artists with physical or intellectual disabilities do we see or have we seen perform in tablaos? How many have starred in *Carmen, El amor brujo*, or *El sombrero de tres picos*? What would a "cripped corps de ballet" look like? Can big companies afford to give up a particular model of choreographic and kinesthetic beauty to open up to the expressiveness of a greater number of bodies? Could we sell foreign tourists flamenco with footwork with prosthetic limbs or no footwork at all? Is the limit to inclusion, as Paul B. Preciado points out, a mere question of productivity? Are disabled bodies capable of dancing but unable to sell (themselves) beyond their zoologization?

The notion of disability is a modern notion that arises with the expansion of industrial capitalism at the end of the seventeenth century. The disabled body will be thought of in two different ways based on the division between production and reproduction (between public space and domestic space) established by the disciplinary regime. Thus, male disability will be seen as a dysfunction in the face of production, while the disabled female body is conceived as a place to manage a reproductive problem.[92]

If the LGTBIQ-F (à la flamenco) "revolution" happens in connection with the revolution of other minoritarian movements, it is precisely because we all share, with nuances, the same space of historical marginality and exclusion, because we are, as Pedro G. Romero stated in the synopsis of Israel Galván's show "*Lo real*," about the Gitano holocaust, "bedfellows," but absolutely "strange," rather old acquaintances. This is how Preciado explains it:

> At the same time that the notion of disability appears, another notion arises, which is that of *infirme*, a French word that one could translate into Spanish [or English] as "weak" or "sickly" or, in a literal sense, as "one who is not firm." The notion of *infirme* is in opposition to the notion of *malade* [sick person] since in the latter, their "dysfunctionality" is conceived as provisional and their process of insertion in the hospital institution is imagined as a therapeutic process (that is, curing). In contrast, the infirm person, whose "dysfunctionality" is perceived as constitutive, is distributed through an institutional series of confinements whose main reference model is prison. In this way, throughout the eighteenth and nineteenth centuries, the subspecies of the "infirmed" multiplied—the malformed, insane, syphilitic, plague ridden, cretins (that is, the mentally weak), homosexuals, hysterics—along with the totality of institutions in which they were incarcerated—insane asylums, correctional facilities (the quintessential confinement space for homosexuals and hysterics), orphanages, old-age asylums, . . . Institutions that, in reality, are interconnected since it was not uncommon for a person to go from the orphanage to the correctional facility, from the correctional facility to the prison or insane asylum, and from these to the old-age asylum.

Gitano Issues

On the verge of ending our dance, we are making a decision here to talk about Gitano activism in the history of flamenco dance. We must cite *Lo real* (2013), by Israel Galván, and *Romnia* (2015) and *Persecución* (2018), by Belén Maya. The cast of the first work includes Israel Galván, Isabel Bayón, and Belén Maya—who already coincided as dancers in the Compañía Andaluza de Danza under the direction of Mario Maya, the father of the latter and creator of *Camelamos naquerar*, a pioneering work in Gitano dance activism. The second piece in our timeline is a solo by Belén Maya in which she somehow offers a gallery of portraits of various Gitana women, through whom she seems to want to rediscover an important part of her identity while discovering unexplored areas for herself. In the third of these works, we find Belén Maya again, this time not as a performer, but as a choreographic director, accompanied by the archival and theatrical counsel of Gitano researcher Miguel Ángel Vargas.

The particularity of this last work resides in the fact that it proposes a panoramic experience in which the spectator sees from above what is happening in the scene and what is below. It also uses the floor as a screen on which various kinds of images are projected (photographs, moving maps, etc.) with which the dancing bodies are in dialogue. Based on the homonymous album released in 1976 by singer Juan Peña, "El Lebrijano," and poet and flamencologist Félix Grande, it narrates the persecution, harassment, and systematic mistreatment suffered by Gitanos in Spain since the times of the Catholic Monarchs, a moment in which the Real Pragmática de 1499 [pragmatic decree of 1499] forces them to abandon their nomadic life:

> We hereby notify the "Egyptians" (*los egipcianos*) who roam our kingdoms and regions with their wives and children ... that within sixty days from the day that this law was proclaimed and announced by our Court, and to the towns, localities, and cities that are not judicial district centres, each of them shall earn a living from known trades for which they are well suited and travel to places where they shall agree to settle or accept accommodation from Masters whom they will serve and who will provide for their needs, and they shall not go travelling together throughout our kingdom as they have. Otherwise, within another sixty days, they must leave our kingdom and never return under penalty that, should they be captured or imprisoned without masters, together, after the aforementioned time period has passed, each one shall receive one hundred lashes the first time and be permanently banished from this kingdom. On the

second offense, their ears will be cut off, and they shall spend 60 days chained and once again be expelled, as previously stated. And on the third occasion, those who took part shall be imprisoned for life.[93]

It is not the only historical fact depicted in *Persecución* by El Lebrijano. In his martinete, entitled "En el siglo XVIII," he gives an account of the Gran Redada de Julio de 1749 [Great Raid of July 1749]—also known as the General Imprisonment of Gitanos—with which Felipe V began the project of arresting and exterminating Gitanos:

> Some nine thousand Gitanos, according to Campomanes, suffered deportation and imprisonment for years in the eighteenth century as a result of the mass persecution raid designed by the Marqués de la Ensenada in the summer of 1749, a figure that rises to twelve thousand if you count the Gitanos who were already incarcerated in the prisons and arsenals of the kingdom.[94]

Returning to *Lo real*, a piece that seemed to renew choreographic interest in the "Gitano issue" in the 2010s, we provide the text by Pedro G. Romero that accompanies the piece's program. In it, the author offers us many references that give us clues about the musical, textual, and cinematographic "citations" that feed the imaginary of the piece. However, what is most interesting about it is that he formulates some of the concerns that a non-Gitano researcher like me cannot help but notice in a "queer" text like this, even though I am not the right person to give them the treatment they deserve, nor is this the textual space to delve into them, since the focus is on other predicaments. "The Gitanos have not told their story; they have not told it in history," Pedro G. warns us, also illuminating us on the necessary intersectionality of the struggles (perhaps without realizing it himself) when he says, surprised, "strange bedfellows: Jews, homosexuals, Jehovah's Witnesses, communists, and Gitanos."

> It is not really a work with a plot. Of course, things happen, and many at the same time, appealing to different levels of signification. Like the layers of an onion, the storylines overlap rather than follow one another. Then what follows is a program, rather than a list of events, like a series of questions we can ask ourselves while we see what is materializing onstage.

Prologue
The air is cut off.
The flamenco point of view. Presentation of the witness and his tools.
First part
A man: Flowers grow from the dead.
A woman: the sky trembles and falls.
Flamenco is what speaks, sings, dances: *granaínas*, malagueñas, verdiales. A kind of exorcism, the evil that grows inside of me. Has anyone questioned why "Hitler in my Heart," the composition by AHOHNI and The Johnsons, is a fandango? Fandango, *fado*, predetermination, destiny . . .

The same positive sciences that helped make flamenco known built the racist extermination machine. Prior to modernity, our Middle Ages. Anachronism: Gitanos were always persecuted.

A degenerate art. Tomás de Perrate puts Hugo Ball's "Karawane" to *tonás*. What does it mean to be from the East? Strange bedfellows: Jews, homosexuals, Jehovah's Witnesses, communists, and Gitanos. What meaning, then, can we give to Orientalism? Metastasis: where Xenakis, an anti-fascist wounded by his own allies, precisely defines the shape of the anomaly.

Music that comes from there, what in Europe is called the criminal classes. They called us petty thieves, always on the attack from the bullpen. It is possible to imagine flamenco and the Nazis at the same time. Tony Gatlif's first film, *Canta gitano*: the maestro Mario Maya dances in the concentration camp, Manuel de Paula sings in *cabales*, burn the earth because I want to die . . .
Intermission
Carmen, the bedbug and the flea
And that strange fascination? A nationalist emblem, Tiefland, in which Leni Riefenstahl plays a bailaora while the Gitanos represent the unholy inhabitants of the lowlands.

And Goebbels's passion for our Gitano-like film stars, for patriotic folklore. Beyond the propaganda, they announce a world that makes men and their goods equal.

Carmen, "La de Triana" or Mariquilla Terremoto. Nietzsche against Wagner: not only Carmen, Bizet's African music, I never listened to such sincere music, that "Jota de los ratas" that Chueca throws in the face of the world from Gran Vía!

Weird stories: a Dutch Jew saves her life thanks to her portrait as a Gitana bailaora; Hannah's flamenco drawings in the Terezin barracks; in the countryside, Madame Fifi, the dancer, naked before the Gestapo officer, grabs his pistol, kills him, then commits suicide. Is there judgment at the end of the story?
Last station:
Death is a welcome teacher.
But what is a concentration camp? The first time they detained us, they took us to the countryside, just like my father, like our grandparents, like always our people. The Gitanos have not told their story; they have not counted in history. Put Gitano voices in Steve Reich's *Different Trains.*

How do we begin telling our (his)story without being absorbed by the great History? How can we continue saying that we are a people without aspiring to be a nation? Is that what the flamenco voice can offer to Gitanos?

Prayer: the band of Jews and Gitanos interprets "La muerte es un maestro venido de Alemania," the tango by Paul Celan. Feet against geography. The earth is not a country. The soil knows no maps. For ghosts, representation is not a problem.

We who are nobody; we who have no name.

The clap of a hand against the body, broken knee against the wooden floor, a dampened clap, stuttering breath, sound of air leaving the throat. On the side of a highway, by the wayside, lost, a wagon of dead and living bodies. Trying to demolish historical time by altering its rhythm, another way of counting.

Nothing is seen. One, two, three. One, two, three. Four, five, six. Four, five, six. Seven.

Beyond the issues related to cultural appropriation (of "Gitano-ness" by non-Gitanos) and self-exoticization (as a form of instrumentalization by Gitanos of their own culture, ethnicity, and family legacy), we can ask ourselves at what level of analysis the "Gitano issue" would be situated in dance. On a statistical level, that would account for the number of professional Gitano artists? In the configuration of work groups (companies, tablao cuadros, etc.), in which we would find both fully Gitano groups—often configured around family nuclei—as well as mixed groups and completely non-Gitano groups?

Perhaps in the theme of the pieces on the History of Gitano people, of which we have spoken and whose material about oppression and social exclusion coincides with other forms of identity exclusion based on gender, sexuality, or political opinion?

Is it about the genetic-familial transmission of gestures and compás, which would lead us to inscribe the genetic learning "from the blood" and the "suckled" art within the broader context of a History of flamenco pedagogies that would have to talk about the differences and similarities between the formal learning of conservatories, the informal education of academies, and the learning of "participant observers" in private contexts, as well as the experiences of "scopic apprentices," who integrate into their studies both the shows seen live and the memorization through videos available on the internet?

Perhaps in relation to the choice of certain song styles (seguiriya, soleá, bulerías...) over others considered non-Gitano? In relation to an aesthetic binary according to which the *baile gitano* [Gitano style of dancing] would be more explosive, wild, or Dionysian than the *baile payo* [non-Gitano style of dancing], more controlled, academic, or Apollonian? Related to this point, are we not tired of showing that there are non-Gitanos who "dance Gitano-like" and vice versa? Are we not tired of deconstructing these categories to show that they are insufficient labels to account for the complexity of each artist's "choreographic signature" and its mobility through the different song styles, performance contexts, and stages of life? Do we expand our consciousness in dance by resorting to these categories? Can we do without them? And, what is most important, will we be capable of treating the "Gitano issue" with accuracy, sensitivity, and solidarity in such a way that it encourages all of us not to create more exclusions in areas—such as this text—motivated by a will to open to the other?

Gitano-ness, Flamenco-ness, and Queerness

Artists like Noelia Heredia, "La Negri" (Madrid, 1980), singer and percussionist, Gitana and lesbian ("diverse," as she defines herself), literally string together two flags in their concerts: the rainbow LGTBIQ flag and the Gitano flag, light green and blue behind a scarlet-colored wheel. This communion seems to be the target of a crossfire between the non-Gitanocentrism of the LGTBIQ movement, which turns Gitanos into a minoritized subgroup within another minoritized community, and the homophobia existing in certain Gitano sectors, who see the sexual diversity of "La Negri" as a factor that "diminishes Gitano-ness."

In that vibrant space between convergent struggles and different perspectives, nevertheless and without a doubt, "the realness" (*lo real*) of our identity and our struggle is found. Unfortunately, what seems to be far away is that type of flamenco prior to its nationalist use that Francoism made of it and that I have tried to describe in this book, in which, as Pedro G. Romero argues, flamenco art was a space for "disidentification," a refuge and breeding ground for social and artistic heterodoxy, that allows the author of the article "El flamenco es un género" to state, quoting Janek, that "flamenco and Gitano-ness are the same. Gitano-ness and Roma-ness are the same. But flamenco-ness (*flamencura*) and Roma-ness have their distinctions."[95]

Aside from sharing the fact that they were initially insults, as Romero maintains, "flamenco-ness" and "queerness" share a concern for the loss of authenticity, the nostalgia of no longer being what they originally were and what it is, moreover, that they should be, which not only generates nostalgia but also a slight feeling of guilt. The price of the institutional, academic, and artistic appropriation of one another has often engendered an inert distrust and a certain pessimism. However, it can also create a healthy critical distance that preserves a duration of time to reflect on the practices that are being done at present and, beyond the ruckus that recognition and visibility produce, to analyze in which direction it is going and what the aesthetic, ethical, and political implications are of that which is proposed.

Are, then, "flamenco" and "queer" in some sense the same thing? Do they share something more than the original insult and concern for the loss of authenticity? Is it incidental that the Los Canasteros tablao, in the Chueca neighborhood, later became the Polana gay nightclub, and its stage became a dance floor? After its closure in the 1980s, is it a coincidence that the Las Brujas tablao, which had previously been a wine store, became what is today the Paraíso gay sauna? There you can still recognize the brick vault of the main corridor, where, on the left, there are four tiles made by the company Cerámicas Villa de Madrid, signed by Cecilio Calabaza S., Julián Santacruz, and Alfonso Montes. The images on the tiles represent, respectively, the Cibeles fountain in Madrid; a group of male and female bolero dancers with castanets in the center of a group of people who accompany them with clapping; a snack in Virgen del Puerto, on the banks of the Manzanares River; and a final scene in front of the Las Ventas bullring, in which we find a picador on horseback, two bullfighters, and a man dressed in a long black cape and hat. In front of these tiles, some

Andalusian-style bars can also be seen on the facade of the sauna, and, between them, passersby dressed only in a towel around their waists who observe each other without stopping to look at the traditional scenes on the tiles, in turn creating other scenes. Can we deduce something prudent from this (through) line from lament to wail? Anything about the architecture of intimate spaces, about the dramaturgy of desire, about vaulted ceilings, clayey materials, darkness, and humidity? Maybe something about the covens, full of magic and sexuality, that the owner of Las Brujas wanted to emulate in his tablao?

Conclusion
A Revolution?

Without a doubt, the Spanish feminist and LGTBIQ movement is positively transforming the flamenco world and, hopefully, will continue to do so in the near future. The achievements of activism in its variety of forms have permeated an artistic environment that is sometimes too free for its own members, whether they are singers, guitarists, dancers, or fans. This has generated unnecessary aesthetic and social barriers that have produced nothing but violence, pain, frustration, and misunderstandings everywhere and that we can still see and hear in different contexts, especially that of the press conglomerates, in which we witness the resistance of some journalists to take responsibility for the consequences of a cultural machismo in which we have all grown up and whose criticisms by artists, such as Huelva-born singer Rocío Márquez, are contemptuously branded as *feminijondismos* [pejorative view of feminist concerns from flamenco artists].[1]

That feminism that Bohórquez criticizes has also taught us that one can fight by lowering one's arms and listening to the other (both of these profoundly flamenco gestures) and that beyond frontism there is a space in which we all fit because there are no borders. This space is full of creative possibilities and new forms of coexistence, some of which we still do not dare to imagine.

If it is absolutely indisputable that the feminist and LGTBIQ movements have transformed the flamenco universe, it is also possible to look at the other side of the coin. With its consequences, both positive and negative, flamenco has become part of what we could call Spanish culture and, above all, part of the imaginary that several generations have had and still have about what it means to go to the theater to listen to music and see dancing. Its power, therefore, as a "shared code" is by no means insignificant when it comes to using it to convey messages to groups of people who are perhaps more conservative or simply disconnected from contemporary art, where these issues are often raised for an already-convinced audience. Flamenco allows you to explain things to your grandmother, your aunt, that other artistic languages could not because the communication codes are too different to produce a "common" ground of understanding.

That was my experience when I took "Bailar en hombre" to distant places, such as the Venezuelan city of Maracaibo, but also to other closer ones, such as the Centro Cultural Villaverde in Madrid and, thanks to the project *Teoría de conjuntos*, to the Manuel Núñez de Arenas public school in El Pozo del Tío Raimundo, part of the Vallecas district. In the latter context, I adapted the staged piece to the format of a dance conference, in which I explained to the boys and girls, with a high percentage of Gitano ethnicity, what it had meant for me to be an eleven-year-old boy whose biggest dream was to dance in a neighborhood where dancing was "a thing for girls and fairies (*mariquitas*)." My T-shirt, which had the word *MARICA* written on it, also allowed them to ask me, not without some sarcasm, if "I was one," normalizing a topic of conversation in which the answer was "Yes, why?" My annual collaborations with this school have allowed me to see how flamenco was, in this and other contexts, a tool for social transformation that served not only to teach boys and girls to clap but also to touch on themes of great importance, like gender identity, sexuality, and ecology.

Furthermore, flamenco has historically served as a therapeutic refuge for many who have had no more support than what they could give themselves, and perhaps we should begin to appreciate its healing effect, especially during the decades of psychological isolation and social and political ostracism that precede us. We will talk, then, about how Bambino's rumbas have unblocked torrents of tears that we had held back; how Fernanda de Utrera has made us feel less alone in our sadness because there is no sorrow greater than her sorrow; how we have flown with the jumps of Antonio, "El Bailarín," letting go of extra weight and feeling the lightness of the earth, flexible as a trampoline. About how Carmen Amaya has taught us to draw strength from weakness to "pull ourselves up" and set boundaries for those who have overstepped with us. About how El Güito, with his soleá, made us understand that speed changes everything and that life must be "danced slowly."

About how *aje* [artistic command and presence] has taught us the sacred value of a *juerga* and the Eucharist of a *pellizco* [sudden movement quality in flamenco as if the body gets pinched]. About how compás has shown us that in order to communicate with one another, we must speak a language that we all understand, even if we stray from it from time to time, to make rhythmic excursions. About how, ultimately, flamenco has made us understand, starting from the flesh, what it means to be human, that we are all here trying to be a little bit happy, and that sadness is as much a part of life as joy because, as Ocaña would say, "Crying is like laughing."

Notes

Translator's Note

1. Gayatri Chakravorty Spivak, "The Politics of Translation," in *Outside in the Teaching Machine* (New York: Routledge, 1993), 205.
2. For a substantial elaboration on the contexts and usage of the term "Gitano," refer to "Introduction" in K. Meira Goldberg, Ninotchka Bennahum, and Michelle Heffner Hayes, "Introduction," in *Flamenco on the Global Stage: Historical, Critical, and Theoretical Perspectives*, ed. K. Meira Goldberg, Ninotchka Bennahum, and Michelle Heffner Hayes (Jefferson, NC: McFarland, 2015), 9–13.
3. Joseph M. Pierce, "I Monster: Embodying Trans and *Travesti* Resistance in Latin America," *Latin American Research Review* 55, no. 2 (2020): 306.
4. The following sources were particularly influential and informative: Lawrence La Fountain-Stokes, *Translocas: The Politics of Puerto Rican Drag and Trans Performance* (Ann Arbor: University of Michigan Press, 2021); Camila Sosa Villada, *Bad Girls: A Novel*, trans. Kit Maude (New York: Other Press, 2022); M. Myrta Leslie Santana, "*Transformista, Travesti, Transgénero*: Performing Sexual Subjectivity in Cuba," *Small Axe* 26, no. 2 (July 2022): 46–59; Marlene Wayar, *Furia travesti: Diccionario de la T a la T* (Buenos Aires: Paidós, 2021); and Pierce, "I Monster."
5. For more on the usage and evolution of this term, see Carrie Sandahl, "Queering the Crip or Cripping the Queer? Intersections of Queer and Crip Identities in Solo Autobiographical Performance," *GLQ* 9, nos. 1–2 (2003): 25–56; Robert McRuer, *Crip Theory: Cultural Signs of Queerness and Disability* (New York: New York University Press, 2006); and Alison Kafer, *Feminist, Queer, Crip* (Bloomington: Indiana University Press, 2013).
6. K. Meira Goldberg, *Sonidos Negros: Sobre la negritud del flamenco*, trans. Kiko Mora (Granada: Libargo, 2022).

Introduction

1. Gilles Deleuze and Félix Guattari, *What Is Philosophy?*, trans. Graham Burchell and Hugh Tomlinson (New York: Verso, 1994), 1–2.

2. Giorgio Agamben, *Nudities*, trans. David Kishik and Stefan Pedatella (Stanford: Stanford University Press, 2011), 16.

3. [See the "Translator's Note" in the front matter for translation choices and usages of *travesti, travestismo, transformismo,* and *marica,* in particular.]

4. [Consult the "Translator's Note" for the rationale behind the usage of *Gitano* and not lowercased *gitano,* "Gypsy," or Roma.]

5. I am referencing Jack Halberstam's *The Queer Art of Failure* (Durham: Duke University Press, 2011).

Chapter 1

1. José Álvarez Junco, *Mater dolorosa: La idea de España en el siglo XIX* (Madrid: Taurus, 2001), 153.

2. Julio Caro Baroja, *Temas castizos* (Madrid: Isthmus, 1980), 99.

3. [This condensed understanding of *casticismo* comes from Javier Irigoyen-García, *The Spanish Arcadia: Sheep Herding, Pastoral Discourse, and Ethnicity in Early Modern Spain* (Toronto: University of Toronto Press, 2014), 3. I am including flamenco scholar K. Meira Goldberg's brief introduction on the subject as additional context for those unfamiliar with its history: "Casticismo comes from the word *casta,* meaning chaste, or caste. If, in early modern Spain, *raza,* or race, signified the stain of Blackness, casta signified and certified nobility and purity of blood—Whiteness. Eighteenth-century majismo asserted its untainted Castillian national essence by dressing up as a dark Other, whose Semitic and south-Saharan African antecedents were now wrapped within an imaginary Gitano." Goldberg, *Sonidos Negros,* 48.—TRANSLATOR]

4. José Luis Navarro García, *Historia del baile flamenco,* vol. 1 (Seville: Signatura, 2010), 137.

5. Pierre Bourdieu, *Language and Symbolic Power,* ed. John B. Thompson, trans. Gino Raymond and Matthew Adamson (Cambridge: Harvard University Press, 1991), 100.

6. Alain Gobin, *Le flamenco: Que sais-je?* (Paris: Presses Universitaires de France, 1975), 106.

7. *Free flow* is sometimes used in moments of climax, in which the hands, arms, and head move in a proliferation of gestures that do not, however, spread to the rest of the body, which remains solidly anchored to the ground. The *flexible space,* which allows us to enter into relation with the entire area without focusing on a precise point, sometimes appears at the opening moments of dances, in which the bailaor is seen listening to the singing before executing a *remate* [phrase closer]. It also appears in more relaxed choreographic passages, such as *falsetas* [accompanying melodic phrases], in which the movement of the bailaor is not directed by the rhythm but by the pattern of the melody. Finally, the *gentle weight* is used to relax the firm weight, both in the upper part of the body and in the lower part, as well as to create accents, that is, to generate gaps between the downbeats.

8. According to Laban, there are other actions derived from the main action verbs, which would be for "punching," *shove, kick, poke;* for "flicking," *flip, jerk, flap;* for "pressing," *crush, cut, squeeze,* and for "wringing," *pluck, pull,* and *stretch.* All of these from

Rudolf von Laban, *The Mastery of Movement*, 3rd ed., ed. Lisa Ullmann (Boston: Plays, 1971), 77.

9. The footwork step called a *látigo* begins and ends with a strong downward heel from the foot opposite to the one that executes the main back-and-forth movement that very quickly drags the sole of the foot along the ground "as if it were erasing something."

10. Ludwig Wittgenstein, "Proposition 5.6," in *Tractatus Logico-Philosophicus*, trans. C. K. Ogden (London: Kegan Paul, Trench, Trubner, 1922), 74.

11. Laban, *The Mastery of Movement*, 145.

12. Isabelle Launay, *Les danses d'après*, vol. 2, *Cultures de l'oubli et citation* (Pantin: Centre National de la Danse, 2018), 142.

13. *El Alabardero*, no. 677, Seville, November 13, 1884, cited in José Luis Ortiz Nuevo, *¿Se sabe algo? Viaje al conocimiento del arte flamenco en la prensa sevillana del XIX* (Seville: El Carro de la Nieve, 1990), 425.

14. Fernando López Rodríguez, *De puertas para adentro: Disidencia sexual y disconformidad de género en la tradición flamenca* (Madrid: Egales, 2017), 34.

15. Alberto Mira, *De Sodoma a Chueca: Una historia cultural de la homosexualidad en España en el siglo XX* (Madrid: Egales, 2007).

16. Richard Cleminson and Francisco Vásquez Garcia, *"Los Invisibles": A History of Male Homosexuality in Spain, 1850–1940* (Cardiff: University of Wales Press, 2007).

17. Andrés Moreno Mengíbar and Francisco Vázquez García, *Sexo y razón: Una genealogía de la moral sexual en España (siglos XVI–XX)* (Madrid: Akal, 1997), 123.

18. José Otero Aranda, *Tratado de bailes de sociedad, regionales españoles, especialmente andaluces, con su historia y modo de ejecutarlos* (Seville: Tip. de la Guía Oficial, 1912), 98.

19. Otero Aranda, *Tratado de bailes*, 128–129.

20. Ramiro de Maeztu, *Hacia otra España* (Madrid: Biblioteca Nueva, 1997 [1899]), 165; Lucas Mallada, *Los males de la patria* (Madrid: Alianza Editorial, 1994 [1890]), 165; Lucas Mallada, *La futura revolución española y otros escritos regeneracionistas* (Madrid: Biblioteca Nueva, 1998 [1897]), 207; Rafael Altamira, *Psicología del pueblo español* (Madrid: Biblioteca Nueva, 1997 [1902]), 183; and Ricardo Macías Picavea, *El problema nacional* (Madrid: Biblioteca Nueva, 1996 [1899]), 105 and 119.

21. [For further English-language context on the notion of *flamenquismo* or *nacionalflamenquismo*, I offer William Washabaugh's definition: "the sneering name [dissident artists and scholars] gave to the *franquista* [Franco regime's] promotion of meretricious spectacles that celebrated the richness of Spanish art while hiding both the poverty and the regional allegiances of the artists." *Flamenco: Passion, Politics, and Popular Culture* (Oxford: Berg, 1996), 103. I also address this concept in relation to the construction of the ideal masculinity for bailaores during the Franco regime in Ryan Rockmore, "Dancing the Ideal Masculinity," in *Flamenco on the Global Stage: Historical, Critical, and Theoretical Perspectives*, ed. K. Meira Goldberg, Ninotchka Bennahum, and Michelle Heffner Hayes (Jefferson, NC: McFarland, 2015), 239.—TRANSLATOR]

22. [This quotation was provided using a combination of English text from the original Cleminson and Vázquez García, *"Los Invisibles,"* 211 n. 59, as well as translation into English from the Spanish edition, which included major revisions to the language in the footnote: Richard Cleminson and Francisco Vázquez García, *Los invisibles: Una historia de la homosexualidad masculina en España, 1850–1939* (Granada: Comares, 2011), 189 n. 83.—Translator]

23. *Journal des débats politiques et littéraires*, March 2, 1840, cited in Hélène Marquié, *Non, la danse n'est pas un truc de filles: Essai sur le genre en danse* (Toulouse: Éd. de l'Attribut, 2016), 178–179.

24. Marquié, *Non, la danse*, 170, 172–173.

25. Description collected by Javier Sáez, *Teoría queer y psicoanálisis* (Madrid: Síntesis, 2008), 24.

26. Sáez, *Teoría queer*, 24–25.

27. ABC, "Una pieza del Arqueológico revela que la primera mujer torera es del siglo XVII," *ABC Cultura*, December 26, 2014, https://www.abc.es/cultura/arte/201410 25/abci-pieza-arqueologico-revela-primera-201412251630.html

28. To learn more about the history of female bullfighting, consult Muriel Feiner, *La mujer en el mundo del toro* (Madrid: Alianza, 1995).

29. José Blas Vega, *Cincuenta años de flamencología* (Madrid: El Flamenco Vive, 2007), 30.

30. *La independencia española*, June 5, 1870; Ángeles Cruzado, "1879, el salto a la Villa y Corte," in *La valiente: Trinidad Huertas "La Cuenca"*, by José Luis Ortiz Nuevo, Ángeles Cruzado, and Kiko Mora (Seville: Libros con Duende, 2016), 24.

31. Navarro García, *Historia del baile flamenco*, 307.

32. Navarro García, *Historia del baile flamenco*, 308.

33. Cristina Cruces Roldán, *Más allá de la música. Antropología y flamenco (II): Identidad, género y trabajo* (Seville: Signatura, 2003), 133.

34. "The soleá was the flamenco counterpoint to festive dances.... In it, women—because the soleá used to be an exclusive dance for women—could develop all her artistic creativity. In this dance, reminiscences of the old *jaleos* blended with aspects of those known in *soleares de Arcas*, a style that is another essential link in the gestation of the flamenco soleá, to form a more relaxed rhythm. According to José Otero, Trinidad Huertas, "La Cuenca," from Málaga, interpreted these melodic-rhythmic styles and was the first to give them a flamenco feeling and introduce footwork into them," Cruces Roldán, *Más allá de la música*, 311.

35. Cruces Roldán, *Más allá de la música*, 325.

36. Navarro García, *Historia del baile flamenco*, 295.

37. José Manuel Gamboa, *Una historia del flamenco* (Barcelona: Espasa, 2004), 321.

38. Cristina Cruces Roldán, "'De cintura para arriba': Hipercorporeidad y sexuación en el flamenco," *Proceedings from Entretejiendo saberes: Actas del IV seminario de la Asociación Universitaria de Estudios de Mujeres (AUDEM)* 1 (2003): 1–2.

39. Ramón Martínez, *La cultura de la homofobia y cómo acabar con ella* (Madrid: Egales, 2016).

40. I am referencing the canonical work on this matter: Monique Wittig, *The Straight Mind and Other Essays* (Boston: Beacon Press, 1992).

41. In the first volume of his *Historia del baile flamenco*, José Luis Navarro García collects newspaper reviews and texts written by foreign travelers from the eighteenth century, in which the erotic nature of the dances is always pointed out as something fundamental.

42. The interpretation that I propose here is based on the notion of the "scopic drive" or "gaze drive," created by Jacques Lacan in his seminar from 1973. *The Four Fundamental Concepts of Psychoanalysis: The Seminar of Jacques Lacan Book XI*, ed. Jacques-Alain

Miller, trans. Alan Sheridan (New York: Norton, 1998). In it, the author distinguishes drives from biological needs. In opposition to these needs, drives do not have as their principle the range of their objective but rather that of following their tension, gravitating around the object: the pleasure the gaze offers does not reside in anything other than the repetitive movement of the desire itself. According to Lacanian psychoanalysis, the paths of the drive are structured by three grammatical voices: active (*looking*), reflexive (*seeing oneself*), and passive (*being seen*). If we make these three paths converge with the postulates of our analysis, according to which the active role is occupied by the man and the passive role by the woman, then the man will position himself in the place of the one who looks, while the woman will position herself in the place of the one that is observed. Far from being original, this perspective of the "male gaze" as a privileged gaze of the heterosexual man was worked on by John Berger in 1972 in his work *Ways of Seeing* and evolved in the 2000s to become, in the words of film researcher E. Ann Kaplan, the "imperial gaze." John Berger, *Ways of Seeing* (London: British Broadcasting Corporation and Penguin Books, 1972) and E. Ann Kaplan, *Looking for the Other: Feminism, Film, and the Imperial Gaze* (New York: Routledge, 1997). This "imperial gaze" reflects the importance of analyzing the dynamics of the gaze from the intersectional, gendered, and ethnic-geographic point of view of the heterosexual male subject who is also white and Western.

43. Cruces Roldán, *Más allá de la música*, 45 n. 23.

44. Edward G. Kendrew, "Dancers in Spain," *Variety*, December 1, 1912, 61.

45. José Luis Ortiz Nuevo, *Yo tenía mu güeña estrella: Anica la Periñaca* (La Puebla de Cazalla: Barataria, 2012), 53–54.

46. Pierre Louÿs, *Woman and Puppet*, trans. unknown (New York: Pierre Louÿs Society, 1927), 189–200.

47. Although the author speaks about a jota, given the description of the performer's movements (including footwork), it seems to be about a flamenco dance.

48. ochopajaritos, "Isabel Bayón Compañía Flamenca. LA MUJER Y EL PELELE," YouTube video, 10:32, June 3, 2009, https://www.youtube.com/watch?v=fM0rHZneRGI

49. Sal De Velilla, *Sodoma y lesbos modernas: Pederastas y safistas, estudiados en la clínica, en los libros y en la historia* (Barcelona: Carlos Ameler, 1932), 140.

50. Lily Litvak, *Antología de la novela corta erótica española de entreguerras (1918–1936)* (Madrid: Taurus, 1993), 16.

51. To learn more about this character, consult historian Juan Carlos Usó, *Gloria laguna: Ingenio castizo, mito literario y lesbianismo chic* (Santander: El Desvelo, 2018).

52. José Blas Vega, *Los cafés cantantes de Madrid (1846–1936)* (Madrid: Guillermo Blázquez, 2006), 92–95.

53. First, in its location on Alcalá Street, which disappeared due to refurbishment work on the Puerta del Sol area around 1857, and then simultaneously at number 5 of this plaza and, very close to there, at number 15 on Arenal Street.

54. Litvak, *Antología*, 16.

55. José Blas Vega, *Vida y cante de Antonio Chacón: La edad de oro del flamenco (1869–1929)* (Córdoba: Ayuntamiento de Córdoba, 1986), 82.

56. Mario Gómez, dir., *Rito y geografía del cante flamenco*, Season 1, episode 95, "Lorca y el flamenco," aired September 24, 1973, RTVE, https://www.rtve.es/play/videos/rito-y-geografia-del-cante/rito-geografia-del-cante-lorca-flamenco/5478378/

57. Juan Carlos Usó, *Orgullo travestido* (Santander: El Desvelo, 2017), 38.
58. Antonio Escribano, *Y Madrid se hizo flamenco* (Madrid: Avapiés, 1990), 63.
59. Diego López Moya, *La Argentinita: Libro de confidencias* (Madrid: J. Yagües, 1914), 61.
60. Interview conducted by Sánchez Carrére, cited in José Javier León, *El duende: Hallazgo y cliché* (Seville: Athenaica, 2018), 218.
61. We found the complete text of Muñoz Seca's monologue and some photographs of La Argentinita copying the poses she did during it in an issue of *La Esfera* magazine from March 29, 1924. Pedro Muños Seca, "¡Ay, se me cae!," *La Esfera* 11, no. 534 (March 29, 1924): 27.
62. León, *El duende*, 210.
63. Eulalia Pablo Lozano, *Mujeres guitarristas* (Seville: Signatura, 2009), 130–132.
64. Ángeles Cruzado, "Amalia Molina, el arte y la gracia de Sevilla que conquistan al mundo (VIII)," *Flamencas por derecho*, July 4, 2014, https://www.flamencasporderecho.com/amalia-molina-viii/
65. An article that appeared in *El blanco y negro* on September 26, 1926, discussed Molina's reaction to an American businessman requesting that she dance without stockings: "But what do you take me for? I don't need to undress for them to admire me!" she exclaimed indignantly. Ángeles Cruzado, "Amalia Molina, el arte y la gracia de Sevilla que conquistan al mundo (X)," *Flamencas por derecho*, July 18, 2014, https://www.flamencasporderecho.com/amalia-molina-x/
66. Antonio Gómez, "Tres cuplés feministas de La Argentinita," *Memoria músico-festiva de un jubilado tocapelotas*, November 6, 2017, https://aplomez.blogspot.com/2017/11/antologia-de-cuples-2-tres-cuples.html
67. Gómez, "Tres cuplés."
68. Gómez, "Tres cuplés."
69. Alicia H. Puleo García, "Introducción al concepto género," in *Género y comunicación*, ed. Juan F. Plaza Sánchez and Carmen Delgado Álvarez (Madrid: Fundamentos, 2007), 188. Paul B. Preciado elaborated on an essential critical analysis of this concept of gender in a short text, "Biopolítica del género," in *Conversaciones feministas: Biopolítica* (Buenos Aires: Ají de Pollo, 2009), and his extensive work *Testo Junkie: Sex, Drugs, and Biopolitics in the Pharmacopornographic Era*, trans. Bruce Benderson (New York: Feminist Press, 2013).
70. As would happen with the notion of feminism, although in a different sense, and as will also happen to the idea of *transvestism* (*travestismo*). Remember that the latter did not disappear from the *Diagnostic and Statistical Manual of Mental Disorders*, or *DSM*, until its fifth edition, published on May 18, 2013. American Psychiatric Association, *Diagnostic and Statistical Manual of Mental Disorders*, 5th ed. (Arlington, VA: American Psychiatric Publishing, 2013).
71. John Money, "Hermaphroditism, Gender and Precocity in Hyperadrenocorticism: Psychological Findings," *Bulletin of the Johns Hopkins Hospital*, no. 96 (1955): 253–264.
72. I am referencing both the *performativity* of gender, inherited by Butler from Austin, and the notion of *habitus*, coined by French sociologist Pierre Bourdieu, not without a certain Aristotelian aftertaste. If the first notion denaturalizes gender and announces it as the result of a quotidian theatricalization, the second insists upon the unconscious

nature, to the point of achieving automation, of the incorporation or embodiment of different gender codes.

73. Magnus Hirschfeld, *Transvestites: The Erotic Drive to Cross-Dress*, trans. Michael A. Lombardi-Nash (Buffalo, NY: Prometheus Books, 1991 [1910]).

74. Cleveland Plain Dealer, "Queen of the Ring," *Cleveland Plain Dealer*, July 13, 1888.

75. Susan Stryker, *Transgender History: The Roots of Today's Revolution* (New York: Seal Press, 2008).

76. Kiko Mora, "Nueva York, entre La Habana y París; 1889," in *La valiente: Trinidad Huertas "La Cuenca"*, by José Luis Ortiz Nuevo, Ángeles Cruzado, and Kiko Mora (Seville: Libros con Duende, 2016), 263.

77. Ninotchka Devorah Bennahum, "Early Spanish Dancers on the New York Stage," in *100 Years of Flamenco in New York City*, ed. Ninotchka Bennahum and K. Meira Goldberg (New York: New York Public Library for the Performing Arts, 2003), 46.

78. José Luis Navarro García, "Algunas novedades en torno a La Cuenca," *Revista de investigación sobre flamenco la madruga*, no. 2 (June 2010): 1–24.

79. Ángeles Cruzado, "Carmencita Dauset, la reina de Broadway (II)," *Flamencas por derecho*, October 24, 2014, https://www.flamencasporderecho.com/carmencita-dauset-ii/

80. Ángeles Cruzado, "Carmencita Dauset, la reina de Broadway (I)," *Flamencas por derecho*, October 17, 2014, https://www.flamencasporderecho.com/carmencita-dauset-i/

81. Library of Congress, "Carmencita," YouTube video, 0:38, March 26, 2009, https://www.youtube.com/watch?v=-15jwb1ZTMA

82. I am referencing Loïe Fuller's "Danse Serpentine," filmed by the Lumière brothers around 1897. spitfaya123, "Loie Fuller—Danse Serpentine by Lumière Brother[s]," YouTube video, 6:12, January 22, 2011, https://www.youtube.com/watch?v=YNZ4WCFJGPc

83. José Otero attests to this in his *Tratado de bailes*, 152–156.

84. An extensive and detailed history of female bullfighting can be found in Feiner, *La mujer en el mundo del toro*.

85. Natalio Rivas, "Las mujeres en la tauromaquía," in *Toreros del romanticismo: Anecdotario taurino* (Madrid: Aguilar, 1987), 286–293.

86. Ángeles Cruzado, "La Estrella de Andalucía, reina del zapateado (IV)," *Flamencas por derecho*, May 27, 2016, https://www.flamencasporderecho.com/la-estrella-de-andalucia-iv/

87. Cruzado, "La Estrella de Andalucía."

88. Fernando Rodríguez Gómez, *Arte y artistas flamencos* (Madrid: Extramuros, 1935), 132.

89. Álvaro Retana, *Historia del arte frívolo* (Madrid: Tesoro, 1964), 35.

90. Retana, *Historia del arte frívolo*, 42.

91. Retana, *Historia del arte frívolo*, 125.

92. Retana, *Historia del arte frívolo*, 35.

93. Ángeles Cruzado, "Dora la Gitana, la transgresora reina del garrotín (y V)," *Flamencas por derecho*, January 1, 2016, https://www.flamencasporderecho.com/dora-la-gitana-v/

94. Ramón Regidor Arribas, "El travestismo en la zarzuela," in *Gigantes y cabezudos / la viejecita* (Madrid: Teatro de la Zarzuela, 1998), 31–32.
95. Usó, *Orgullo travestido*, 11.
96. Usó, *Orgullo travestido*, 76.
97. I thank Ángeles Cruzado for posting this excerpt on her Facebook wall.
98. El Derecho, "Los cafés cantantes," *El Derecho*, October 16, 1886, available on Ángeles Cruzado's Facebook, https://www.facebook.com/photo/?fbid=10155901067356570
99. Rodríguez Gómez, *Arte y artistas flamencos*, 104.
100. pie flamenco, "Julien Duvivier, La Bandera, 1935," YouTube video, 4:32, November 13, 2013, https://www.youtube.com/watch?v=LTwpWuh8BaU
101. To learn more about the life of Lluís Serracant, "Flor de Otoño," consult L'armari Obert, "Lluiset Serracant, Flor de Otoño, y el travestismo barcelonés años 20–30," *Leopoldest*, March 2016, https://leopoldest.blogspot.com/2016/03/lluiset-serracant-flor-de-otono-y-el.html
102. This refers to the Spanish Penal Code, 1954, Ley de vagos y maleantes de 1954, https://www.boe.es/datos/pdfs/BOE/1954/198/A04862-04862.pdf
103. Cruzado, "Dora la Gitana."
104. Retana, *Historia del arte frívolo*, 111.
105. Retana, *Historia del arte frívolo*, 17.
106. Gorka Elorrieta, "Madrid oculto: Una historia curiosa de la ciudad cada día," *TimeOut*, March 24, 2020, https://www.timeout.es/madrid/es/noticias/madrid-oculto-una-historia-curiosa-de-la-ciudad-cada-dia-032420
107. Collected by Pablo Lozano, *Mujeres guitarristas*, 116.
108. César González-Ruano, *Memorias: Mi medio siglo se confiesa a medias* (Madrid: Tebas, 1970), 70.
109. José Blas Vega, *El flamenco en Madrid* (Seville: Almuzara, 2006), 145.
110. Escribano, *Y Madrid*, 87.
111. Consult episodes 53 and 54, dedicated to Manolo Caracol, in the documentary series *Rito y geografía del cante* (1972), in which the singer and owner of the Los Canasteros tablao offers his reasoning to position himself against this devaluation of dancing and the tablao. Mario Gómez, dir., *Rito y geografía del cante flamenco*, Season 1, episode 53, "Manolo Caracol (I)," aired November 20, 1972, RTVE, https://www.rtve.es/play/videos/rito-y-geografia-del-cante/rito-geografia-del-cante-manolo-caracol/1898471/, and Season 1, episode 54, "Manolo Caracol (II)," aired November 27, 1972, RTVE, https://www.rtve.es/play/videos/rito-y-geografia-del-cante/rito-geografia-del-cante-manolo-caracol-ii/1898615/
112. Ana Isabel Elvira Esteban, "Tiempo de Mariemma, tiempo de festivales: La danza y los festivales de España (1960–1969) o como se llamen esas cosas que a nadie le importan," in *Mariemma y su tiempo*, ed. Rosa Ruiz Celaá, Antonio Álvarez Cañibano, and Paula De Castro Fernández (Madrid: Centro de Documentación de Música y Danza, 2018), 215.
113. Gamboa, *Una historia*, 156.
114. Enrique Moradiellos, *La España de Franco (1939–1975)* (Madrid: Síntesis, 2000), 138.
115. To find out more about tablaos in other Spanish cities, such as Seville, see point

Notes to Pages 48–51   175

6.5.3.1, "Los Tablaos," in Carmen Penélope Pulpón, "Bailaoras de Sevilla: Aprendizaje, profesión y género en el flamenco del franquismo y la transición. Estudio histórico-etnográfico de casos (1950–1980)," PhD diss., Universidad de Sevilla, 2015. The dissertation talks about tablaos, such as El Patio Andaluz, La Cochera, Los Gallos, La Trocha, El Arenal, and Los Caireles, in Seville; El Zoco and El Cordobés, in Córdoba; El Jaleo, in Torremolinos; Los Tarantos, in Barcelona; La Guitarra and El Flamenco, in Tokyo; El Setenta y Siete, in Mexico City; or El Chato Madrid, in New York.

116. Elvira Esteban, "Tiempo de Mariemma," 216.
117. Elvira Esteban, "Tiempo de Mariemma," 236–245.
118. Elvira Esteban, "Tiempo de Mariemma," 246–249.
119. Elvira Esteban, "Tiempo de Mariemma," 246.
120. According to flamencologist Juan Verguillos, the term *Bolero school* (*escuela bolera*) designates, starting in the 1940s, the bolero dances danced—among others, by the Pericet family—during the eighteenth and nineteenth centuries. Juan Verguillos, "30 años de 'Danza y tronío,'" *Diario de Sevilla*, March 30, 2014, https://www.diariodesevilla.es/ocio/anos-Danza-tronio_0_793421105.html

121. On the idea of Spain promoted by the Spanish Falange, consult its initial points in a publication from December 7, 1933. Falange Española, "Puntos iniciales," *Filosofia.org*, December 7, 1933, https://www.filosofia.org/hem/193/fes/fe0106.htm

122. To learn more about the nationalist use of flamenco by the Franco dictatorship, consult Cristina Cruces Roldán, "Entre el anonimato, el exhibicionismo y la propaganda: Mujeres del flamenco y del baile español en el NO-DO del primer franquismo (1943–1958)," in *Dance, Ideology and Power in Francoist Spain (1938–1968)*, ed. Beatriz Martínez del Fresco and Belén Vega Pichaco (Turnhout, Belgium: Brepols, 2017), 285–322.

123. Ilitur-gitano Lisardo, "Grabación histórica—Encarnación López 'La Argentinita.' (La caña) Gtr.-Manolo de Huelva," YouTube video, 4:00, January 16, 2015, https://www.youtube.com/watch?v=IrASRTHANaA

124. Despite the existing consensus around Vicente Escudero as the first choreographer of the seguiriya, we should mention another film from 1935 in which we see a small hand dance by La Argentinita, who does not dance the seguiriya with her entire body but offers an interesting choreography in which we see her feet marking the rhythm with stomps on the ground and her hands, first clapping and then making circular gestures with her fingers and hands. José Luna, "La Argentinita Seguiriyas 1935," YouTube video, 2:36, May 11, 2013, https://www.youtube.com/watch?v=-anQKU-SVlU

125. Alexandra Arnaud-Bestieu and Gilles Arnaud, *La danse flamenco: Techniques et esthétiques* (Paris: L'Harmattan, 2013), 43–44.

126. Paco Sevilla, "The Spanish Tablao," *Jaleo* 1, no. 3 (October 1977): 2–3, http://www.elitedynamics.com/jaleomagazine/JALEO-1977-10.pdf

127. Juan Rondón Rodríguez, *Recuerdos y confesiones del cantaor Rafael Pareja de Triana* (Córdoba: La Posada, 2001).

128. For this translation, the site MeasuringWorth was used to calculate pesetas to euros from 1910 to 2021, using the Historic Standard of Living value, which "measures the purchasing power of an income or wealth in its relative ability to purchase a (fixed over time) bundle of goods and services such as food, clothing, shelter, etc., that an average household would buy. This bundle does not change over time. This measure uses

the CPI." The year 1910 was chosen because of relative birth/death dates of mentioned artists. Then the euro to USD exchange rate in 2021 was calculated (the latest peseta data are available), which hovered around 1 euro to 1.20 USD, according to the *Wall Street Journal*'s euro-USD historical prices index. *MeasuringWorth—Measures of Worth, Inflation Rates, and Purchasing Power.* Accessed November 11, 2023. https://www.measurin gworth.com/

129. Eduardo Murillo Saborido, "Los tablaos flamencos en Madrid entre 1954-1973: Una aproximación académica a su escena musical," MA thesis, Universidad Complutense de Madrid, 2017.

130. Antonio Burgos, "Los jornaleros del flamenco," *Triunfo* 27, no. 506 (June 10, 1972): 23-25.

131. Sevilla, "The Spanish Tablao," 2.

132. I am thinking of the dominant model of the family during the Franco regime, based on the Nationalist-Catholic ideology, in which heterosexual marriage established a strict distribution of roles between the male producer and the female housewife. For more information, see Alfonso Botti, *Cielo y dinero: El nacionalcatolicismo en España (1881-1975)* (Madrid: Alianza, 1992).

133. José Luis Castillo-Puche, "Madrid, cátedra del flamenco: Visita sentimental y pintoresca a los 'tablaos' más famosos de la villa y corte," *Blanco y Negro*, no. 2644 (January 1963): 36-53.

134. Sevilla, "The Spanish Tablao," 2.

135. Cruces Roldán, "'De cintura para arriba,'" 167.

136. An exercise similar to the one I am carrying out here with these press articles has been done by Eulalia Pablo in her rereading of the text Gómez, *Arte y artistas flamencos*, published in 1935, taking up some of the author's descriptions of female artists, which look beyond artistic talent and focus on the physical beauty of women. The following serves as an example: "[La Paca]. A second-rate dancer, but the sight of her beauty was dizzying." Pablo Lozano, *Mujeres guitarristas*, 61.

137. Castillo-Puche, "Madrid, cátedra del flamenco."

138. Edgar Neville, "Las Brujas," *ABC*, February 27, 1965.

139. Francisco Diéguez, *Historia de un tablao: Las Brujas. Sus gentes, sus artistas y su época* (Cadiz: Absalon, 2008), 192.

140. Edgar Neville, "Los Canasteros," *ABC*, March 13, 1965, https://www.abc.es/arch ivo/periodicos/abc-madrid-19650313-123.html. November 18, 2023.

141. Diéguez, *Historia de un tablao*, 68.

142. Murillo Saborido, "Los tablaos flamencos en Madrid."

143. Pulpón, "Bailaoras de Sevilla," 438.

144. René Descartes, "Rules for the Direction of the Mind," in *The Philosophical Writings of Descartes*, trans. John Cottingham, Robert Stoothoff, and Dugald Murdoch (Cambridge: Cambridge University Press, 1984), 7-78.

145. Jacques Derrida, *On Touching—Jean-Luc Nancy*, trans. Christine Irizarry (Stanford: Stanford University Press, 2005).

146. Victoria Mateos de Manuel, "'Bailar en hombre': Una ortopedia del cuerpo nacional," unpublished paper for Instituto de Filosofía, CCHS-CSIC, 2015.

147. Edgar Neville, "El duende," *ABC*, March 3, 1965, https://www.abc.es/archivo/pe riodicos/abc-madrid-19650303-88.html. November 18, 2023.

148. For more on this topic, consult the work of dance philosopher Frédéric Pouillaude, *Le désoeuvrement chorégraphique: Étude sur la notion d'oeuvre en danse* (Paris: Vrin, 2009).

149. Diéguez, *Historia de un tablao*, 342.

150. Rocío Plaza Orellana, "El baile, la empresa y el espectáculo: Historias de encuentros y desencuentros en los teatros europeos," lecture given at Universidad Internacional de Andalucía, Seville, November 30, 2006, https://vimeo.com/85140318

151. Regarding Pohren's biography and his encounter with flamenco, the references that Nazario Luque makes to him in the second part of his autobiography, *Sevilla y la Casita de las Pirañas*, are of great interest (Barcelona: Anagrama, 2018, 62–63 and 76–77).

152. D. E. Pohren, *The Art of Flamenco* (Jerez de la Frontera: Jerez Industrial, 1962), 60–64.

153. The analysis of this alchemy of the effeminate gesture appears in my previous book, *De puertas para adentro*, in which I comment on the pas de deux by Antonio Ruiz Soler and Rosario in the 1944 film *Hollywood Canteen* (p. 60), the sevillanas of the eighteenth century danced and sung by Miguel de Molina together with a group of dancers in the 1952 film *Ésta es mi Vida* (p. 65), the performance of Pedrito Rico in the 1958 film *El Ángel de España* (p. 68), and the soleá por bulerías by El Güito and Mario Maya at the Café de Chinitas in Madrid (p. 115). López Rodríguez, *De puertas para adentro*.

154. Daniel Da Silva, "El Guito y Mario Maya por bulerias," YouTube video, 1:40, July 28, 2015, https://www.youtube.com/watch?v=shUYm9ZCpCc

155. Filmoteca Histórica Flamenca, "Bambino—no me des guerra (Años 70)," YouTube video, 2:13, July 4, 2016, https://www.youtube.com/watch?v=jInrcZ1JEZQ

156. Isabel y Emilio, "Antonio por 'Martinete' 'Duende y misterio del flamenco' 1952," YouTube video, 3:28, February 4, 2020, https://www.youtube.com/watch?v=H_I-0bTBuXU

157. Mario Gómez, dir., *Rito y geografía del cante flamenco*, Season 1, episode 64, "Fernanda de Utrera," aired February 5, 1973, RTVE, https://www.rtve.es/play/videos/rito-y-geografia-del-cante/rito-geografia-del-cante-fernanda-utrera/5276018/

158. Mario Gómez, dir., *Rito y geografía del cante flamenco*, Season 1, episode 65, "Bernarda de Utrera," aired February 12, 1973, RTVE, https://www.rtve.es/play/videos/rito-y-geografia-del-cante/rito-geografia-del-cante-bernarda-utrera/5130507/

159. Cristina Cruces Roldán and Assumpta Sabuco Cantó, *Las mujeres flamencas: Etnicidad, educación y empleo ante los nuevos retos profesionales* (Seville: Universidad de Sevilla, 2005), 138.

160. Mario Gómez, dir., *Rito y geografía del cante flamenco*, Season 1, episode 77, "La Paquera de Jerez," aired May 14, 1973, RTVE, https://www.rtve.es/play/videos/rito-y-geografia-del-cante/rito-geografia-del-cante-paquera-jerez/1786640/

161. Spanish Penal Code, Ley de vagos.

162. Spanish Penal Code, 1970, Ley de peligrosidad y rehabilitación social, https://www.boe.es/buscar/doc.php?id=BOE-A-1970-854

163. Pedro G. Romero, "El flamenco es un género," *El País*, March 16, 2018, https://elpais.com/cultura/2018/03/16/babelia/1521201640_215414.html

164. Pulpón, "Bailaoras de Sevilla."

165. Washabaugh, *Flamenco*, 153.

166. Michelle Heffner Hayes, *Flamenco: Conflicting Histories of the Dance* (Jefferson, NC: McFarland, 2009), 40–41.
167. Richard Wright, *Pagan Spain* (New York: Harper & Brothers, 1957).
168. José Racero, interview in Madrid, summer 2018.
169. Antonio Zori, interview in Madrid, summer 2018.
170. Diéguez, *Historia de un tablao*, 90.
171. Diéguez, *Historia de un tablao*, 105.
172. Pulpón, "Bailaoras de Sevilla," 463.
173. Pulpón, "Bailaoras de Sevilla," 439.
174. Retana, *Historia del arte frívolo*, 127.
175. Ana María Díaz Olaya, "Los cafés cantantes y su influencia en la actividad musical de la sociedad española de finales del siglo XIX y principios del siglo XX. El núcleo minero de Linares como ejemplo de avance cultural y artístico," *Boletín del Instituto de Estudios Giennenses*, no. 205 (2012): 243.

176. asalutes, "Manolo Caracol y Francisco Franco-España en la memoria," YouTube video, 3:39, March 4, 2010, https://www.youtube.com/watch?v=mLSq_tHvLgo

177. Jesús Alcalde and Ricardo J. Barceló, *Celtiberia gay* (Barcelona: Personas, 1976), 128.

178. In article 1, prostitution is declared *tráfico ilícito* [illicit traffic], and in article 2 *mancebías y casas de tolerancia* [houses of ill repute and brothels] are prohibited throughout the territory, without taking into account the denomination and apparently licit objectives that hide their true activity. The criminal reform, and not only administrative, appears in the Código Penal de 1963 [Penal Code of 1963] as a consequence of the Spanish adhesion one year earlier to the UN Convention of March 21, 1950, to suppress human trafficking and the exploitation of prostitution. Decreto 168/1963, Spanish Penal Code, 1963, https://www.boe.es/buscar/doc.php?id=BOE-A-1963-2618

179. Rafael Alcaide González, "Guereña, Jean-Louis. La prostitución de la España contemporánea," review of *La prostitución de la España contemporánea*, by Jean-Louis Guereña, *Revista bibliográfica de geografía y ciencias sociales* 9, no. 508 (May 2004), https://www.ub.edu/geocrit/b3w-508.htm

180. Report on prostitution in Spain (154/9) presented in the Congreso de los Diputados [the equivalent of the US House of Representatives] on April 11, 2007. Cortes Generales, "Informe de la ponencia sobre la prostitución en nuestro país (154/9)," Comisión Mixta de los Derechos de la Mujer y de la Igualdad de Oportunidades, March 13, 2007, http://www.lourdesmunozsantamaria.cat/IMG/pdf/INFORME_PONENCIA_PROSTITUCION.pdf

181. Vidas Ejemplares, "Lola Flores y el sexo," YouTube video, 2:56, May 28, 2010, https://www.youtube.com/watch?v=v5hgoTCaOTQ

182. Oscar Guasch and Eduardo Lizardo, *Chaperos: Precariado y prostitución homosexual* (Barcelona: Bellaterra, 2017), 20.

183. Guasch and Lizardo, *Chaperos*, 20.

184. The rumba "Viviendo sin freno," sung by Migue Benítez, is a musical example in flamenco that deals with the consumption of this substance. J, "Migue Benitez y El Torta—viviendo sin frenos," YouTube video, 4:42, July 19, 2011, https://www.youtube.com/watch?v=p3GGAt0ybAk

185. Usó, *Orgullo travestido*, 36.
186. Blanca Ávila Moreno, interview in Madrid, winter 2017.
187. Ávila Moreno, interview.
188. Ávila Moreno, interview.
189. Francisca Sadornil Ruiz, interview in Madrid, winter 2018.
190. Cristina Amich Elías, "El trabajo de los menores de edad en la dictadura franquista en historia contemporánea," *Historia contemporánea*, no. 36 (2011): 177.
191. Navarro García, *Historia del baile flamenco*, 298.
192. ABC, "Reagan hizo entrega al jefe del estado de un mensaje personal de presidente Nixon," *ABC*, July 12, 1972, https://www.abc.es/archivo/periodicos/abc-madrid-19720712-23.html
193. ABC, "Ellas y ellos: 'El Santo,' por bulerías," *ABC: Blanco y negro*, November 16, 1974, 11.
194. Paréntesis, "Rudolf Nureyev baila en Madrid," *ABC: Blanco y negro*, September 27, 1975, 64.
195. "At half past eight in the evening, a reception was held at the Italian Embassy. The cocktail hour was offered in honor of the illustrious personalities from Italy and was offered by the ambassador, Mr. Pellegrino Chici, who was accompanied by the minister of the press, Mr. Rafaello Patuelli, Count Ranieri Paulucci di Calboni Barone; Lieutenant Colonel Sommella, Captain Angelo Cabrini and Mr. Bascone, Mr. Mareri, Mr. Giacomelli and Mr. Pagliai, as well as Italian and Spanish journalists who had carried out the '*Caravelle*' flight and editors from Madrid newspapers. Among the personalities who attended the event were the general director of the press, Mr. Adolfo Muñoz Alonso, and tourism, Duke of Luna; deputy director of the diplomatic information office, Mr. Martín Martín, and Madrid's tourism delegate, Mrs. Calamai. At night, they were offered a meal in the Corral de la Morería . . ." (ABC, "Recepción en la embajada de Italia," *ABC*, April 3, 1962, 48, https://www.abc.es/archivo/periodicos/abc-madrid-19620403-48.html
196. Unknown reference shared by Cristina Cruces Roldan on her Facebook account in 2018.
197. NO-DO, producer, *Madrid de noche*, January 1, 1959, https://www.rtve.es/play/videos/documentales-b-n/madrid-noche/2846380/
198. NO-DO, producer, *Madrid*, January 1, 1974, https://www.rtve.es/play/videos/documentales-color/madrid/2903196/
199. NO-DO, producer, *Diccionario turístico español*, January 1, 1972, https://www.rtve.es/play/videos/documentales-color/diccionario-turistico-espanol/2898346/
200. Fernando Olmeda, *El látigo y la pluma: Homosexuales en la España de Franco* (Madrid: Anaya, 2004), 30.
201. Olmeda, *El látigo y la pluma*, 42.
202. Olmeda, *El látigo y la pluma*, 161.
203. A first version of these alegrías appears in the film *Original Gypsy Dances*, recorded in the United States in 1941. Emmanuel GAYET, "1941 'ORIGINAL GYPSY DANCES,'" YouTube video, 8:38, April 16, 2018, https://www.youtube.com/watch?v=dkTgXbGwJVk
204. pie flamenco, "Fernanda Romero Tarantos," YouTube video, 7:07, September 3, 2015, https://www.youtube.com/watch?v=ibnJFOUMa6U

Chapter 2

1. Teresa M. Vilarós, *El mono del desencanto: Una crítica cultural de la transición española (1973–1993)* (Madrid: Espasa, 1998), 38–39.
2. Vilarós, *El mono del desencanto*, 295.
3. Kerman Calvo Borobia, *¿Revolución o reforma? La transformación de la identidad política del movimiento LGTB en España, 1970–2005* (Madrid: CSIC, 2017), 200.
4. Regarding this topic, consult Víctor Mora Gaspar, *Al margen de la naturaleza: La persecución de la homosexualidad durante el franquismo. Leyes, terapias y condenas* (Barcelona: Debate, 2016) and the collective book Víctor Mora Gaspar and Geoffroy Huard, eds., *40 años después: La despenalización de la homosexualidad en España. Investigación, memoria y experiencias* (Madrid: Egales, 2019).
5. To learn more about this issue, consult Ramón Martínez, *Lo nuestro sí que es mundial: Una introducción a la historia del movimiento LGTB en España* (Madrid: Egales, 2017).
6. See the documentary *Bajo el sol de Torremolinos* for more on the Pasaje Begoña and the city of Torremolinos during 1960–1970. Ana Pastor, producer, "Bajo el sol de Torremolinos," Crónicas, aired April 15, 2012, RTVE, https://www.rtve.es/play/videos/cronicas/cronicas-bajo-sol-torremolinos/1133477/
7. Víctor Berzal de Miguel, "Pasaje Begoña: Respeto a la diversidad, truncado por la represión franquista," *Cultura diversa*, March 3, 2019, https://culturadiversa.es/2019/03/pasaje-begona-torremolinos-lgtbi.html
8. "'Lejos de los árboles,' Jacinto Esteva (1963–1971)," *Reina d'Àfrica*, YouTube video, 99:36, April 8, 2013, https://www.youtube.com/watch?v=1TKmaYeth5w, 96:00.
9. Researcher Valeria Vegas states in her work *Vestidas de azul: Análisis social y cinematográfico de la mujer transexual en los años de la transición española* (Madrid: Dos Bigotes, 2019) that the decline of this type of cabaret can be dated to 1984 with the closure of Madrid's Gay Club, the most well known in the capital.
10. Joaquín Arbide, dir., *"La Esmeralda"*, 1970, http://rtv.joaquinarbide.com/tv/pelis/esmeralda.html
11. Alcalde and Barceló, *Celtiberia gay*, 42.
12. A television performance of this song dated to the 1990s is available on the internet. alex28lp, "PACO ESPAÑA," YouTube video, 4:32, June 15, 2018, https://www.youtube.com/watch?v=axegkfiKkpY
13. The lyrics of this song, not without a certain dark humor, evoke the world of flamenco tablaos in the following way: "Oh, Paca, cold Paca / I kicked her to death / to show that chick / that I also knew how / to dance a zapateado / . . . I danced on top of her / as if she were a tablao / I cheered her on myself / I cheered her on myself / until she kicked the bucket." Alcalde and Barceló, *Celtiberia gay*, 54.
14. Alcalde and Barceló, *Celtiberia gay*, 56.
15. Vegas, *Vestidas de azul*, 155.
16. ABC, "Multa a Lola Flores de 255 pesetas," *ABC*, September 10, 1977, 73 and ABC, "Quince días de carcel para Lola Flores," *ABC*, October 27, 1977, 59.
17. ABC, "Multa a Lola Flores," 73.
18. ABC, "Quince días de carcel," 59.

19. Carla Antonelli, "Pierrot: Memorias trans (2) / Ultimo capítulo," Carla Antonelli, 2009, https://www.carlaantonelli.com/memorias-trans2-9.htm
20. ABC, "Del mundo del espectáculo," *ABC*, November 25, 1978, 61.
21. The film was based on the play of the same name written by José María Rodríguez Méndez in 1973. This play, which could not be performed until 1982 due to censorship, narrates the life of a real character mentioned earlier, Flor de Otoño.
22. David Zamajón París, "Carmen de Mairena—un repaso a su vida INÉDITO," YouTube video, 11:12, August 10, 2012, https://www.youtube.com/watch?v=HcGm-ojfv30
23. Antonelli, "Pierrot."
24. In addition to artistic fields, Ocaña has been one of the most studied figures in the field of academia. It is worth noting the chapters dedicated to him in Mira, *De Sodoma a Chueca*; Rafael M. Mérida Jiménez, *Transbarcelonas: Cultura, género y sexualidad en la España del siglo XX* (Barcelona: Bellaterra, 2016); and López Rodríguez, *De puertas para adentro*, up to the recent collective work Rafael M. Mérida Jiménez, ed., *Ocaña: Voces, ecos y distorsiones* (Barcelona: Bellaterra, 2018), without forgetting the texts by Pedro G. Romero and Paul B. Preciado collected in the exhibition catalog edited by Pedro G. Romero, *Ocaña, 1973–1983: Acciones, actuaciones, activismo* (Barcelona: Polígrafa, 2011).
25. See the analysis of this scene in my previous book, *De puertas para adentro*, 87–91.
26. See the detailed analysis of this scene in my chapter "Ocaña: Tradición sin tradicionalismo," in *Ocaña: Voces, ecos y distorsiones*, ed. Rafael M. Mérida Jiménez, 52–66 (Barcelona: Bellaterra, 2018).
27. Agamben, *Nudities*, 65.
28. The reflections expressed in this last excerpt were presented for the first time at the "Jornada de Estudios Ocaña Magna," held at the University of Seville in December 2019. I thank Rafael M. Mérida for counting on me again for this Ocaña-style adventure.
29. José Luis Ortiz Nuevo, *De las danzas y andanzas de Enrique el Cojo* (Seville: Athenaica, 2017), 79–80.
30. Extracted from the artist's personal archive, a video of a 2007 gala at the Velá de San Pablo is available on the internet, in which La Esmeralda and La Otra Pantoja appear. Maria José Navarro, "María José la Otra Pantoja—Velá San Pablo 2007," YouTube video, 58:02, November 28, 2017, https://www.youtube.com/watch?v=TH7moJIwKtE
31. For more on these two figures of flamenco, consult the chapter "Flamenco y transexualidad" in my book *De puertas para adentro*, 97.
32. Raúl Solís Galván, *La doble transición* (Jaén: Libros.com, 2019), 70–71.
33. Solís Galván, *La doble transición*, 79.
34. Solís Galván, *La doble transición*, 110.
35. Vegas, *Vestidas de azul*, 205.
36. Vegas, *Vestidas de azul*, 208.
37. Vegas, *Vestidas de azul*, 215.
38. A detailed analysis of the origins and evolution of this dance appears in my work *Espejismos de la identidad coreográfica: Estética y transformaciones de la farruca* (Madrid: Los Libros de la Academia, 2015).
39. Julio Bravo, "Sara Baras: 'No pretendo gustar a todo el mundo,'" *ABC*, August

12, 2004, https://www.abc.es/estilo/gente/abci-sara-baras-no-pretendo-gustar-todo-mundo-200408120300-9623044643980_noticia.html

40. JJGabarre, "SARA BARAS farruca," YouTube video, 6:55, September 3, 2016, https://www.youtube.com/watch?v=z9DyXigL-LU

41. In her show "Perspectivas." canalFlamenco, "Flamenco TV—Mercedes Ruiz enfervorizó con su farruca," YouTube video, 3:00, January 13, 2012, https://www.youtube.com/watch?v=YBFQgGP3jg0

42. In her show "Utopía." GUITARRACORDOBATV, "María Pagés 'Utopía'—Córdoba Guitar Festival 2014," YouTube video, 10:24, July 9, 2014, https://www.youtube.com/watch?v=v4_vdY5zwAQ, 5:40.

43. In her show "Simplemente flamenco." Concha Jareño, "Concha Jareño Farruca 'SIMPLEMENTE FLAMENCO'," YouTube video, 10:00, October 22, 2010, https://www.youtube.com/watch?v=w2dsyoV0kfs

44. A more detailed analysis appears in my work *Espejismos de la identidad coreográfica*, 56–64.

45. [For more information in English about the history of the bata de cola and its contemporary queer usages, I humbly recommend my publication as a useful resource: Ryan Rockmore, "Queering the Tale of the Skirt: The Masculine Presence, Archival Histories, and Queer Future of the *Bata de Cola*," in *Celebrating Flamenco's Tangled Roots: The Body Questions*, ed. K. Meira Goldberg and Antoni Pizà (Newcastle upon Tyne: Cambridge Scholars Publishing, 2022), 101–125.—TRANSLATOR]

46. fckat3, "BALLET TEATRO ESPANOL DE Rafael Aguilar—CARMEN-6," YouTube video, 16:48, December 5, 2012, https://www.youtube.com/watch?v=NykcLSVKDlM

47. Miguel Ángel Villena, "Canales y Pasqual montan un espectáculo de danza sobre Bernarda Alba," *El País*, November 15, 1997, https://elpais.com/diario/1997/11/15/cultura/879548413_850215.html

48. Kika Lorace, "PARTIDO DE LA AMISTAD—KIKA LORACE Y SATÍN GRECO (LOLA FLORES)," YouTube video, 3:29, December 3, 2015, https://www.youtube.com/watch?v=_fbx0zBJnDE

49. Nacha la Macha, "Nacha La Macha—eres cobarde (Video Oficial)," YouTube video, 6:06, June 2, 2018, https://www.youtube.com/watch?v=8fU5RZy0RJo

50. CBO Andalucía, "LOLA FLORES (Sevillanas rocieras con pito y tamboril)—SEVILLANAS, de Carlos Saura," YouTube video, 2:49, July 4, 2018, https://www.youtube.com/watch?v=Twc44pQ_ARQ

51. Nacha LA MACHA, "Nacha la Macha—Como la Copla no hay Ná. VIDEOCLIP," YouTube video, 4:43, April 7, 2015, https://www.youtube.com/watch?v=a7VRXTfR4UA

52. Nacha la Macha, "Nacha La Macha—Mañana Muérete feat. Miguel Garena (Video Oficial)," YouTube video, 7:19, March 18, 2019, https://www.youtube.com/watch?v=MEz1zAseMjM

53. Vilarós, *El mono del desencanto*, 18–19.

54. In Madrid, despite the closure of Zambra, Los Canasteros, and Las Brujas, other new tablaos have opened their doors: Candela (1982), Casa Patas (1987), Cardamomo (1994), Las Carboneras (2000), Las Tablas (2003), etc.

55. To find out more about this show, consult María Isabel Díez Torres, "Entre cante y baile: El flamenco protesta de Quejío (1972) de Salvador Távora y La Cuadra de Sevilla," in *La investigación en danza, Sevilla 2018*, ed. Carmen Giménez Morte, Virginia

Soprano Manzo, Amparo Bayarri Furió, María Dolores Tena Medialdea, and Serafín Mesa Garcia (Valencia: Mahali, 2018), 433–436.

56. María Lejárraga, "La mujer española ante la república: Realidad," lecture delivered at the Ateneo de Madrid, May 4, 1931 (Seville: Instituto Andaluz de la Mujer, 2003 [1931]).

57. María Lejárraga, "La mujer española ante la república: Libertad," lecture delivered at the Ateneo de Madrid, May 11, 1931 (Seville: Instituto Andaluz de la Mujer, 2003 [1931]).

58. José Varela Ortega, Fernando Rodríguez Lafuente, and Andrea Donofrío, eds., *La mirada del otro: La imagen de España ayer y hoy* (Madrid: Fórcola, 2016), 84.

59. For more on this topic, consult Iván Jiménez, "Une Carmen en cache une autre Moscou-Cuba, 1967," in *Danse ren 68: Perspectives internationales*, ed. Isabelle Launay, Sylviane Pages, Mélanie Pain, and Guillaume Sintès (Paris: Deuxième Époque, 2018), 211–230.

60. In Javier Sáez and Fefa Vila, eds., *El libro del buen amor: Sexualidades raras y políticas extrañas* (Madrid: Traficantes de Sueños, 2019), 46.

61. Sáez and Vila, *El libro del buen amor*, 46.

62. Sáez and Vila, *El libro del buen amor*, 47.

63. Sáez and Vila, *El libro del buen amor*, 47.

64. I am speaking here about "one" single set for each of the tablaos, even though the atmosphere of each one of them is different. At the same time, this difference does not change the scenic design either since none of the artists interacts with the decorative elements of each tablao as dramaturgical elements of their shows. Without going so far as to include the extensive description of the different Madrid tablaos here and their different poetics of space that I carried out for my doctoral dissertation, I would like to point out that we can distinguish at least three fundamental types of sets: the Orientalist, present, for example, in Villarrosa and Torres Bermejas; the nineteenth-century (café cantante feel), present in El Corral de la Morería, La Taberna de Mr. Pinkleton, and Casa Patas; and the artistic (the tablao as a *museo del flamenco* [flamenco museum] or tablao-gallery with painting and sculpture exhibitions), such as Las Carboneras, Las Tablas, and Cardamomo.

65. Daniel Bernabé, *La trampa de la diversidad: Cómo el neoliberalismo fragmentó la identidad de la clase trabajadora* (Madrid: Akal, 2018), 215.

66. Bernabé, *La trampa de la diversidad*, 127–128.

67. Bernabé, *La trampa de la diversidad*, 99.

68. A detailed triple analysis of the emergence of "contemporary flamenco dance" from a historical, anthropological, and aesthetic perspective is part of the doctoral dissertation that gave rise to this book and was published as an essay. Fernando López Rodríguez, "Bailar en tiempos de crisis: El flamenco contemporáneo," in *Historia de la danza contemporánea en España*, vol. 3, *De la crisis económica de 2008 a la crisis sanitaria de 2020*, ed. Carmen Giménez Morte (Madrid: Academia de las Artes Escénicas de España, 2021).

69. David Halperin, *How to Be Gay* (Cambridge: Belknap Press, 2012), 243. First quotation is by Berger. The second two are directly from Halperin.

70. Marcos Medina and Jonathan González, dirs., *Flamencas: Mujeres, fuerza y duende* (Arbolé Producciones, 2013), documentary, 97:00, https://www.canalsurmas.es

184 Notes to Pages 103–12

/en/videos/detail/42321-documentales-flamencasmujeres-fuerza-y-duendesi-satintern
et-09032022
71. José Luis Moreno Pestaña, *La cara oscura del capital erótico: Capitalización del cuerpo y trastornos alimentarios* (Madrid: Akal, 2016), 94.
72. Moreno Pestaña, *La cara oscura*, 278.
73. Moreno Pestaña, *La cara oscura*, 278.
74. Hayes, *Flamenco*, 167.
75. Hayes, *Flamenco*, 175.
76. Hayes, *Flamenco*, 180.
77. Hayes, *Flamenco*, 171.
78. José Luna, "La Argentinita. Bulerías 1935," YouTube video, 2:32, May 11, 2013, https://www.youtube.com/watch?v=bH__SK3Nr5g
79. Choreographic final touch or coded series of movements that is used to start or end a choreographic passage directed by the singing.
80. Ilitur-gitano Lisardo, "Dos fenómenos-Manuela Carrasco y Juan Villar (Bulerias) Los Canateros 196," YouTube video, 2:43, May 12, 2014, https://www.youtube.com/watch?v=uERIwqQ4FGY
81. Luis Fernando Dueñas, "Eva Yerbabuena—corte lluvia flamenco.flv," YouTube video, 7:36, November 8, 2012, https://www.youtube.com/watch?v=gNe_jF7hm4M

Chapter 3

1. Under the Royal Decree (*Real Decreto*) of December 29, 2018, this tax was reduced again to 10 percent, but only for individuals and not companies. Real Decreto-ley 28/2018, Royal Decree, 2018, https://www.boe.es/buscar/doc.php?id=BOE-A-2018-17992
2. Jaume Colomer, *Análisis de la situación económica de las artes escénicas en España* (Madrid: Los Libros de la Academia, 2016).
3. Fátima Anillo, unpublished lecture for Federación Estatal de Compañías y Empresas de Danza (Centro Danza Canal, Madrid, December 19, 2018).
4. Jonatan Miró, interview in Madrid, winter 2017.
5. Sadornil, interview, 2018.
6. Teresa Marín García, "Frente a la precariedad laboral en las artes: Situación y tentativas colectivas (en el estado español)," in *Producción artística en tiempos de precariado laboral*, ed. Juan Vicente Aliaga and Carmen Navarrete (Madrid: Tierradenadie, 2017), 70.
7. Melody Nicholls, interview in Madrid, winter 2017.
8. Carolina Fernández Oliva, interview in Madrid, winter 2017.
9. Miró, interview, 2017.
10. Tasha González, interview in Madrid, winter 2017.
11. Tasha González, interview in Madrid, winter 2017.
12. Miró, interview, 2017.
13. Politikon, *El muro invisible: Las dificultades de ser joven en España* (Barcelona: Penguin Random House, 2017), 174.
14. Sadornil Ruiz, interview, 2018.

15. Isabelle Launay, *Les danses d'après*, vol. 1, *Poétiques et politiques des répertoires* (Pantin: Centre National de la Danse, 2017), 166.
16. Launay, *Les danses d'après*, 1:166.
17. "Without being bound to the fulfillment of promises, we would never be able to achieve that amount of identity and continuity which together produce the 'person' about whom a story can be told; each of us would be condemned to wander helplessly and without direction in the darkness of his own lonely heart, caught in its ever changing moods, contradictions, and equivalities. This subjective identity, achieved through binding oneself in promises, must be distinguished from the 'objective,' i.e., object-related, identity that arises out of being confronted with the sameness of the world which I mentioned in the discussion of work. In this respect, forgiving and making promises are like control mechanisms built into the very faculty to start new and unending processes." Hannah Arendt, "Labor, Work, Action," in *Amor Mundi: Explorations in the Faith and Thought of Hannah Arendt*, ed. James W. Bernauer (Boston: Martinus Nijhoff Publishers, 1987), 42.
18. Cruces Roldán, *Más allá de la música*, 24–29.
19. Remedios Zafra, *El entusiasmo: Precariedad y trabajo creativo en la era digital* (Barcelona: Anagrama, 2017), 14.
20. Zafra, *El entusiasmo*, 14.
21. Pedro, interview conducted over the phone, summer 2018. Since we are dealing with collaborators who expose a situation of relative fragility, I have chosen to blur their profiles by removing their last names, city of residence, and origins to avoid overexposing them. Their work in the street is or has been transitory for all of them.
22. Ander, interview conducted over the phone, summer 2018.
23. Lidia, interview conducted over the phone, summer 2018.
24. Pedro, interview, 2018.
25. Ander, interview, 2018.
26. Lidia, interview, 2018.
27. Pedro, interview, 2018.
28. Pedro, interview, 2018.
29. [American flamenco scholar Joshua Brown has written considerably about the performance protests of Flo6x8. I highlight his work here as further context for English-language readers. Joshua Brown, "'The Banks Are Our Stages': Flo 6x8 and Flamenco Performance as Protest in Southern Spain," *Popular Music and Society* 42, no. 2 (2019): 230–252, https://doi.org/10.1080/03007766.2018.1448249—Translator]
30. Juan Carlos Lérida, "La liturgia de las horas. 2018–2021," Juan Carlos Lérida, https://juancarloslerida.com/project/la-liturgia-las-horas/
31. Nando Cruz, "Flamenco patas arriba," *El Periódico*, January 28, 2020, https://www.elperiodico.com/es/ocio-y-cultura/20200128/mundos-paralelos-ruta-flamenco-barcelona-raval-poble-sec-sant-antoni-7825958
32. Silvia Cruz Lapeña, *Crónica jonda* (Madrid: Libros del K.O., 2017), 64–65.
33. Antonia Moya, interview in Madrid, winter 2017.
34. Pilar Trenas, "Noche de flamenco y arte en 'Los Cabales,'" *ABC*, October 1, 1972, https://www.abc.es/archivo/periodicos/abc-madrid-19721001-119.html
35. Fernández Oliva, interview, 2017.
36. Cruces Roldán, Más allá de la música, 210–211.

37. Pierre Bourdieu, *The Bachelors' Ball: The Crisis of Peasant Society in Béarn*, trans. Richard Nice (Cambridge: Polity, 2008), 177.

38. Martínez, *Lo nuestro*.

39. [Again, see Rockmore, "Queering the Tale" for histories and queer perspectives on the bata de cola.—TRANSLATOR]

40. Eulalia Pablo Lozano, "La bata de cola: Un capricho de la majeza," *Candil*, no. 128 (2015): 3874–3876, https://elecodelamemoria.blogspot.com/2015/03/la-bata-de-co la-un-capricho-de-la-majeza.html

41. [Contemporary performing arts scholar Daniel Valtueña has published and curated extensively on Niño de Elche in English. For more information on the artist, please see Daniel Valtueña, "Niño de Elche, a Heterotopian (Flamencx) Voice," in *Celebrating Flamenco's Tangled Roots: The Body Questions*, ed. K. Meira Goldberg and Antoni Pizà (Newcastle upon Tyne: Cambridge Scholars Publishing, 2022), 126–136.—TRANSLATOR]

42. [The entire fragment, except for the translator's choice to preserve García Lorca's usage of *maricas* in lieu of the slur in English, comes from Federico García Lorca, "Poet in New York," in *Selected Verse: Revised Bilingual Edition*, ed. Christopher Maurer, trans. Greg Simon and Steven F. White (New York: Farrar, Straus and Giroux, 2004), 277–279.—TRANSLATOR]

43. R. Joy Littlewood, *A Commentary on Ovid: Fasti Book VI* (Oxford: Oxford University Press, 2006), 73; and T. P. Wiseman, *Remus: A Roman Myth* (Cambridge: Cambridge University Press, 1995), 61.

44. I have carried out broader research on this topic, presented in Veracruz (Mexico) in April 2019 within the context of the "Indígenas, Africanos, Roma y Europeos: Ritmos Transatlánticos en Música, Canto y Baile" international conference. Fernando López Rodríguez, "Gestos de ida y vuelta: Antonia Mercé, 1929–Kazuo Ohno, 1977," *Música oral del sur* 17 (December 2020): 439–448, http://www.centrodedocumentacion musicaldeandalucia.es/ojs/index.php/mos/article/view/369

45. For more on these two pieces, consult the chapter "Ceder a la fragilidad: Bailar en primera persona" in my book *De puertas para adentro*, 129–137.

46. UNESCO, "El flamenco," *UNESCO Patrimonio Cultural Inmaterial*, accessed November 11, 2023, https://ich.unesco.org/es/RL/el-flamenco-00363. [I chose to translate from Spanish since the English version of the website changes the language substantially, especially related to sensuality and sexuality: "Flamenco *baile* is a dance of passion, courtship, expressing a wide range of situations ranging from sadness to joy. The technique is complex, differing depending on whether the performer is male (heavier use of the feet) or female (gentler, more sensual movements)."—TRANSLATOR]

47. To learn more about the life of this artist, I recommend reading his autobiography, José Greco and Harvey Ardman, *The Gypsy in My Soul: The Autobiography of José Greco* (Garden City, NY: Doubleday, 1977).

48. In this regard, Marta Carrasco's article is interesting. "Oh! Fascinados por el flamenco," *Revista de la Academia de las Artes Escénicas*, no. 7 (June 2017): 45–47, https:// academiadelasartesescenicas.es/revista/16/artescenicas-7

49. [Washabaugh thoroughly examines the roots and impacts of *gitanismo*, explaining it as follows: "Just as the Black Power movement in North America was promoted through the celebration of a distinctive Black aesthetic in the 1950s and 1960s, so too

the 'Gitano Power' movement of Spain in the 1950s and 1960s was promoted through an analogous Gitano aesthetic, primarily rooted in flamenco music." Washabaugh, *Flamenco*, 16.—TRANSLATOR]

50. La Meri, *Spanish Dancing*, 2nd ed. (Pittsfield, MA: Eagle Printing and Binding, 1967).

51. Godard Hubert, "El gesto y su percepción," *Estudis escènics: Quaderns de l'Institut del Teatre de la Diputació de Barcelona*, no. 32 (2007): 335–344.

52. Nancy Lee Ruyter, "La Meri and the World of Dance," *Anales del Instituto de Investigaciones Estéticas* 22, no. 77 (2000): 177.

53. Mahalia Lassibille, "La danse africaine: Una catégorie anthropologisée," *EspacesTemps.net*, August 22, 2016, https://www.espacestemps.net/articles/la-danse-africaine-une-categorie%20anthropologisee

54. According to the previously cited article by Nancy Lee Ruyter, this must have been around 1916. Lee Ruyter, "La Meri."

55. Carlos Mansó, "Notas para el periodista Pablo Suero: Buenos Aires, 1935," in *La Argentina, fue Antonia Mercé* (Buenos Aires: Devenir, 1993), 60.

56. Ana Alberdi Alonso, "Los doce años de Mariemma y los Ballets Espagnols," in *Mariemma y su tiempo*, ed. Rosa Ruiz Celaá, Antonio Álvarez Cañibano, and Paula De Castro Fernández (Madrid: Centro de Documentación de Música y Danza, 2018), 185.

57. Antonia Mercé y Luque, Original program from Tokyo recitals. Accessed at Juan March Foundation in Madrid. Imperial Theater, Tokyo, January 26–30, 1929.

58. Maria Callas died in Paris on September 16, 1977, that is, a month and a half before the premiere of *Admiring La Argentina*, which took place on November 1 of that same year at the Daimii Seimei Hall in Tokyo.

59. Toshio Mizohata, unpublished lecture delivered at Spanish Embassy, Tokyo, February 15, 2019. Delivered in the context of the ninetieth anniversary of the Mercé recital in the Japanese capital.

60. Source: photo album gifted by the Mercé family to the Ohno family. Viewed at the Spanish Embassy in Tokyo in February 2019.

61. For the analysis of the piece, I have used the notes from Mizohata's lecture, as well as the video of the piece, displayed in Madrid (Reina Sofía Museum) and in Tokyo (Spanish Embassy in Japan). Mizohata, unpublished lecture.

62. In her work *Le butô en France: Malentendus et fascination* (Pantin: Centre National de la Danse, 2017), 263, Sylviane Pagès lists the different places where Ohno performed in France—in addition to London and Stockholm—on that first European tour: the Nancy Festival, the Saint-Jacques Church in Paris, the Quatre Temps in La Défense, the Comédie de Caen, and the TNS in Strasbourg.

63. Kazuo Ohno, choreographer, *La Argentina*, Maison de la Danse, Lyon, 2018, https://www.numeridanse.tv/videotheque-danse/hommage-la-argentina?s

64. Pagès, *Le butô*, 263.

65. Pagès, *Le butô*, 265.

66. López Rodríguez, "Gestos de ida y vuelta."

67. Fernando López Rodríguez, "La Argentina, ¿por dónde? Fascinación y filiación escópica en O Senseï (2012) y Ôno-Sensation (2019)," in *Actas de la jornada de estudios sobre Los Ballets Españoles de Antonia Mercé La Argentina*, conference proceedings (Madrid: CSIC, November 2019).

68. For more information about this piece, consult Fernando López Rodríguez, "H2-Ohno: Autoetnografía de un proceso creativo en danza," *Revista Acotaciones* 43 (July–December 2019): 257–275, https://doi.org/10.32621/acotaciones.2019.43.10

69. Pauline Le Boulba, "Les bords de l'oeuvre: Réceptions performées et critiques affectées en danse," PhD diss., l'Université Paris VIII–Vincennes–Saint Denis, 2019. [English translation from Spanish translation of French by Fernando López Rodríguez.—Translator]

70. Isabella Ginot, *Dominique Bagouet, un labyrinthe dansé* (Pantin: CND, 1999), 266.

71. Ina Sport, "Danse avec la Compagnie Dominique Bagouet 'Necessito'—Archive vidéo INA," YouTube video, 2:14, June 12, 2012, https://www.youtube.com/watch?v=P4tR8fJA_Wc

72. Ginot, *Dominique Bagouet*, 100–101.

73. Gilles Deleuze, *Francis Bacon: The Logic of Sensation*, trans. Daniel W. Smith (New York: Continuum, 2003), 50.

74. Deleuze, *Francis Bacon*, 51.

75. I am grateful to bailaora and choreographer Carmen Muñoz Jiménez for offering me this pathway in connection with her piece "Bailes de histéricas" (2019).

76. K. Meira Goldberg, Walter Aaron Clark, and Antoni Pizà, Eds., *Transatlantic Malagueñas and Zapateados in Music, Song and Dance* (Newcastle upon Tyne: Cambridge Scholars Publishing, 2019).

77. Francisca Reyes Tolentino (1899–1983) in her classic *Philippine Folk Dances and Games* (New York: Silver, Burdet, 1927) and Basilio Esteban S. Villaruz in works like *Treading Through: 45 Years of Philippine Dance* (Quezon City: University of the Philippines Press, 2006) and in various articles that can be found online, such as "Philippine Dance in the Spanish Period," Manila: National Commission for Culture and the Arts, June 2, 2015, https://ncca.gov.ph/about-ncca-3/subcommissions/subcommission-on-the-arts-sca/dance/philippine-dance-in-the-spanish-period/

78. Juan Manuel Suárez-Japón, "Algunas ideas sobre las relaciones entre flamenco y poder," in *Acts del V Congreso Internacional Universitario de Investigación sobre Flamenco* (Murcia: Universidad Católica San Antonio, 2015), 11–20.

79. In the current education sphere, in addition to José Galán's *Flamenco inclusivo* project, we should mention Isabel Olavide's school in Madrid, which has also produced shows with people with disabilities, such as "Al revuelo de tus volantes," "De mi . . . pá ti," "Rumbo al sur," and "A nuestro ritmo," or Tanja Sattler's modest but interesting project in Germany, which works with people with visual impairments, about which I carried out a research project published in the form of an article in Fernando López Rodríguez, "Estrategias de representación de cuerpos frágiles en el flamenco: Un estudio de campo llevado a cabo en Bensheim (Alemania)," in *La investigación en danza 2016*, ed. Carmen Giménez Morte (Valencia: Mahali, 2016).

80. José María Ruiz Fuentes, "El Loco Mateo," *El arte de vivir el flamenco*, n.d., https://elartedevivirelflamenco.com/cantaores260.html

81. Ángeles Cruzado, "La Ciega de Jerez, jondura y sentimiento (I)," *Flamencas por derecho*, July 29, 2016, https://www.flamencaspoderecho.com/la-ciega-de-jerez-i/

82. José María Ruiz Fuentes, "La Ciega de Jerez," *El arte de vivir el flamenco*, n.d., https://elartedevivirelflamenco.com/cantaores679.html

83. Diéguez, *Historia de un tablao*, 221.
84. On the relationship between flamenco from Extremadura and Gitano-Portuguese songs, we must highlight chapter 93 of the documentary series *Rito y geografía del cante*. Mario Gómez, dir., *Rito y geografía del cante flamenco*, Season 1, episode 92, "Extremadura y Portugal," aired September 3, 1973, RTVE, https://www.rtve.es/play/videos/rito-y-geografia-del-cante/rito-geografia-del-cante-extremadura-portugal/545 1510/
85. Manuel Bohórquez, "De patito feo a cisne del baile," *La gazapera flamenco*, April 11, 2011, https://manuelbohorquez.com/la-gazapera-flamenca/de-patito-feo-a-cisne-del-baile/
86. Diario de Jerez, "Las primeras grandes figuras del baile (1)," *Diario de Jerez*, February 25, 2012, https://www.diariodejerez.es/festivaldejerez/primeras-grandes-figuras-baile_0_564243591.html
87. José Luis Navarro García, *Vicente Escudero: Un bailaor cubista* (Seville: Libros con Duende, 2012), 194.
88. Navarro García, *Vicente Escudero*, 289.
89. Interview with Enrique, "El Cojo." Ortiz Nuevo, *De las danzas*, 64.
90. Interview with Enrique, "El Cojo." Ortiz Nuevo, *De las danzas*, 87–88.
91. Roberto Bermejo, "Baile por Alegrías de Cádiz de Enrique el Cojo," YouTube video, 7:16, August 21, 2008, https://www.youtube.com/watch?v=yEVKfpMGwhA
92. Paul B. Preciado, "Revoluciones somatopolíticas: Cuerpos feministas, queer, trans y cripple-queer," lecture given in seminar "Cuerpo impropio: Guía de modelos somatopolíticos y de sus posibles usos desviados," Universidad Internacional de Andalucía, 2011.
93. Real Pragmática de 1499, Royal Pragmatic Decree, 1499, trans. Jesús Salinas, https://www.museuvirtualgitano.cat/en/history/first-pragmatic-decree/
94. José Luis Gómez Urdáñez, "Los gitanos, al borde del genocidio," *La aventura de la historia* 45 (2002): 38–43.
95. Romero, "El flamenco."

Conclusion

1. I am referencing the article Manuel Bohórquez, "Rocío Márquez y el feminijondismo," *El correo de Andalucía*, March 8, 2019, https://elcorreoweb.es/cultura/rocio-marquez-y-el-feminijondismo-KJ5092873

Bibliography

ABC. "Del mundo del espectáculo." *ABC*, November 25, 1978.
ABC. "Ellas y ellos: 'El Santo,' por bulerías." *ABC: Blanco y negro*, November 16, 1974.
ABC. "Multa a Lola Flores de 255 pesetas." *ABC*, September 10, 1977.
ABC. "Quince días de carcel para Lola Flores." *ABC*, October 27, 1977.
ABC. "Reagan hizo entrega al jefe del estado de un mensaje personal de presidente Nixon." *ABC*, July 12, 1972. https://www.abc.es/archivo/periodicos/abc-madrid-197 20712-23.html
ABC. "Recepción en la embajada de Italia." *ABC*, April 3, 1962. https://www.abc.es/arch ivo/periodicos/abc-madrid-19620403-48.html
ABC. "Una pieza del Arqueológico revela que la primera mujer torera es del siglo XVII." *ABC cultura*, December 26, 2014. https://www.abc.es/cultura/arte/20141025/abci-pi eza-arqueologico-revela-primera-201412251630.html
Agamben, Giorgio. *Nudities*. Translated by David Kishik and Stefan Pedatella. Stanford: Stanford University Press, 2011.
Alberdi Alonso, Ana. "Los doce años de Mariemma y los Ballets Espagnols." In *Mariemma y su tiempo*, edited by Rosa Ruiz Celaá, Antonio Álvarez Cañibano, and Paula De Castro Fernández. Madrid: Centro de Documentación de Música y Danza, 2018.
Alcaide González, Rafael. "Guereña, Jean-Louis. *La prostitución de la España contemporánea*." Review of *La prostitución de la España contemporánea*, by Jean-Louis Guereña. *Revista bibliográfica de geografía y ciencias sociales* 9, no. 508 (May 2004). https://www.ub.edu/geocrit/b3w-508.htm
Alcalde, Jesús, and Ricardo J. Barceló. *Celtiberia gay*. Barcelona: Personas, 1976. alex28lp.
"PACO ESPAÑA." YouTube video, 4:32. June 15, 2018. https://www.youtube.com/watch ?v=axegkfiKkpY
Altamira, Rafael. *Psicología del pueblo español*. Madrid: Biblioteca Nueva, 1997 [1902].
Álvarez Junco, José. *Mater dolorosa: La idea de España en el siglo XIX*. Madrid: Taurus, 2001.
American Psychiatric Association. *Diagnostic and Statistical Manual of Mental Disorders*. 5th ed. Arlington, VA: American Psychiatric Publishing, 2013.
Amich Elías, Cristina. "El trabajo de los menores de edad en la dictadura franquista en historia contemporánea." *Historia contemporánea*, no. 36 (2011): 163-192.
Anillo, Fátima. Unpublished lecture for Federación Estatal de Compañías y Empresas de Danza. Centro Danza Canal, Madrid, December 19, 2018.

Bibliography

Antonelli, Carla. "Pierrot. Memorias trans (2) / Ultimo capítulo." *Web Carla Antonelli*, 2009. Accessed January 16, 2024. https://www.carlaantonelli.com/memorias-trans2-9.htm

Arbide, Joaquín, dir. "*La Esmeralda*." 1970. http://rtv.joaquinarbide.com/tv/pelis/esmeralda.html

Arendt, Hannah. "Labor, Work, Action." In *Amor Mundi: Explorations in the Faith and Thought of Hannah Arendt*, edited by James W. Bernauer, 29–42. Boston: Martinus Nijhoff Publishers, 1987.

Arnaud-Bestieu, Alexandra, and Gilles Arnaud. *La danse flamenco: Techniques et esthétiques*. Paris: L'Harmattan, 2013.

asalutes. "Manolo Caracol y Francisco Franco-España en la Memoria." YouTube video, 3:39. March 4, 2010. https://www.youtube.com/watch?v=mLSq_tHvLgo

Bennahum, Ninotchka Devorah. "Early Spanish Dancers on the New York Stage." In *100 Years of Flamenco in New York City*, edited by Ninotchka Bennahum and K. Meira Goldberg, 26–57. New York: New York Public Library for the Performing Arts, 2003.

Berger, John. *Ways of Seeing*. London: British Broadcasting Corporation and Penguin Books, 1972.

Bernabé, Daniel. *La trampa de la diversidad: Cómo el neoliberalismo fragmentó la identidad de la clase trabajadora*. Madrid: Akal, 2018.

Berzal de Miguel, Víctor. "Pasaje Begoña: Respeto a la diversidad, truncado por la represión franquista." *Cultura diversa*, March 3, 2019. https://culturadiversa.es/2019/03/pasaje-begona-torremolinos-lgtbi.html

Blas Vega, José. *Cincuenta años de flamencología*. Madrid: El Flamenco Vive, 2007.

Blas Vega, José. *El flamenco en Madrid*. Seville: Almuzara, 2006.

Blas Vega, José. *Los cafés cantantes de Madrid (1846–1936)*. Madrid: Guillermo Blázquez, 2006.

Blas Vega, José. *Vida y cante de Antonio Chacón: La edad de oro del flamenco (1869–1929)*. Córdoba: Ayuntamiento de Córdoba, 1986.

Bohórquez, Manuel. "De patito feo a cisne del baile." *La gazapera flamenco*, April 11, 2011. https://manuelbohorquez.com/la-gazapera-flamenca/de-patito-feo-a-cisne-del-baile/

Bohórquez, Manuel. "Rocío Márquez y el feminijondismo." *El correo de Andalucía*, March 8, 2019. https://elcorreoweb.es/cultura/rocio-marquez-y-el-feminijondismo-KJ5092873

Botti, Alfonso. *Cielo y dinero: El nacionalcatolicismo en España (1881–1975)*. Madrid: Alianza, 1992.

Bourdieu, Pierre. *The Bachelors' Ball: The Crisis of Peasant Society in Béarn*. Translated by Richard Nice. Cambridge: Polity, 2008.

Bourdieu, Pierre. *Language and Symbolic Power*. Edited by John B. Thompson. Translated by Gino Raymond and Matthew Adamson. Cambridge: Harvard University Press, 1991.

Bravo, Julio. "Sara Baras: 'No pretendo gustar a todo el mundo.'" *ABC*, August 12, 2004. https://www.abc.es/estilo/gente/abci-sara-baras-no-pretendo-gustar-todo-mundo-200408120300-9623044643980_noticia.html

Brown, Joshua. "'The Banks Are Our Stages': Flo 6x8 and Flamenco Performance as Protest in Southern Spain." *Popular Music and Society* 42, no. 2 (2019): 230–252. https://doi.org/10.1080/03007766.2018.1448249

Burgos, Antonio. "Los jornaleros del flamenco." *Triunfo* 27, no. 506 (June 10, 1972): 23–25.
Calvo Borobia, Kerman. *¿Revolución o reforma? La transformación de la identidad política del movimiento LGTB en España, 1970–2005*. Madrid: CSIC, 2017.
canalFlamenco. "Flamenco TV—Mercedes Ruiz enfervorizó con su farruca." YouTube video, 3:00. January 13, 2012. https://www.youtube.com/watch?v=YBFQgGP3jg0
Caro Baroja, Julio. *Temas castizos*. Madrid: Isthmus, 1980.
Carrasco, Marta. "Oh! Fascinados por el flamenco." *Revista de la Academia de las Artes Escénicas*, no. 7 (June 2017): 45–47. https://academiadelasartesescenicas.es/revista/16/artescenicas-7
Castillo-Puche, José Luis. "Madrid, cátedra del flamenco: Visita sentimental y pintoresca a los 'tablaos' más famosos de la villa y corte." *Blanco y negro*, no. 2644 (January 1963): 36–53.
CBO Andalucía. "LOLA FLORES (Sevillanas rocieras con pito y tamboril)—SEVILLANAS, de Carlos Saura." YouTube video, 2:49. July 4, 2018. https://www.youtube.com/watch?v=Twc44pQ_ARQ
Cleminson, Richard, and Francisco Vásquez García. *"Los Invisibles": A History of Male Homosexuality in Spain, 1850–1940*. Cardiff: University of Wales Press, 2007.
Cleminson, Richard, and Francisco Vásquez García. *Los invisibles: Una historia de la homosexualidad masculina en España, 1850–1939*. Granada: Comares, 2011.
Cleveland Plain Dealer. "Queen of the Ring." *Cleveland Plain Dealer*, July 13, 1888.
Colomer, Jaume. *Análisis de la situación económica de las artes escénicas en España*. Madrid: Los Libros de la Academia, 2016.
Concha Jareño. "Concha Jareño Farruca 'SIMPLEMENTE FLAMENCO.'" YouTube video, 10:00. October 22, 2010. https://www.youtube.com/watch?v=w2dsyoV0kfs
Cortes Generales. "Informe de la ponencia sobre la prostitución en nuestro país (154/9)." *Comisión mixta de los derechos de la mujer y de la igualdad de oportunidades*, March 13, 2007. http://www.lourdesmunozsantamaria.cat/IMG/pdf/INFORME_PONENCIA_PROSTITUCION.pdf
Cruces Roldán, Cristina. "'De cintura para arriba': Hipercorporeidad y sexuación en el flamenco." Proceedings from *Entretejiendo saberes: Actas del IV seminario de la Asociación Universitaria de Estudios de Mujeres (AUDEM)* 1 (2003): 1–2.
Cruces Roldán, Cristina. "Entre el anonimato, el exhibicionismo y la propaganda: Mujeres del flamenco y del baile español en el NO-DO del primer franquismo (1943–1958)." In *Dance, Ideology and Power in Francoist Spain (1938–1968)*, edited by Beatriz Martínez del Fresco and Belén Vega Pichaco, 285–322. Turnhout, Belgium: Brepols, 2017.
Cruces Roldán, Cristina. *Más allá de la música. Antropología y flamenco (II): Identidad, género y trabajo*. Seville: Signatura, 2003.
Cruces Roldán, Cristina, and Assumpta Sabuco Cantó. *Las mujeres flamencas: Etnicidad, educación y empleo ante los nuevos retos profesionales*. Seville: Universidad de Sevilla, 2005.
Cruz, Nando. "Flamenco patas arriba." *El Periódico*, January 28, 2020. https://www.elperiodico.com/es/ocio-y-cultura/20200128/mundos-paralelos-ruta-flamenco-barcelona-raval-poble-sec-sant-antoni-7825958
Cruz Lapeña, Silvia. *Crónica jonda*. Madrid: Libros del K.O., 2017.
Cruzado, Ángeles. "Amalia Molina, el arte y la gracia de Sevilla que conquistan al mundo

(VIII)." *Flamencas por derecho*, July 4, 2014. https://www.flamencasporderecho.com/amalia-molina-viii/

Cruzado, Ángeles. "Amalia Molina, el arte y la gracia de Sevilla que conquistan al mundo (X)." *Flamencas por derecho*, July 18, 2014. https://www.flamencasporderecho.com/amalia-molina-x/

Cruzado, Ángeles. "Carmencita Dauset, la reina de Broadway (I)." *Flamencas por derecho*, October 17, 2014. https://www.flamencasporderecho.com/carmencita-dauset-i/

Cruzado, Ángeles. "Carmencita Dauset, la reina de Broadway (II)." *Flamencas por derecho*, October 24, 2014. https://www.flamencasporderecho.com/carmencita-dauset-ii/

Cruzado, Ángeles. "Dora la Gitana, la transgresora reina del garrotín (y V)." *Flamencas por derecho*, January 1, 2016. https://www.flamencasporderecho.com/dora-la-gitana-v/

Cruzado, Ángeles. "1879, el salto a la Villa y Corte." In *La valiente: Trinidad Huertas "La Cuenca,"* by José Luis Ortiz Nuevo, Ángeles Cruzado, and Kiko Mora, 21–36. Seville: Libros con Duende, 2016.

Cruzado, Ángeles. "La Ciega de Jerez, jondura y sentimiento (I)." *Flamencas por derecho*, July 29, 2016. https://www.flamencasporderecho.com/la-ciega-de-jerez-i/

Cruzado, Ángeles. "La Estrella de Andalucía, reina del zapateado (IV)." *Flamencas por derecho*, May 27, 2016. https://www.flamencasporderecho.com/la-estrella-de-andalucia-iv/

Daniel Da Silva. "El Guito y Mario Maya por bulerias." YouTube video, 1:40. July 28, 2015. https://www.youtube.com/watch?v=shUYm9ZCpCc

David Zamajón París. "Carmen de Mairena—un repaso a su vida INÉDITO." YouTube video, 11:12. August 10, 2012. https://www.youtube.com/watch?v=HcGm-ojfv30

De Maeztu, Ramiro. *Hacia otra España*. Madrid: Biblioteca Nueva, 1997 [1899].

De Velilla, Sal. *Sodoma y lesbos modernas: Pederastas y safistas, estudiados en la clínica, en los libros y en la historia*. Barcelona: Carlos Ameler, 1932.

Deleuze, Gilles. *Francis Bacon: The Logic of Sensation*. Translated by Daniel W. Smith. New York: Continuum, 2003.

Deleuze, Gilles, and Félix Guattari. *What Is Philosophy?* Translated by Graham Burchell and Hugh Tomlinson. New York: Verso, 1994.

Derrida, Jacques. *On Touching—Jean-Luc Nancy*. Translated by Christine Irizarry. Stanford: Stanford University Press, 2005.

Descartes, René. "Rules for the Direction of the Mind." In *The Philosophical Writings of Descartes*, translated by John Cottingham, Robert Stoothoff, and Dugald Murdoch, 7–78. Cambridge: Cambridge University Press, 1984.

Diario de Jerez. "Las primeras grandes figuras del baile (1)." *Diara de Jerez*, February 25, 2012. https://www.diariodejerez.es/festivaldejerez/primeras-grandes-figuras-baile_0_564243591.html

Díaz Olaya, Ana María. "Los cafés cantantes y su influencia en la actividad musical de la sociedad española de finales del siglo XIX y principios del siglo XX. El núcleo minero de Linares como ejemplo de avance cultural y artístico." *Boletín del Instituto de Estudios Giennenses*, no. 205 (2012): 243.

Diéguez, Francisco. *Historia de un tablao: Las Brujas. Sus gentes, sus artistas y su época*. Cadiz: Absalon, 2008.

Díez Torres, María Isabel. "Entre cante y baile: El flamenco protesta de *Quejío* (1972) de Salvador Távora y La Cuadra de Sevilla." In *La investigación en danza, Sevilla 2018*, edited by Carmen Giménez-Morte, Virginia Soprano Manzo, Amparo Bayarri Furió, María Dolores Tena Medialdea, and Serafín Mesa Garcia, 433–436. Valencia: Mahali, 2018.
El Derecho. "Los cafés cantantes." *El Derecho*, October 16, 1886. Available at Ángeles Cruzado's Facebook. https://www.facebook.com/photo/?fbid=10155901067356570
Elorrieta, Gorka. "Madrid oculto: Una historia curiosa de la ciudad cada día." *TimeOut*, March 24, 2020. https://www.timeout.es/madrid/es/noticias/madrid-oculto-una-hi storia-curiosa-de-la-ciudad-cada-dia-032420
Elvira Esteban, Ana Isabel. "Tiempo de Mariemma, tiempo de festivales: La danza y los festivales de España (1960–1969) o como se llamen esas cosas que a nadie le importan." In *Mariemma y su tiempo*, edited by Rosa Ruiz Celaá, Antonio Álvarez Cañibano, and Paula De Castro Fernández, 211–249. Madrid: Centro de Documentación de Música y Danza, 2018.
Emmanuel Gayet. "1941 'ORIGINAL GYPSY DANCES.'" YouTube video, 8:38. April 16, 2018. https://www.youtube.com/watch?v=dkTgXbGwJVk
Escribano, Antonio. *Y Madrid se hizo flamenco*. Madrid: Avapiés, 1990.
Falange Española. "Puntos iniciales." *Filosofia.org*, December 7, 1933. https://www.filoso fia.org/hem/193/fes/fe0106.htm
fckat3. "BALLET TEATRO ESPANOL DE Rafael Aguilar—CARMEN-6." YouTube video, 16:48. December 5, 2012. https://www.youtube.com/watch?v=NykcLSVKDlM
Feiner, Muriel. *La mujer en el mundo del toro*. Madrid: Alianza, 1995.
Filmoteca Histórica Flamenca. "Bambino—no me des guerra (años 70)." YouTube video, 2:13. July 4, 2016. https://www.youtube.com/watch?v=jInrcZ1JEZQ
Gamboa, José Manuel. *Una historia del flamenco*. Barcelona: Espasa, 2004.
García Lorca, Federico. "Poet in New York." In *Selected Verse: Revised Bilingual Edition*, edited by Christopher Maurer, 277–279. Translated by Greg Simon and Steven F. White. New York: Farrar, Straus and Giroux, 2004.
Ginot, Isabella. *Dominique Bagouet, un labyrinthe dansé*. Pantin: CND, 1999.
Gobin, Alain. *Le flamenco: Que sais-je?* Paris: Presses Universitaires de France, 1975.
Goldberg, K. Meira. *Sonidos Negros: On the Blackness of Flamenco*. New York: Oxford University Press, 2019.
Goldberg, K. Meira. *Sonidos negros: Sobre la negritud del flamenco*. Translated by Kiko Mora. Granada: Libargo, 2022.
Goldberg, K. Meira, Ninotchka Bennahum, and Michelle Heffner Hayes. "Introduction." In *Flamenco on the Global Stage: Historical, Critical, and Theoretical Perspectives*, edited by K. Meira Goldberg, Ninotchka Bennahum, and Michelle Heffner Hayes, 1–22. Jefferson, NC: McFarland, 2015.
Goldberg, K. Meira, Walter Aaron Clark, and Antoni Pizà, eds. *Transatlantic Malagueñas and Zapateados in Music, Song and Dance*. Castle upon Tyne: Cambridge Scholars Publishing, 2019.
Gómez, Antonio. "Tres cuplés feministas de La Argentinita." *Memoria músico-festiva de un jubilado tocapelotas*, November 6, 2017. https://aplomez.blogspot.com/2017/11 /antologia-de-cuples-2-tres-cuples.html
Gómez, Mario, dir. *Rito y geografía del cante flamenco*. Season 1, episode 53, "Manolo

Caracol (I)." Aired November 20, 1972, RTVE. https://www.rtve.es/play/videos/rito-y-geografia-del-cante/rito-geografia-del-cante-manolo-caracol/1898471/

Gómez, Mario, dir. *Rito y geografía del cante flamenco.* Season 1, episode 54, "Manolo Caracol (II)." Aired November 27, 1972, RTVE. https://www.rtve.es/play/videos/rito-y-geografia-del-cante/rito-geografia-del-cante-manolo-caracol-ii/1898615/

Gómez, Mario, dir. *Rito y geografía del cante flamenco.* Season 1, episode 64, "Fernanda de Utrera." Aired February 5, 1973, RTVE. https://www.rtve.es/play/videos/rito-y-geografia-del-cante/rito-geografia-del-cante-fernanda-utrera/5276018/

Gómez, Mario, dir. *Rito y geografía del cante flamenco.* Season 1, episode 65, "Bernarda de Utrera." Aired February 12, 1973, RTVE. https://www.rtve.es/play/videos/rito-y-geografia-del-cante/rito-geografia-del-cante-bernarda-utrera/5130507/

Gómez, Mario, dir. *Rito y geografía del cante flamenco.* Season 1, episode 77, "La Paquera de Jerez." Aired May 14, 1973, RTVE. https://www.rtve.es/play/videos/rito-y-geografia-del-cante/rito-geografia-del-cante-paquera-jerez/1786640/

Gómez, Mario, dir. *Rito y geografía del cante flamenco.* Season 1, episode 92, "Extremadura y Portugal." Aired September 3, 1973, RTVE. https://www.rtve.es/play/videos/rito-y-geografia-del-cante/rito-geografia-del-cante-extremadura-portugal/5451510/

Gómez Urdáñez, José Luis. "Los Gitanos, al borde del genocidio." *La aventura de la historia* 45 (2002): 38–43.

González-Ruano, César. *Memorias: Mi medio siglo se confiesa a medias.* Madrid: Tebas, 1970.

Greco, José, and Harvey Ardman. *The Gypsy in My Soul: The Autobiography of José Greco.* Garden City, NY: Doubleday, 1977.

Guasch, Oscar, and Eduardo Lizardo. *Chaperos: Precariado y prostitución homosexual.* Barcelona: Bellaterra, 2017.

GUITARRACORDOBATV. "María Pagés 'Utopía'—Córdoba Guitar Festival 2014." YouTube video, 10:24. July 9, 2014. https://www.youtube.com/watch?v=v4_vdY5zwAQ

Halberstam, Jack. *The Queer Art of Failure.* Durham: Duke University Press, 2011.

Halperin, David. *How to Be Gay.* Cambridge: Belknap Press, 2012.

Hayes, Michelle Heffner. *Flamenco: Conflicting Histories of the Dance.* Jefferson, NC: McFarland, 2009.

Hirschfeld, Magnus. *Transvestites: The Erotic Drive to Cross-Dress.* Translated by Michael A. Lombardi-Nash. Buffalo, NY: Prometheus Books, 1991 [1910].

Hubert, Godard. "El gesto y su percepción." *Estudis escènics: Quaderns de l'Institut del Teatre de la Diputació de Barcelona,* no. 32 (2007): 335–344.

Ilitur-gitano Lisardo. "Dos fenómenos—Manuela Carrasco y Juan Villar (Bulerías) Los Canateros 196." YouTube video, 2:43. May 12, 2014. https://www.youtube.com/watch?v=uERIwqQ4FGY

Ilitur-gitano Lisardo. "Grabación histórica—Encarnación Lopéz 'La Argentinita.' (La caña) Gtr.-Manolo de Huelva." YouTube video, 4:00. January 16, 2015. https://www.youtube.com/watch?v=IrASRTHANaA

Ina Sport. "Danse avec la Compagnie Dominique Bagouet 'Necessito'—archive vidéo INA." YouTube video, 2:14. June 12, 2012. https://www.youtube.com/watch?v=P4tR8fJA_Wc

Isabel y Emilio. "Antonio por 'Martinete' 'Duende y misterio del flamenco' 1952." YouTube video, 3:28. February 4, 2020. https://www.youtube.com/watch?v=H_I-0bTBuXU

Bibliography 197

J. "Migue Benitez y El Torta—viviendo sin frenos." YouTube video, 4:42. July 19, 2011. https://www.youtube.com/watch?v=p3GGAt0ybAk
Jiménez, Iván. "Une Carmen en cache une autre Moscou-Cuba, 1967." In *Danse ren 68: Perspectives internationales*, edited by Isabelle Launay, Sylviane Pages, Mélanie Pain, and Guillaume Sintès, 211–230. Paris: Deuxième Époque, 2018.
JJGabarre. "SARA BARAS farruca." YouTube video, 6:55. September 3, 2016. https://www.youtube.com/watch?v=z9DyXigL-LU
José Luna. "La Argentinita seguiriyas 1935." YouTube video, 2:36. May 11, 2013. https://www.youtube.com/watch?v=-anQKU-SVlU
José Luna. "La Argentinita. Bulerías 1935." YouTube video, 2:32. May 11, 2013. https://www.youtube.com/watch?v=bH__SK3Nr5g
Kafer, Alison. *Feminist, Queer, Crip*. Bloomington: Indiana University Press, 2013.
Kaplan, E. Ann. *Looking for the Other: Feminism, Film, and the Imperial Gaze*. New York: Routledge, 1997.
Kendrew, Edward G. "Dancers in Spain." *Variety*, December 1, 1912.
Kika Lorace. "PARTIDO DE LA AMISTAD—KIKA LORACE Y SATÍN GRECO (LOLA FLORES)." YouTube video, 3:29. December 3, 2015. https://www.youtube.com/watch?v=_fbx0z BJnDE
La Fountain-Stokes, Lawrence. *Translocas: The Politics of Puerto Rican Drag and Trans Performance*. Ann Arbor: University of Michigan Press, 2021.
La Meri. *Spanish Dancing*. 2nd ed. Pittsfield, MA: Eagle Printing and Binding, 1967.
Laban, Rudolf von. *The Mastery of Movement*. 3rd ed. Edited by Lisa Ullmann. Boston: Plays, 1971.
Lacan, Jacques. *The Four Fundamental Concepts of Psychoanalysis: The Seminar of Jacques Lacan Book XI*. Edited by Jacques-Alain Miller. Translated by Alan Sheridan. New York: Norton, 1998.
Lassibille, Mahalia. "La danse africaine: Una catégorie anthropologisée." *EspacesTemps.net*, August 22, 2016. https://www.espacestemps.net/articles/la-danse-africaine-une-categorie%20anthropologisee
Launay, Isabelle. *Les danses d'après*. Vol. 1, *Poétiques et politiques des répertoires*. Pantin: Centre National de la Danse, 2017.
Launay, Isabelle. *Les danses d'après*. Vol. 2, *Cultures de l'oubli et citation*. Pantin: Centre National de la Danse, 2018.
Le Boulba, Pauline. "Les bords de l'oeuvre: Réceptions performées et critiques affectées en danse." PhD diss., l'Université Paris VIII–Vincennes–Saint Denis, 2019.
Lee Ruyter, Nancy. "La Meri and the World of Dance." *Anales del Instituto de Investigaciones Estéticas* 22, no. 77 (2000): 169–188.
Lejárraga, María. "La mujer española ante la república: Libertad." Lecture delivered at the Ateneo de Madrid, May 11, 1931. Seville: Instituto Andaluz de la Mujer, 2003 [1931].
Lejárraga, María. "La mujer española ante la república: Realidad." Lecture delivered at the Ateneo de Madrid, May 4, 1931. Seville: Instituto Andaluz de la Mujer, 2003 [1931].
León, José Javier. *El duende: Hallazgo y cliché*. Seville: Athenaica, 2018.
Lérida, Juan Carlos. "La liturgia de las horas. 2018–2021." *Juan Carlos Lérida*. https://juancarloslerida.com/project/la-liturgia-las-horas/

Library of Congress. "Carmencita." YouTube video, 0:38. March 26, 2009. https://www.youtube.com/watch?v=-15jwb1ZTMA
Littlewood, R. Joy. *A Commentary on Ovid: Fasti Book VI*. Oxford: Oxford University Press, 2006.
Litvak, Lily. *Antología de la novela corta erótica española de entreguerras (1918–1936)*. Madrid: Taurus, 1993.
López Moya, Diego. *La Argentinita: Libro de confidencias*. Madrid: J. Yagües, 1914.
López Rodríguez, Fernando. "Bailar en tiempos de crisis: El flamenco contemporáneo." In *Historia de la danza contemporánea en España*, vol. 3, *De la crisis económica de 2008 a la crisis sanitaria de 2020*, edited by Carmen Giménez-Morte, 82–99. Madrid: Academia de las Artes Escénicas de España, 2021.
López Rodríguez, Fernando. *De puertas para adentro: Disidencia sexual y disconformidad de género en la tradición flamenca*. Madrid: Egales, 2017.
López Rodríguez, Fernando. *Espejismos de la identidad coreográfica: Estética y transformaciones de la farruca*. Madrid: Los Libros de la Academia, 2015.
López Rodríguez, Fernando. "Estrategias de representación de cuerpos frágiles en el flamenco: Un estudio de campo llevado a cabo en Bensheim (Alemania)." In *La investigación en danza 2016*, vol. 1, edited by Carmen Giménez Morte, 329–334. Valencia: Mahali, 2016.
López Rodríguez, Fernando. "Gestos de ida y vuelta: Antonia Mercé, 1929–Kazuo Ohno, 1977." *Música oral del sur*, no. 17 (December 2020): 439–448. http://www.centrodedocumentacionmusicaldeandalucia.es/ojs/index.php/mos/article/view/369
López Rodríguez, Fernando. "H2-Ohno: Autoetnografía de un proceso creativo en danza." *Revista Acotaciones*, no. 43 (July–December 2019): 257–275. https://doi.org/10.32621/acotaciones.2019.43.10
López Rodríguez, Fernando. "La Argentina, ¿por dónde? Fascinación y filiación escópica en *O Senseï* (2012) y *Ôno-Sensation* (2019)." In *Actas de la jornada de estudios sobre Los Ballets Españoles de Antonia Mercé La Argentina*. Conference proceedings. Madrid: CSIC, November 2019.
López Rodríguez, Fernando. "Ocaña: Tradición sin tradicionalismo." In *Ocaña: Voces, ecos y distorsiones*, edited by Rafael M. Mérida Jiménez, 52–66. Barcelona: Bellaterra, 2018.
Louÿs, Pierre. *Woman and Puppet*. Translator unknown. New York: Pierre Louÿs Society, 1927.
Luis Fernando Dueñas. "Eva Yerbabuena—corte lluvia flamenco.flv." YouTube video, 7:36. November 8, 2012. https://www.youtube.com/watch?v=gNe_jF7hm4M
Luque, Nazario. *Sevilla y la Casita de las Pirañas*. Barcelona: Anagrama, 2018.
Macías Picavea, Ricardo. *El problema nacional*. Madrid: Biblioteca Nueva, 1996 [1899].
Mallada, Lucas. *La futura revolución española y otros escritos regeneracionistas*. Madrid: Biblioteca Nueva, 1998 [1897].
Mallada, Lucas. *Los males de la patria*. Madrid: Alianza Editorial, 1994 [1890].
Mansó, Carlos. "Notas para el periodista Pablo Suero: Buenos Aires, 1935." In *La Argentina, fue Antonia Mercé*. Buenos Aires: Devenir, 1993.
Maria José Navarro. "María José la Otra Pantoja—Velá San Pablo 2007." YouTube video, 58:02. November 28, 2017. https://www.youtube.com/watch?v=TH7moJIwKtE
Marín García, Teresa. "Frente a la precariedad laboral en las artes: Situación y tentativas

colectivas (en el estado español)." In *Producción artística en tiempos de precariado laboral*, edited by Juan Vicente Aliaga and Carmen Navarrete, 67-90. Madrid: Tierradenadie, 2017.
Marquié, Hélène. *Non, la danse n'est pas un truc de filles: Essai sur le genre en danse*. Toulouse: Éd. de l'Attribut, 2016.
Martínez, Ramón. *La cultura de la homofobia y cómo acabar con ella*. Madrid: Egales, 2016.
Martínez, Ramón. *Lo nuestro sí que es mundial: Una introducción a la historia del movimiento LGTB en España*. Madrid: Egales, 2017.
Mateos de Manuel, Victoria. "'Bailar en hombre': Una ortopedia del cuerpo nacional." Unpublished paper for Instituto de Filosofía, CCHS-CSIC, 2015.
McRuer, Robert. *Crip Theory: Cultural Signs of Queerness and Disability*. New York: New York University Press, 2006.
MeasuringWorth. "MeasuringWorth—Measures of Worth, Inflation Rates, and Purchasing Power." Accessed November 11, 2023. https://www.measuringworth.com/
Medina, Marcos, and Jonathan González, dirs. *Flamencas: Mujeres, fuerza y duende*. Arbolé Producciones. 2013. Documentary, 97:00. https://www.canalsurmas.es/en/videos/detail/42321-documentales-flamencasmujeres-fuerza-y-duendesi-satinternet-09032022
Mercé y Luque, Antonia. Original program from Tokyo recitals. Accessed at Juan March Foundation in Madrid. Imperial Theater, Tokyo, January 26–30, 1929.
Mérida Jiménez, Rafael M., ed. *Ocaña: Voces, ecos y distorsiones*. Barcelona: Bellaterra, 2018.
Mérida Jiménez, Rafael M. *Transbarcelonas: Cultura, género y sexualidad en la España del siglo XX*. Barcelona: Bellaterra, 2016.
Mira, Alberto. *De Sodoma a Chueca: Una historia cultural de la homosexualidad en España en el siglo XX*. Madrid: Egales, 2007.
Mizohata, Toshio. Unpublished lecture delivered at Spanish embassy, Tokyo, February 15, 2019.
Money, John. "Hermaphroditism, Gender and Precocity in Hyperadrenocorticism: Psychological Findings." *Bulletin of the Johns Hopkins Hospital*, no. 96 (1955): 253–264.
Mora Gaspar, Víctor. *Al margen de la naturaleza: La persecución de la homosexualidad durante el franquismo. Leyes, terapias y condenas*. Barcelona: Debate, 2016.
Mora Gaspar, Víctor, and Geoffroy Huard, eds. *40 años después: La despenalización de la homosexualidad en España. Investigación, memoria y experiencias*. Madrid: Egales, 2019.
Mora, Kiko. "Nueva York, entre La Habana y París; 1889." In *La valiente: Trinidad Huertas "La Cuenca"*, by José Luis Ortiz Nuevo, Ángeles Cruzado, and Kiko Mora, 262–264. Seville: Libros con Duende, 2016.
Moradiellos, Enrique. *La España de Franco (1939–1975)*. Madrid: Síntesis, 2000.
Moreno Mengíbar, Andrés, and Francisco Vázquez García. *Sexo y razón: Una genealogía de la moral sexual en España (siglos XVI–XX)*. Madrid: Akal, 1997.
Moreno Pestaña, José Luis. *La cara oscura del capital erótico: Capitalización del cuerpo y trastornos alimentarios*. Madrid: Akal, 2016.
Muños Seca, Pedro. "¡Ay, se me cae!" *La Esfera* 11, no. 534 (March 29, 1924): 27.
Murillo Saborido, Eduardo. "Los tablaos flamencos en Madrid entre 1954–1973: Una

aproximación académica a su escena musical." MA thesis, Universidad Complutense de Madrid, 2017.
Nacha la Macha. "Nacha la Macha—Como la Copla no hay Ná. VIDEOCLIP." YouTube video, 4:43. April 7, 2015. https://www.youtube.com/watch?v=a7VRXTfR4UA
Nacha la Macha. "Nacha La Macha—Eres Cobarde (Video Oficial)." YouTube video, 6:06. June 2, 2018. https://www.youtube.com/watch?v=8fU5RZy0RJo
Nacha la Macha. "Nacha La Macha—Mañana Muérete feat. Miguel Garena (Video Oficial)." YouTube video, 7:19. March 18, 2019. https://www.youtube.com/watch?v=MEz1zAseMjM
Navarro García, José Luis. *Historia del baile flamenco*. Vol. 1. Seville: Signatura, 2010.
Navarro García, José Luis. "Algunas novedades en torno a La Cuenca." *Revista de investigación sobre flamenco la madruga*, no. 2 (June 2010), 1-24.
Navarro Garcia, José Luis. *Vicente Escudero: Un bailaor cubista*. Seville: Libros con Duende, 2012.
Neville, Edgar. "El Duende." *ABC*, March 3, 1965.
Neville, Edgar. "Las Brujas." *ABC*, February 27, 1965.
Neville, Edgar. "Los Canasteros." *ABC*, March 13, 1965.
NO-DO, producer. *Diccionario turístico español*. January 1, 1972. https://www.rtve.es/play/videos/documentales-color/diccionario-turistico-espanol/2898346/
NO-DO, producer. *Madrid*. January 1, 1974. https://www.rtve.es/play/videos/documentales-color/madrid/2903196/
NO-DO, producer. *Madrid de noche*. January 1, 1959. https://www.rtve.es/play/videos/documentales-b-n/madrid-noche/2846380/
Obert, L'armari. "Lluiset Serracant, Flor de Otoño, y el travestismo barcelonés años 20–30." *Leopoldest*, March 2016. https://leopoldest.blogspot.com/2016/03/lluiset-serracant-flor-de-otono-y-el.html
ochopajaritos. "Isabel Bayón Compañía Flamenca. LA MUJER Y EL PELELE." YouTube video, 10:32. June 3, 2009. https://www.youtube.com/watch?v=fM0rHZneRGI
Ohno, Kazuo, chor. *La Argentina*. Maison de la danse, Lyon, 2018. https://www.numeridanse.tv/videotheque-danse/hommage-la-argentina?s
Olmeda, Fernando. *El látigo y la pluma: Homosexuales en la España de Franco*. Madrid: Anaya, 2004.
Ortiz Nuevo, José Luis. *De las danzas y andanzas de Enrique el Cojo*. Seville: Athenaica, 2017.
Ortiz Nuevo, José Luis. *¿Se sabe algo? Viaje al conocimiento del arte flamenco en la prensa sevillana del XIX*. Seville: El Carro de la Nieve, 1990.
Ortiz Nuevo, José Luis. *Yo tenía mu güeña estrella: Anica la Periñaca*. La Puebla de Cazalla: Barataria, 2012.
Otero Aranda, José. *Tratado de bailes de sociedad, regionales españoles, especialmente andaluces, con su historia y modo de ejecutarlos*. Seville: Tip. de la Guía Oficial, 1912.
Pablo Lozano, Eulalia. "La bata de cola: Un capricho de la majeza." *Candil*, no. 128 (2015): 3874–3876. https://elecodelamemoria.blogspot.com/2015/03/la-bata-de-cola-un-capricho-de-la-majeza.html
Pablo Lozano, Eulalia. *Mujeres guitarristas*. Seville: Signatura, 2009.
Pagès, Sylviane. *Le butô en France: Malentendus et fascination*. Pantin: Centre National de la Danse, 2017.

Paréntesis. "Rudolf Nureyev baila en Madrid." *ABC: Blanco y negro*, September 27, 1975.
Pastor, Ana, producer. *Crónicas*. "Bajo el sol de Torremolinos." Aired April 15, 2012, RTVE. https://www.rtve.es/play/videos/cronicas/cronicas-bajo-sol-torremolinos /1133477/
pie flamenco. "Fernanda Romero Tarantos." YouTube video, 7:07. September 3, 2015. https://www.youtube.com/watch?v=ibnJFOUMa6U
pie flamenco. "Julien Duvivier, La Bandera, 1935." YouTube video, 4:32. November 13, 2013. https://www.youtube.com/watch?v=LTwpWuh8BaU
Pierce, Joseph M. "I Monster: Embodying Trans and *Travesti* Resistance in Latin America." *Latin American Research Review* 55, no. 2 (2020): 305–321.
Plaza Orellana, Rocío. "El baile, la empresa y el espectáculo: Historias de encuentros y desencuentros en los teatros europeos." Lecture given at Universidad Internacional de Andalucía, Seville, November 30, 2006. https://vimeo.com/85140318
Pohren, D. E. *The Art of Flamenco*. Jerez de la Frontera: Jerez Industrial, 1962.
Politikon. *El muro invisible: Las dificultades de ser joven en España*. Barcelona: Penguin Random House, 2017.
Pouillaude, Frédéric. *Le désoeuvrement chorégraphique: Étude sur la notion d'oeuvre en danse*. Paris: Vrin, 2009.
Preciado, Paul B. "Biopolítica del género." In *Conversaciones feministas: Biopolítica*. Buenos Aires: Ají de Pollo, 2009.
Preciado, Paul B. "Revoluciones somatopolíticas: Cuerpos feministas, queer, trans y cripple-queer." Lecture given at the seminar "Cuerpo impropio: Guía de modelos somatopolíticos y de sus posibles usos desviados." Universidad Internacional de Andalucía, 2011.
Preciado, Paul B. *Testo Junkie: Sex, Drugs, and Biopolitics in the Pharmacopornographic Era*. Translated by Bruce Benderson. New York: Feminist Press, 2013.
Puleo García, Alicia H. "Introducción al concepto género." In *Género y comunicación*, edited by Juan F. Plaza Sánchez and Carmen Delgado Álvarez, 13–32. Madrid: Fundamentos, 2007.
Pulpón, Carmen Penélope. "Bailaoras de Sevilla: Aprendizaje, profesión y género en el flamenco del franquismo y la transición: Estudio histórico-etnográfico de casos (1950–1980)." PhD diss., Universidad de Sevilla, 2015.
Regidor Arribas, Ramón. "El travestismo en la zarzuela." In *Gigantes y cabezudos / la viejecita*, 31–32. Madrid: Teatro de la Zarzuela, 1998.
Reina d'Àfrica. "'Lejos de los árboles', Jacinto Esteva.(1963–1971)." YouTube video, 99:36. April 8, 2013. https://www.youtube.com/watch?v=1TKmaYeth5w
Retana, Álvaro. *Historia del arte frívolo*. Madrid: Tesoro, 1964.
Reyes Tolentino, Francisca. *Philippine Folk Dances and Games*. New York: Silver, Burdett, 1927.
Rivas, Natalio. "Las mujeres en la tauromaquía." In *Toreros del romanticismo: Anecdotario taurino*, 286–293. Madrid: Aguilar, 1987.
Roberto Bermejo. "Baile por Alegrías de Cádiz de Enrique el Cojo." YouTube video, 7:16. August 21, 2008. https://www.youtube.com/watch?v=yEVKfpMGwhA
Rockmore, Ryan. "Dancing the Ideal Masculinity." In *Flamenco on the Global Stage: Historical, Critical, and Theoretical Perspectives*, edited by K. Meira Goldberg, Ninotchka Bennahum, and Michelle Heffner Hayes, 234–243. Jefferson, NC: McFarland, 2015.

Bibliography

Rockmore, Ryan. "Queering the Tale of the Skirt: The Masculine Presence, Archival Histories, and Queer Future of the *Bata de Cola*." In *Celebrating Flamenco's Tangled Roots: The Body Questions*, edited by K. Meira Goldberg and Antoni Pizà, 101–125. Newcastle upon Tyne: Cambridge Scholars Publishing, 2022.

Rodríguez Gómez, Fernando. *Arte y artistas flamencos*. Madrid: Extramuros, 1935.

Romero, Pedro G. "El flamenco es un género." *El País*, March 16, 2018. https://elpais.com/cultura/2018/03/16/babelia/1521201640_215414.html

Romero, Pedro G., ed. *Ocaña, 1973–1983: Acciones, actuaciones, activismo*. Barcelona: Polígrafa, 2011.

Rondón Rodríguez, Juan. *Recuerdos y confesiones del cantaor Rafael Pareja de Triana*. Córdoba: La Posada, 2001.

Ruiz Fuentes, José María. "El Loco Mateo." *El arte de vivir el flamenco*. Accessed January 18, 2024. https://elartedevivirelflamenco.com/cantaores260.html

Ruiz Fuentes, José María. "La Ciega de Jerez." *El arte de vivir el flamenco*. Accessed January 18, 2024. https://elartedevivirelflamenco.com/cantaores679.html

Sáez, Javier. *Teoría queer y psicoanálisis*. Madrid: Síntesis, 2008.

Sáez, Javier, and Fefa Vila, eds. *El libro del buen amor: Sexualidades raras y políticas extrañas*. Madrid: Traficantes de Sueños, 2019.

Sandahl, Carrie. "Queering the Crip or Cripping the Queer? Intersections of Queer and Crip Identities in Solo Autobiographical Performance." *GLQ* 9, nos. 1–2 (2003): 25–56.

Santana, M. Myrta Leslie. "*Transformista, Travesti, Transgénero*: Performing Sexual Subjectivity in Cuba." *Small Axe* 26, no. 2 (July 2022): 46–59.

Sevilla, Paco. "The Spanish Tablao." *Jaleo* 1, no. 3 (October 1977): 2–3. http://www.elitedynamics.com/jaleomagazine/JALEO-1977-10.pdf

Solís Galván, Raúl. *La doble transición*. Jaén: Libros.com, 2019.

Sosa Villada, Camila. *Bad Girls: A Novel*. Translated by Kit Maude. New York: Other Press, 2022.

spitfaya123. "Loie Fuller—Danse Serpentine by Lumière Brother[s]." YouTube video, 6:12. January 22, 2011. https://www.youtube.com/watch?v=YNZ4WCFJGPc

Spivak, Gayatri Chakravorty. "The Politics of Translation." In *Outside in the Teaching Machine*, 200–225. New York: Routledge, 1993.

Stryker, Susan. *Transgender History: The Roots of Today's Revolution*. New York: Seal Press, 2008.

Suárez-Japón, Juan Manuel. "Algunas ideas sobre las relaciones entre flamenco y poder." In *Acts del V Congreso Internacional Universitario de Investigación sobre Flamenco*, 11–20. Murcia: Universidad Católica San Antonio, 2015.

Trenas, Pilar. "Noche de flamenco y arte en 'Los Cabales.'" *ABC*, October 1, 1972. https://www.abc.es/archivo/periodicos/abc-madrid-19721001-119.html

UNESCO. "El flamenco." *UNESCO Patrimonio Cultural Inmaterial*. Accessed November 11, 2023. https://ich.unesco.org/es/RL/el-flamenco-00363

Usó, Juan Carlos. *Gloria laguna: Ingenio castizo, mito literario y lesbianismo chic*. Santander: El Desvelo, 2018.

Usó, Juan Carlos. *Orgullo travestido*. Santander: El Desvelo, 2017.

Valtueña, Daniel. "Niño de Elche, a Heterotopian (Flamencx) Voice." In *Celebrating Flamenco's Tangled Roots: The Body Questions*, edited by K. Meira Goldberg and Antoni Pizà, 126–136. Newcastle upon Tyne: Cambridge Scholars Publishing, 2022.

Varela Ortega, José, Fernando Rodríguez Lafuente, and Andrea Donofrío, eds. *La mirada del otro: La imagen de España ayer y hoy*. Madrid: Fórcola, 2016.
Vegas, Valeria. *Vestidas de azul: Análisis social y cinematográfico de la mujer transexual en los años de la transición española*. Madrid: Dos Bigotes, 2019.
Verguillos, Juan. "30 años de 'Danza y tronío.'" *Diario de Sevilla*, March 30, 2014. https://www.diariodesevilla.es/ocio/anos-Danza-tronio_0_793421105.html
Vidas Ejemplares. "Lola Flores y el sexo." YouTube video, 2:56. May 28, 2010. https://www.youtube.com/watch?v=v5hgoTCaOTQ
Vilarós, Teresa M. *El mono del desencanto: Una crítica cultural de la transición española (1973–1993)*. Madrid: Espasa, 1998.
Villaruz, Basilio Esteban S. "Philippine Dance in the Spanish Period." Manila: National Commission for Culture and the Arts, June 2, 2015. https://ncca.gov.ph/about-ncca-3/subcommissions/subcommission-on-the-arts-sca/dance/philippine-dance-in-the-spanish-period/
Villaruz, Basilio Esteban S. *Treading Through: 45 Years of Philippine Dance*. Quezon City: University of the Philippines Press, 2006.
Villena, Miguel Ángel. "Canales y Pasqual montan un espectáculo de danza sobre Bernarda Alba." *El País*, November 15, 1997. https://elpais.com/diario/1997/11/15/cultura/879548413_850215.html
Washabaugh, William. *Flamenco: Passion, Politics, and Popular Culture*. Oxford: Berg, 1996.
Wayar, Marlene. *Furia travesti: Diccionario de la T a la T*. Buenos Aires: Paidós, 2021.
Wiseman, T. P. *Remus: A Roman Myth*. Cambridge: Cambridge University Press, 1995.
Wittgenstein, Ludwig. "Proposition 5.6." In *Tractatus Logico-Philosophicus*, 74. Translated by C. K. Ogden. London: Kegan Paul, Trench, Trubner, 1922.
Wittig, Monique. *The Straight Mind and Other Essays*. Boston: Beacon Press, 1992.
Wright, Richard. *Pagan Spain*. New York: Harper & Brothers, 1957.
Zafra, Remedios. *El entusiasmo: Precariedad y trabajo creativo en la era digital*. Barcelona: Anagrama, 2017.

Acknowledgments

First, thank you to my thesis advisers, Isabel Launay and Mahalia Lassibille, for their unwavering faith and for following the galloping rhythm required to work with me. Thank you as well to Isabelle Ginot and all the doctoral students in the Department of Dance at the University of Paris VIII, with whom I have had the enormous luck of chatting regularly about our research. The multiple points of view and the exchange of ideas have been a considerable help to me.

To Elia Rodière, for reading and correcting the French version of my dissertation; for working with me since I arrived in Paris in 2011; and for her listening ear, advice, support, and encouragement: thanks for continuing to want to fly with me.

Thank you to Alicia Sánchez and Estefanía López, my Spanish friends who lived with me in Paris during my doctoral years and welcomed me so often in their homes. Thanks for filling my Parisian life with laughs; "Paris was a party" with both of you.

To my family, for being an indisputable place of support. And to my husband, Jaime Iglesias: I waited many years for you, and you appeared; I would wait another hundred lifetimes for you if necessary.

Thanks to all the flamenco artists who helped me develop this research, especially Juan Carlos Lérida and Belén Maya, whose friendship has been an absolute comfort.

Thanks also to the community of researchers in Spain, who, from the beginning, received my contributions to the field of dance with such enthusiasm and care. Also, thanks to my committee members for reading, commenting on, nuancing, and broadening my dissertation. Cristina Cruces, Ana María Díaz, Carmen Giménez, Hélène Marquié, and Philippe Guisgand—your time and glances are greatly appreciated!

Lastly, thank you, Mili Hernández, for placing your trust in me again to make my small contribution to the changing field of LGBTQ+ studies.

Index

accessories: *bata de cola*, 17–18, 19, 75, 90, 92, 106, 127–28, 133, 148; castanets, 128, 132–33, 136, 141, 142, 161; fans, 18; hats, 18; men's use of feminine accessories, 90; in womanly dancing, 18. *See also* shawls
activism: achievements of, 163; *Gitano* activism in history of flamenco dance, 155–60, 186n48; space(s) for, 119. *See also* LGTBIQ movement
"*Admiring La Argentina*" (piece) (Ohno), 134, 140–43, 187n57
aesthetics: aesthetic experience from flamenco, 144–46; aesthetic hysteria, 146; aesthetic identity, 6; aesthetic judgment, 56–57; Effort theory and, 9–10; feminine gender codes and, 61; limitation of, 10; problems from aesthetic barriers, 163; Spanish Falange and, 49; transition in, 4. *See also* contemporary flamenco dance
aesthetic transitions of flamenco: contemporary flamenco dance, 99–102; decline of *tablao*, 98–100; duets, 95–98; erotic capital of *bailaores* and, 102–6; from Spanish ballet to flamenco ballet, 94–95; the Transition and, 93–94
Agamben, Giorgio, 2, 85
Aguilar, Rafael, 95, 101
Agujetas, 82
AIDS: Bagouet and, 144–45; Tamara and, 89

aje (artistic command and presence), 164–65
Albéniz, Isaac, 132–33, 140
alcohol usage, 3, 4, 16, 41, 45, 68
alegrías, xv, 17, 18, 27, 49, 75, 76, 118, 153, 179n203
Alonso, Rafael Salazar, 14, 37
Álvarez Junco, José, 7
Amargo, Rafael, 101
Amaya, Carmen, 50, 72, 76, 164
Andalusia: aesthetics of, 43, 122; poetry and customs of, 6
andaluz (Andalusian) dialect, xiii, xiv
Ander (interviewee), 116, 117, 118
Anillo, Fátima, 107
anti-Enlightenment values, 7–8
antiguapas (anti-beauties), 104–6
Antología del cante flamenco (Hispavox), 46
Antonio (El de Bilbao), 150–51
Antonio (El Muñeco), 71
Antonio Gades y Su Espectáculo de Arte Español, 48
Arendt, Hannah, 185n17
artists: artistic judgment, 52–58; criticisms by, 163; salaries of, 51
audiences. *See* spectators (consumers)
Aznar, José María, 77–78, 101

The Bachelors' Ball (Bourdieu), 126
Bagouet, Dominique, 144–46; France and, 144–46

207

Index

bailaoras (female flamenco dancers): Amaya, Carmen, 50, 72, 76, 164; Ana María, 55; Baras, Sara, 89–90, 97; Concha la Carbonera, 40; cross-dressing, 76; Cruz, Claudia, 113; España, Trini, 64–65; Fernández Oliva, Carolina, 109, 125; Flores, Lola, 67–68, 75, 80–81, 89, 91–93, 145; Graves, Yinka Esi, 148; Jareño, Concha, 89–90; La Mejorana, 81; La Rubia de Vallecas, 109, 125; La Sordita, 150; La Tati, 71–73, 108, 112; La Uchi, 54; Lezana, Sara, 82, 97, 153; López, Lola, 148, 154; in *Madrid de noche*, 106; Moya, Antonia, 123; Pagés, María, 90, 97, 100, 101; promise of interactions with spectators, 64–66; role distribution and, 4; Ruiz, Mercedes, 90; Tena, Lucero, 74, 75; trans identity and, 89; Trenas on, 54–55; Yerbabuena, Eva, 100, 106

bailaores (male flamenco dancers): aesthetics of, 57, 58; Bambino as, 59–60; Córdova, Rafael de, 82, 97; El Bailarín as, 50, 60, 95; El Cojo as, xiv, 57, 86–88, 87, 151–54; erotic capital of, 102–6; expressiveness of, 58–59; Flores, Marco, 101, 124, 127; Grilo, Joaquín, 105; Heras, Rubén, 134; heterosexual duet by, 59; Liñán, Manuel, xiii, 90, 127–28, 129; Molina as, 60; Pericet, Olga, 101, 124; precarity and, 110–11, 113; Rico as, 60; scarcity of manly, 58–59; unbalanced effeminacies in, 60

"*Bailar en hombre*" (piece) (López Rodríguez), 128, 134, 164

baile de hombre (manly dancing), 17–18, 136

baile de mujer (womanly dancing), 17–18, 136

Ballet: Ballet de la Ópera de París, 97; Ballet de Rafael Aguilar, 90; Ballet de Victor Ullate, 97; Ballet Español de Alberto Portillo, 48; Ballet Español de Antonio, 48; Ballet Español de María Rosa, 48; Ballet Español de Pilar López, 48; Ballet Español de Rafael de Córdova, 48; *ballet flamenco*, 94–95; Ballet Flamenco de Andalucía, 100; Ballet Flamenco de Madrid, 97; Ballet Gitano de Luisa Ortega y Arturo Pavón, 48; Ballet Nacional de Cuba, 97; Ballet Nacional de España, 94–95, 100; Ballets Russes, 150

Bambino (Miguel Vargas Jiménez), 59–60

Baras, Sara, 89–90, 97

Barcelona: Ambos Mundos, 82; Bagdad, 120; Barcelona de Noche, 79, 82; Barcelona de Noche (Barcelona), 83; Barri Xinès (Chinese Quarter), 25, 41–43; Bella Helen in, 89; Bodega Apolo, 82; Cabaret de la Muerte, 120; Café Nuevo, 82; *cafés cantantes* in, 15, 20; Carmen de Mairena in, 82; Ciros, 82; Copacabana, 79, 82, 83; El Cangrejo, 82; El Trascacho, 151; euphoric drug use in, 45; fairy (*mariquita*) shows in, 79; Festival Flamenco Empírico, 101; Flamenco Queer, 134; illegal tablaos, 114–15; Increpación Danza, 100; Jiménez, Pol, 132; La Chana (Antonia Santiago Amador), 154; La Criolla, 41–43; Las Ramblas, 83, 84, 85, 86, 88, 145; La Taberna de Apolo, 79; LGBT protests in, 78, 128; Lido, 82; Mr. Artur in, 81; *Mundos paralelos* project (Lérida), 120; Ocaña's street performances in, 84; Paco España in, 82; Thirty-Fifth Congreso Eucarístico Internacional en Barcelona, 48; 2D1, 100; Whisky Twist, 79, 83

Barcelona de Noche (Barcelona), 79, 82, 83

Barrús Martínez, María (La Niña de Antequera), 62–64

bata de cola, 17–18, 19, 75, 90, 92, 106, 127–28, 133, 148

Bayón, Isabel, 24, 100, 156

beauty: anti-beauties, 104–6; of *bailaor*, 57; of *bailaora*, 53, 57, 176n136; demand for bodily beauty, 103–4; lack of, 28, 151; in male body, 53, 56–57; model of

choreographic and kinesthetic beauty, 154; Ocaña on, 86; privileges of, 60; of solo bodies, 95; thinness and, 103–4
Bella Dora, 39
Bennahum, Ninotchka, xvi, 137
Berger, John, 103, 171n42
Bernarda Alba (character), 91
Bienal de Flamenco de Málaga, 127
Bienal de Flamenco de Sevilla, 100, 119
Bizet, Georges, 24, 90, 96
blackness in flamenco: *casticismo* (Castillian national essence) and, 168n3(ch.1); Graves, Yinka Esi, 148; *Gurumbé* (2016 documentary) (Rosales), 148; *Semillas de ébano* (Ortiz Nuevo), 148; silenced History of, 147–48; *Sonidos Negros* (Goldberg and Mora), xvi, 148
Blas Vega, José, 15, 17, 26
"*Bodas de sangre*" (1971 ballet) (Gades), 95
Bodas de sangre (1981 film) (Saura), 95, 96
body: democratic access of, 103; erotic capital of *bailaores*, 102–6; heterosexuality as embodied ideology of the, 19; hypercorporeality, 52–53, 56, 58; hypocorporeality, 56, 58; inclusion to expressiveness of disabled bodies, 154; kinesthetic contagion, 16; as a medium, 142; objectification of, 4, 103; self-spectacularization of the, 126; teletouch (*teletacto*) and, 56
bolero dance, 17, 19, 20, 35–36, 49, 57, 161, 175n120
bonito soniquete de maricas (BSDM), 134
Bourdieu, Pierre, 8, 126, 172n72
Brau Gou, Miguel (Carmen de Mairena), 60, 81, 82–83
Bries, Edmond de, 26
Brown, Joshua, 185n29
bulerías genre, 61, 69, 105, 106, 148
bullfighters/bullfighting: bullfighting dances, 34–38; Escamillo (character), 96; female bullfighters, 14, 36–37; imagery of, 92, 121, 124, 161; La Reverte, 14; masculinization of, 12, 13, 14; movements of, 102, 142, 143; popularity of, 36; posture of, 145; Rojas, Victor, 81; *transformistas* and, 66–67
Buñuel, Luis, 23
Burgos, Antonio, 51, 79
burlesque, 134

cabarets: Bagouet and, 145–46; Cabaret de la Muerte, 120; decline of, 180n9; drag and, 78, 82, 84; euphoric drug use in, 68; La Criolla (Barcelona), 41–43; La Tati in, 72; Madame Artur (venue), 81; Margot de Salamanca, 66; Molino Rojo, 64; Rosales on, 26;
Cádiz: African dance imported from Havana to, 147; *cafés cantantes* in, 15; LSD in, 69; La Mejorana (Monje, Rosario), 81; La Petróleo, 88; La Salvaora, 88; Quintana and, 6; transatlantic slave trade in, 148
Café de Chinitas (Madrid), 48, 59, 76, 100, 115, 122
Café del Burrero, 40
Café de Silverio (Seville), 25–26, 37
cafés cantantes: as ancestor of *tablao*, 15–25; *cafés-concerts* and, 15; comparisons to, 79; decline of, 44; defined, 4; eroticization of dancers' bodies in, 22–25; explanatory theory on drag, 44; female drag in Zarzuela, 38–39; Flor de Otoño, 42; gender divisions in, 16–19; gender fluid artists, 33–34; La Criolla (Barcelona), 41–43; male prostitution in, 25; men dressed as women, 39–42; multidisciplinary and hybrid artists, 25–27; prostitution and, 66; *transformistas*, 33–34; voyeurism and, 19–20; women, artists, and feminists, 28–33; women dressed as men, 34–38
cafés-concerts, 15
Café Ziryab, 124
Callas, Maria, 140, 141, 187n57
Camarón de la Isla, 70
Camprubí, Mariano, 57–58
Canales, Antonio, 91

210 Index

Candela (trans folk artist), 88
Candela (venue), 121, 182n54
Cano, Carlos, 83–84
cante jondo: after Spanish Civil War, 46; connoisseurs of, 46; La Paquera and, 61; Ocaña and, 84; Ortiz Nuevo on, 11; *RomeroMartin* project and, 131
Caracol, Manolo, 48, 54, 66, 174n111
caracoles, 90, 127
Cardamomo (Madrid), 182n54, 183n64
Carmen (character), 24–25, 90–91, 96–98
Carmen (flamenco) (Aguilar), 90–91, 97
Carmen (flamenco and theater dance) (Távora), 97
Carmen (1975 film) (Diamante), 153
Carmen (1983 film) (Saura), 95, 96, 97, 100, 124
Carmen (novella) (Mérimée), 24–25, 96
Carmen (opera) (Bizet), 24, 96
Carmen de Mairena (Miguel Brau Gou), 60, 81, 82–83
Carmen(s) (piece) (Montalvo), 97
Carmen VS Carmen (Spanish dance) (Compañía Ibérica de Danza (Compañía Ibérica de Danza), 97
Carrasco, Manuela, 106
Carrasco, Rafaela, 100, 101
Carvento, Carlos, 130–31
Casa Patas (Madrid), 110, 123, 131, 182n54, 183n64
castanets, 128, 132–33, 136, 141, 142, 161
casticismo (Castillian national essence), 8, 168n3(ch.1)
Castro, José (Miracielos), 150
Cátedra de Flamencología y de Jerez de la Frontera, 46
Certamen Coreográfico de Danza Española de Madrid, 90, 128
child labor, 3, 4, 73
choreographers: Aguilar, Rafael, 95, 101; Alonso, Alberto, 97; Galván, Pastora, 104; López, Pilar, 94, 95; Mariemma, 48–49, 95; Mercé, Antonia (La Argentina), 95, 134, 139–44, 172n61, 175n124; Petit, Roland, 97; Ruiz Soler, Antonio, 50, 60, 76, 95, 151, 164, 177n153; Sanchís, Paola T., 113; of Spanish dance, 97. See also specific choreographers
choreography, 2–3, 18–19, 50, 60, 175n124
Civil War. See Spanish Civil War
clapping of hands (*palmas*), 9, 18, 52, 55, 75, 105–6, 106, 161, 175
Cleminson, Richard, 11, 12–13, 25, 169n22
codes: aesthetics and, 61; of burlesque, 134; communication codes, 164; dress codes, 118; of expression, 61; feminine gender codes, 61; flamenco as shared code, 105, 164; of flamenco masculinity, 59, 90; gender codes, 135, 173n72; gestures and, 61; heteronormative codes, 79; movement codes for men, 4, 17, 59; movement codes for women, 4, 17; of role distribution, 118; social codes, 85
Código de la escuela sevillana: La importancia de bailar como una mujer (Coral), 135–36
compañías de danza (dance companies): Compañía Andaluza de Danza, 100, 156; Compañía de Rojas y Rodríguez, 128; Compañía Ibérica de Danza, 97; Compañía Ibérica de Danza en Sevilla, 100; Compañía Nacional de Danza de España, 97
compás (rhythmic structure of flamenco), 5, 165
Concha la Carbonera, 40
Concurso Nacional de Arte Flamenco de Córdoba, 46, 61
Conservatorio Superior de Danza María de Ávila, 130
contemporary flamenco dance: birth of, 98–102; category of, 3; emergence of, 4; public space use by, 119–20; research on, xiii, 2
Copacabana (Barcelona), 79, 82, 83
copla genre: Flores, Lola, 91, 92; Jurado, Rocío, 91; Ocaña, José Pérez, 84; Rico, Pedrito, 83
Coral, Matilde, 70, 100, 135

Index   211

Córdova, Rafael de, 82, 97
Cortés, Joaquín, 90, 100, 102
Council of Castile, 14
couples dances: *fandango*, 20, 29, 46, 49, 51, 56, 84, 147; *paso doble*, 29, 145; passage from, 19–20; *rumbas*, 51, 52, 75, 94, 126, 164, 178n184; *seguidillas*, 20, 140. See also *bolero* dance
cripped (*tullido*) history of flamenco, xv–xvi, 3, 5, 148–55, 188n79
crises: artists in times of, 107–13; economic, 4, 107–13; gender-based, 4, 127–33; survival strategies for dancers, 113–27; transcultural revolution, 133–36. See also economic issues; the Transition
Cruces Roldán, Cristina, 17, 18, 52, 56, 104, 114, 126, 170n34
Cruz, Claudia, 113
Cruzado, Ángeles (La Estrella de Andalucía), 37
Cruz Lapeña, Silvia, 122, 128
Cubas, Adela, 28, 45
cultural capital, 9
cuplé genre: La Argentinita and, 27, 31–33; La Asturiana and, 43; La Sillera and, 37; Molina on, 28; origin of, 26; Silvanys, Silvia, 45

dance companies (compañías de danza): Compañía Ibérica de Danza. See compañías de danza (dance companies)
danza estilizada, 49
Dauset Moreno, Carmen (Carmencita), 36
decolonization of Spanish dance, 147–48
Deleuze, Gilles, 2, 146
De Otoño, Flor, 42–43
De puertas para adentro: Disidencia sexual y disconformidad de género en la tradición flamenca (López Rodríguez), 11, 128, 177n153
Descartes, René, 56
Diaghilev, Sergei, 150
Diamante, Julio, 82, 97, 153
Diéguez, Francisco, 54, 57, 64–65, 73

Dietrich, Marlene, 23, 76
Dimas (Madrid), 68–69, 79, 89
disabled people. See cripped (*tullido*) history of flamenco
Doña, Daniel, 101
Dora la Gitana (Antonia Galindo), 37, 38
drag (*transformismo*): between 1936 and 1960, 75–76; explanatory theory on, 44; female drag, 76; female drag after 1990, 89–90; as gender-based dissent, 4; male drag (*travestismo masculino*), 90–91; nostalgia in 2010s and, 91–93; theatrical drag after 1960, 78–81; trans folk artists and, 88–89. See also *transformista* (cross-dresser/drag queen/king)
drug usage in Spain: euphoric drugs, 45, 68; LSD, 69; as social issue, 4; WWI and, 45
Dumas, Alexandre, fils, 33

economic issues: crisis of 2008, 4, 107–13; in *cuadro* and acts division of *tablaos*, 50–52; drugs and, 68; Economic Stabilization Plan, 47; salaries, 51, 175n128; survival strategies for dancers, 113–27; taxation, 184n1; tourism, 47–48, 51
El amor brujo (1986 film) (Saura), 95, 96, 100, 101, 129
El Bailarín (Antonio Ruiz Soler), 50, 60, 76, 95, 151, 164, 177n153
El Burrero (Seville), 81, 124
Elche, Niño de, 131
El Cojo (Enrique Jiménez Fernández), xiv, 57, 86–88, 97, 151–54
El Corral de la Morería (Madrid), 48, 61, 70, 71, 73–75, 106, 121, 122, 128, 183n64
El Corral de la Pacheca (Madrid), 48, 100
El Cortijo (Madrid), 109, 125
El Duende (Madrid), 48, 54, 59, 71
El Güito, 59, 70
El Imparcial (periodial), 45
El Lebrijano (Juan Peña), 156, 157
El Muñeco (Antonio Zorí), 64, 68–69, 71, 72

Index

El Patio Andaluz (Seville), 72, 76
the Enlightenment, 7–8
Enrique "El Cojo" Jiménez Fernández, xiv, 57, 86–88, 150, 151–54
Enrique "El Jorobao," 149, 150
enthologization of Spanish Dance, 137–39
erotic judgment, 52–58
Escribano, Antonio, 27, 46
Escudero, Vicente, 50, 150–51, 175n124
España, Paco, 81
España, Trini, 64
Estatuto de los Trabajadores (Workers' Statute), 73
Ethnologic Dance Center, 137
euphoric drugs, 45, 69. *See also* drug usage in Spain

Faíco, 50
farruca: choreography for the, 50; cross-dressing and, 134; difference from *alegría*, xv; erotic capital and, 102–3; masculine clothing and, 89–90
Farruco, 124
female flamenco dancers (*bailaoras*). *See bailaoras* (female flamenco dancers)
feminism: branding as *feminijondismos*, 163; feminists in flamenco, 3; flamenco tranformation and, 163; Lejárraga Garcí and, 95–96; song lyrics with feminist content, 4, 30–33
feminization of dance: in late nineteenth century Spain, 11–14; singing and, 46–47; in the *tablaos*, 55–58
Férec, Jero, xiii, 2, 134
festivals: Festival Flamenco de Jerez de la Frontera, 90, 101, 127, 128, 129; Festival Flamenco de Madrid, 119; Festival Flamenco Empírico, 101; Festival Internacional de Santander, 48
15M movement, 119, 127
flamenco: anti-Enlightenment values and, 7–8; bullfighting and, 13; burlesque and, 134; as closure element, 74–75; communication of, 164; connoisseurs of, 51; as dance genre, xv;

emergence of, 4; flamenco identity, 8; flamenco-ness, 160–62; gender legislation and, 135–36; golden age of, 121; masculinization of, 62; nationalist use of, 47–50; *100 Years of Flamenco* exhibition, 137; *ópera flamenca* (flamenco opera), 46–47; as shared code, 105, 164; Spanish culture and, 163; state-sponsored tourism and, 47–48; term usage, 6; as UNESCO Intangible Cultural Heritage, 135
flamenco artists: crises and, 107–13; internal artistic criticism, 129–30; promise for, 70–73; survival strategies for, 4, 113–27
flamenco of exchange (*flamenco de cambio*), 15
Flamenco Queer, 134
flamenquismo, 12
Flores, Lola, 67–68, 75, 80–81, 89, 91–93, 145
Flores, Marco, 101, 124, 127
Flo6x8 (group), 119, 185n29
footwork: alternative strategies for, 154; El Bailarín and, 60; El Cojo and, 153–54; of *farruca*, 90, 102; of Grilo, 105; La Cuenca and, 35, 170n34; La Argentina and, 142; La Hija del Ciego and, 38; *látigo* step, 9–10, 169n9; long sequences of, 90; of manly dancing, 17, 58, 127; in masculine repertoire, 18; of Ohno, 141–42; *patá/pataíta* step, 85; predomination of, 35; punching action, 9; space and, 125; of *zapateados*, 17
foreign artists in Spain, 7, 44. *See also furreteos*
France: Bagouet and, 144–46; foreign artists in Spain from, 44; French Enlightenment, 7; French opera, 13; Lejárraga García's exile to, 96; male performers from, 39; Napoleon's invasion of Spain, 7; Ohno in, 142–43, 187n61
Franco, Francisco, 66, 67, 77, 78, 93, 112
Francoism: cultural association with, 93;

nationalist use of flamenco in, 161; *segundo franquismo* (second Francoism) era, 47. *See also* Franco regime
Franco regime: dominant model of family in, 176n132; end of, 77, 93; fairy (*mariquita*) shows after, 79; flamenco drag and, 75–76; flirtation with elites, 4; promotion of spectacle during, 169n21; Spanish Falange and, 49; unity of destiny ideology of, 49. *See also* the Transition
furreteos: defined, 4; toward a guiri History of flamenco, 136–48; toward cripped History of flamenco, 148–55

Gades, Antonio, 70, 71, 80, 89–90, 94–95, 96, 97, 100, 103, 124, 151
Galán, José, 148, 154, 188n79
Galván, Israel, 73, 100, 104, 129, 151, 155, 156
Galván, Pastora, 104
Gamboa, José Manuel, 17
García Lorca, Federico, 26, 84, 96, 131
Gay Club (Madrid), 79, 82, 88, 89
gaze: beauty and, 28, 104; *Carmen* concept and politics of, 97; as disturbing element of aesthetic experience, 126; diverting of, 3–4, 103; erotic objectification and, 103; extending of, 5; filtered through past, 120; as form of teletouch (*teletacto*), 56; heterosexual male gaze, 53, 171n42; imperial gaze, 171n42; Lacan on, 170–71n42; masculine gaze and feminization, 59, 103; paths of, 170n142; playing with, 127; provocative gaze, 18; role of musicians and, 56; solo dance and exposure to, 19–20; of spectators (consumers), 12, 52–53; women in observer role, 103. *See also* scopic drive; spectators (consumers)
gender: appearance of notion of, 33; double normativity of, 58–64; gender crisis, 4, 13, 127–33; gender division in *cafés cantantes*, 16–19; gender expression, 60–62; gender fluid artists, 33–34, 40, 128; gender identity, 6; *género* (gender/genre), 4, 6; hybridity of, 25–27, 28, 40–41, 139; performativity of, 172n72; Preciado on, 172n69; trans folk artists and, 88–89; *transformismo* (cross-dressing) and, 34; transition of, 4. *See also* drag (*transformismo*); feminism; *transformismo* (cross-dressing); *travestis*; *travestismo/transformismo* (cross-dressing)
gender transition in flamenco: Carmen de Mairena and, 82–83; El Cojo and, 86–88; drag (*transformismo*) in flamenco companies, 89–91; drag and nostalgia in 2010s, 91–93; Mr. Artur and, 81–82; Ocaña and, 83–86; Paco España and, 82; theatrical drag after 1960, 78–81; trans flamenco women, 88–89
gesture(s): colors added to, 9; effeminate actions, 177n153; feminine gender codes and, 61; floral theory of gesture, 143–44; history of, 10; *seguiriya* genre, 175n124
Gitano (Spanish Roma) people: activists, 4, 155–56; *baile gitano*, 160; in *cafés cantantes*, 20–21; Carmen and, 98; defined, xv; in flamenco, 3; flamenquismo and, 13; genre of, 6; *Gitano* activism in history of flamenco dance, 155–60, 186n48; *Gitano*-ness, 159, 160–62; marginalization of, xv; persecution of, 156–57; reflections on themes about, 5; self-exoticization, 159
Goldberg, K. Meira, xvi, 137, 148, 168nn3(ch.1)
González, Tasha, 100, 110, 124
Goya Theater (Madrid), 149
Granada: Alhambra Palace, 122; El Muñeco (Antonio Zorí Ramírez), 64, 71; El Polinario café, 25; Lejárraga Garcí, Maria de la O a, 95–96; León, José Javier, 27; Manolete, 101; microtablao shows, 117–19; Primer Festival de Músicas y Danzas Españolas de Granada, 48

Granda Terrón, Manuel (La Pirula), 76
Grande, Félix, 156
Gran Redada de Julio de 1749 (Great Raid of July 1749), 157
Gran Velada Flamenca, 149
Greco, José, 103, 137
Guerrero, Isabel, 110, 123
Guía secreta de Sevilla (Burgos), 79
Guilbert, Yvette, 81
guiris (foreign tourists), 3, 136–37, 139; Bagouet, Dominique, 144–46; decolonization of Spanish dance, 147–48; enthologization of Spanish Dance, 137–39. *See also* La Argentina (Antonia Mercé); Ohno, Kazuo

Hayes, Michelle Heffner, xvi, 64, 104
Heras, Rubén, 134
Heredia, Noelia (La Negri), 160
heterosexuality: as embodied ideology in the body, 19–20; heteronormative codes, 79; heterosexual bailaores, 59; heterosexual male gaze, 53, 171n42
Hirschfeld, Magnus, 34
Holy Innocents' Day happening, 87–88
homosexuality: gender expression and, 58–64; male prostitution in *tablao*, 66–68; Uranians and, 13–14
H2-Ohno (2014), 134, 143
Huertas, Trinidad (La Cuenca), 34–38, 76, 170n34
Hughes, Russell Meriwether (La Meri), 137, 139
hypercorporeality, 52–53, 56, 58

identity: aesthetic identity, 6; anti-Enlightenment values and, 7–8; flamenco identity, 8; gender identity, 6; queer identity and performance, xv, 161; Spanish identity, 8–9; trans identity, 89. *See also* national identity
illegal tablaos, 114–15
Imperio, Pastora, 26–27, 48, 81, 95, 124
Interrogations sur l'art (Lublin), ix
intersectionality of struggles, 157–59, 161

Jareño, Concha, 89–90
Jiménez, Antonia, 128
Jiménez, Pol, 132, 132–33
Jiménez Fernández, Enrique (El Cojo), xiv, 57, 86–88, 97, 151–54
Jiménez Peña, Bernarda (Bernarda de Utrera), 61
Jiménez Peña, Fernando (Fernanda de Utrera), 61
jondo, 11, 17, 46, 50, 61, 84, 131
Juana (La Macarrona) (Juana Vargas Heredia), 51
juergas (flamenco parties), 15, 22, 26, 126, 165
Jumillano, 66
Jurado, Rocío, 69, 70, 80, 91, 92, 93

Kaplan, E. Ann, 171n42
Kendrew, Edward G., 20–22

La Argentina (Antonia Mercé), 95, 134, 139–44, 172n61, 175n124
La Argentinita (Encarnación López), 26, 27, 30–31, 45, 50, 94, 105, 106
Laban, Rudolf von, 9–10, 168n8
"*Laberíntica*" (piece) (Lérida), 127
labor laws, 73
Lacan, Jacques, 170n142
La Carmen (1976 film) (Diamante), 82, 97
La Chana (Antonia Santiago Amador), 154
La Ciega de Jerez (Manuela Domínguez), 149
La Criolla (Barcelona), 41–43
La Cuenca (Trinidad Huertas), 34–38, 76, 170n34
La Escribana (José León), 40
La Hija del Ciego (Salud Rodríguez), 37, 76
La Macarrona (Juana Vargas Heredia), 51
La Meri (Russell Meriwether Hughes), 137–38, 139
La Negri (Noelia Heredia), 160
La Otra Pantoja (María José Navarro), 88
La Petróleo, 88

Index 215

La Polaca, 69
Las Brujas (Madrid), 48, 53–54, 57, 61, 64–65, 73, 161, 162
Las Carboneras (Madrid), 108, 110, 124, 182n54, 183n64
Lasera, Mateo (El Loco Mateo), 149
Las Folclóricas Gaditanas (group), 88
Lassibille, Mahalia, 138–39
Latorre, Javier, 101
Launay, Isabelle, 10, 112
Law of Vagrants and Thugs, 43, 62
Law on Social Danger and Rehabilitation, 62, 67, 78, 128
leftist singers, 4
Lérida, Juan Carlos, 100, 101, 119–20, 127, 132, 148
LGBTIQ+ people: collective imagination, 88; in flamenco, 3; solo projects and, 102
LGTBIQ-F revolution, 155
LGTBIQ movement: Flamenco Diverso festival, 128; flamenco tranformation and, 128, 129, 163; Gitanos and, 160; intergeneration revolution, 130–33; protests in, 78, 127; reactivation of, 127
Lidia (interviewee), 116–18
Liñán, Manuel, xiii, 90, 127–28, 129
López, Encarnación (La Argentinita), 26, 27, 30–31, 50, 94, 105, 106
López, Pilar, 94, 95
López Rodríguez, Fernando, 148; "Apuntes para una historia travesti del flamenco" (lecture), 129; *Bailar en hombre*, 128, 134, 164; in *Caída del cielo* (piece), 128; childhood, 1; *De puertas para adentro: Disidencia sexual y disconformidad de género en la tradición flamenca*, 11, 128, 177n153; "Estrategias de representación de cuerpos frágiles en el flamenco," 188n79; "Mutations of Desire in Dance" (dissertation) (López Rodríguez), 2–3
Los Cabales (Madrid), 48, 54–55, 64, 124
Los Canasteros (Madrid), 48, 59, 61, 66, 106, 161, 174n111, 182n54

Louÿs, Pierre, 22–24, 41
Luisillo, 48, 54, 55

Madrid: Alfil Theater, 82; Arco de Cuchilleros, 48; Arrieritos, 100; Ballet Flamenco de Madrid, 97; Beatriz Theater, 96; Café de Chinitas, 48, 59, 76, 100, 115, 122; Café de Levante, 25; Café del Vapor, 25; *cafés cantantes* in, 15, 20, 26, 81; Camorra, Alfonso, 47; Cardamomo, 182n54, 183n64; Casa Patas, 110, 123, 131, 182n54, 183n64; Centauros, 79, 89; Centro Cultural Villaverde, 164; Centro Danza Canal de Madrid, 130; Certamen Coreográfico de Danza Española de Madrid, 90, 125; Cibeles fountain, 161; Cinema Europa, 149; Circo Price, 149; Conservatorio Superior de Danza María de Ávila, 130; El Corral de la Morería, 48, 61, 71, 73–75, 106, 121, 122, 128, 183n64; El Corral de la Pacheca, 48, 100; El Cortijo, 125; El Duende, 48, 54, 59, 71; *El Espectador*, 6, 15; euphoric drug use in, 45; fairy (*mariquita*) shows in, 79; Festival Flamenco de Madrid, 119; Flamenco Diverso festival, 128; Gay Club, 79, 82, 88, 89; General Regulations for the Management and Reform of Theaters in, 8; Goya Theater, 149; illegal tablaos, 114–15; Las Brujas, 48, 53–54, 57, 61, 64–65, 73, 161, 162; Las Carboneras, 110, 124, 182n54, 183n64; Las Cuevas de Nemesio, 48, 54, 71; Las Cuevas de Nerja, 48, 59; La Taberna de Mr. Pinkleton, 48, 121, 183n64; Las Tablas, 123, 182n54, 183n64; LGBT protests in, 78; Lolailo (theme party) in, 130; Los Cabales, 48, 54–55, 64, 124; Los Canasteros, 48, 59, 61, 66, 106, 161, 174n111, 182n54; Los Gabrieles, 46; LSD in, 69; Madrid City Council, 66; Maxim's, 45; Minotauro, 89; Molino Rojo, 64; Muñoz Seca Theater, 81, 82; Patio Andaluz, 83; performance-

Madrid (continued)
outing in, 120–21; political instrumentalization of the tablao in, 74–75; Puerta del Sol, 92; Sacha's, 79, 89; street tablaos, 117; *tablaos* (flamenco nightclub), 51, 61, 100, 112–13, 121–25, 182n54; Teatro Avenida, 149; Teatro Flamenco de Madrid, 92; Teatro Lara, 95; Teatro Real, 57, 139; Torres Bermejas, 12, 48, 54, 60, 61, 71, 72, 74, 99, 183n64; Trianon Palace, 44; venues around, 89; Villarrosa, 26, 46, 48, 108, 122, 183n64; Vinent in, 25; ¡Viva! (Liñán) in, 129; Zambra, 47–48, 61, 71, 76, 100
Mairena, Antonio, 46
Mairena, Miguel de, 60
Maison de la Danse de Lyon, 142
Málaga: Bienal de Flamenco de Málaga, 127; *cafés cantantes* in, 15; gay tourism in, 79; La Cuenca (Trinidad Huertas), 34–35, 170n34; La Sillera (Antonia Galindo), 37; Molina, Rocío, 101; *verdiales* (folk dance), 113
male dancers: feminization of dance and, 51, 56; from France, 39; in French opera, 13; gradual loss of, 12, 13; homosexuality and, 13; hypocorporeality and, 56, 58; model of masculinity for, 58
male drag (*travestismo masculino*), 90–91
manliness, national concern with, 11–13
manly dancing (*baile de hombre*), 17–18, 90, 136. See also male dancers; *zapateados*
Manolete, 101
marginalization: in flamenco studies, xvi; reclaiming spaces and figures of, 3; shared space of, 155. See also cripped (*tullido*) history of flamenco; *furreteos*; Gitano (Spanish Roma) people; LGBTIQ+ people
marica (faggot), xv, 131–32, 134, 164, 186n41
Mariemma, 48–49, 95

Marín, Andrés, 101, 104, 151
masculinization of flamenco: *farruca* and, 89–90; flamenco masculinity codes, 59, 90; origin of, 6–9; women and, 62
Mathé, Baltasar (El Mate sin Pies), 150
Maura administration, 14, 36
Maya, Belén, 90, 100, 104–5, 106, 128, 156
Maya, Mario, 59, 70, 94, 100, 156
media: cultural machismo in, 163; Gades' coverage by, 95; TV broadcasts, 74–75
Méndez Garrido, Francisca (La Paquera de Jerez), 61
Mercé, Antonia (La Argentina), 95, 134, 139–44, 172n61, 175n124
Mérimée, Prosper, 24, 96, 97
Miró, Jonatan, 108, 109–11
Mizohata, Toshio, 140–41, 187n57
Molina, Amalia, 26, 27, 28–29, 172n65
Molina, Miguel de, 60, 177n153
Molina, Rocío, 101, 104, 128
Money, John, 33
Monje, Rosario (La Mejorana), 81
Mora, Kiko, xvi, 35
Morente, Enrique, 70, 94, 97
Morero García, Francisco (Paco España), 80, 81, 82, 89, 97, 134, 153
movement analysis and codes, 4, 17–18, 52–53, 59–61, 90
Mr. Artur (Modesto Mangas Mateos), 66, 80, 81–82
musicians: in *cuadro*, 51; de Lucía, Paco, 94; El Muñeco (Antonio Zorí), 64, 68–69, 71, 72; Fernández Jarillo, Curro, 154; gaze and role of, 28, 56; Gitano guitarists, 88; Huelva, Manolo de, 50; Montoya, Ramón, 50; Postigo, José Luis, 154; role distribution, 4; salaries of, 51; Sanlúcar, Manolo, 94

Nacha la Macha, 91–92
Napoleon I, 7
Narváez, María Ángeles (La Niña de los Cupones), 150
national identity: creation of, 7; the Enlightenment and, 7–8; flamenco

as part of, 6; Spanishness discourse, 49–50
nationalism: beginning of, 7–8; national use of flamenco, 47–50; patrimonialization of tablao and, 75; Spanish Falange and, 49
Navarro, María José (La Otra Pantoja), 88
Navarro García, José Luis, 16–17, 56, 73, 99, 170n41
Neville, Edgar, 50, 54, 56–57, 60
NO-DO (*Noticiarios y documentales*) (Newscasts and documentaries), 74, 179nn196–98
Nureyev, Rudolf, 74

Ocaña, José Pérez: on sadness, 165; as street artist, 81, 84–86; as *travesti*, 83–86
Ochando, Emilio, 90, 128
Ohno, Kazuo: "Admiring La Argentina," 134, 140–43; floral theory of gesture and, 143–44, 146; in France, 143, 187n61; *H2-Ohno*, 134; Mercé "La Argentina" and, 139–44
ópera flamenca (flamenco opera), 46–47
Orquidia (trans folk artist), 88
Otero, José, 12, 21, 134, 170n34

Pablo, Eulalia, 28
Paco España (Francisco Morero García), 80, 81, 82, 89, 97, 134, 153
Pagés, María, 90, 97, 100, 101
palos: characteristics of, xv; defined, xv
Pantoja, Isabel, 89, 92
Paris: *cafés-concerts* in, 15; Gayté Lyrique Theater, 150; La Cuenca in, 35–36; Madame Artur (venue), 81; Ohno in, 187n61; Paris Opera, 13, 57, 112; Zambra in, 71
Pastora Imperio (Pastora Rojas Monje), 26–27, 48, 81, 95, 124
Patio Andaluz (Madrid), 83
Pedro (interviewee), 116, 118, 185n21
Pericet, Olga, 101, 124
Piquer, Concha, 80, 92

Pohren, D. E., 58–59
political issues: liberals and, 7; marriage equality in Spain, 128; nationalism and, 7–8; political crises, 4; political instrumentalization of the tablao, 74; transition in, 4. *See also* the Transition
Politikon Collective, 111
Pollito de California, 137
Poveda, Miguel, 128, 131–32
Preciado, Paul B., 154–55, 172n69
professionalization, effects of, 13
prostitution: in *cafés cantantes* era, 22–25, 66; euphoric drug use and, 45; male prostitution in, 66–70; male prostitution in *cafés cantantes*, 25–27; prohibition of, 178n178; prostitutes (*cocottes*) from France, 45; Second Republic prohibition of, 67; in *tablaos*, 66
PSOE (Socialist Workers' Party), 95–96
Pulpón, Carmen Penélope, 55, 64, 65–66

queer flamenco: broadening readership of, xiv; diverted gaze and, 3; queerness, 160–62; scholarly research and, xiii, 133–34
queer identity and performance: distorted image of, 3; queer histories, xiv; queerness, 161; translated terms of, xv

Rajoy, Mariano, 107
Real Pragmática de 1499 (pragmatic decree of 1499), 156–57
Rey, Blanca del, 70, 71, 72, 99
Rockmore, Ryan, xiii–xvi, 133
Rodríguez, Agustín (La Reverte), 14, 36
Rodríguez, Salud (La Hija del Ciego), 37, 76
Rojas Monje, Pastora (Pastora Imperio), 26–27, 48, 81, 95, 124
Romero, Álvaro, 2, 131, 134
Romero, Pedro G., 63, 155, 157–59, 161
Rosario, 50, 76, 177n153
Ruiz Soler, Antonio (El Bailarín), 50, 60, 76, 95, 151, 164, 177n153

218   Index

Sadornil Ruiz, Francisca (La Tati), 71–73, 108, 112
Santiago Amador, Antonia (La Chana), 154
Saura, Carlos, 92, 95, 100, 101, 102, 124
scopic drive: aesthetic experience from flamenco, 144–46; of Carmen construct, 97–98; interpretation of, 170n142; objectification of bodies and, 103; participant observers and, 160. *See also* gaze
Second Spanish Republic, 14, 29–30, 36–37, 67
Sevilla, Paco, 51–52
Seville: African dance imported from Havana to, 147; Albarracín, Pilar, 120–21; Bienal de Flamenco de Sevilla, 100, 119; Café de Silverio (Seville), 25–26, 37; *cafés cantantes* in, 15, 20, 26, 81; dancing schools in, 21; El Burrero, 81, 124; El Cojo in, 87; El Patio Andaluz, 72, 76; flamenco in, 23; Gamero Cruces, Alfonso (La Esmeralda de Sevilla), 79; *Gitano* women in, 98; González, Soraya (La del Puente de Triana), 88; Graves in, 148; illegal tablaos, 114–15; Lérida, Juan Carlos, 100; LGBT protests in, 78; LSD in, 69; Navarro, María José (La Otra Pantoja), 88; Salón Oriente, 150; *sevillanas* from, 12; Silverio, 81; street tablaos, 117; *tablaos* in, 64; transatlantic slave trade in, 148; underground venues, 79
Sevillian dance style (*escuela sevillana*), 24, 53, 64, 81, 134, 136, 151. *See also* Otero, José
sex work. *See* prostitution
shawls: at Café de Chinitas, 122; dabbing action and, 9–10; to fill in space, 19; La Argentinita's use of, 105, 106; Liñán's use of, 90, 127–28; at Lolailo parties, 130; Lola López's use of, 148; *mantón de Manila* (fringed shawl), 9–10, 17, 20, 24, 142, 148; Ohno's use of, 142; *tangos* and, 17; Valero's use of, 128; womanly dancing and, 18

sign language, 150
social issues: child labor, 4; consumption of drugs and alcohol, 4; flirtation with Franco regime, 4; gender-based dissent, 4; job insecurity, 4; middle class construct, 101–2; nationalism and, 7–8; objectification of female body, 4; problems from social barriers, 163; sex work, 4
solo dance: self-spectacularization of body in, 126; spectator's gaze and, 19–20; in the *tablaos*, 51, 111–12
space(s): for activism, 119; *cafés cantantes* and, 44–45; for disidentification, 161; flamenco opera and, 46; flexible space, 168n7; of marginality, 155; as motion factor, 9; proximity and reduction of, 16; as reflection of past eras, 121–26; streets as stages, 119–21; street tablaos, 115–19. *See also cafés cantantes* (flamenco venues); *tablaos* (flamenco nightclub)
Spanish ballets: flamenco ballets and, 94–95; flamenco dance in mixed programs of, 48; male dancers in, 58
Spanish Civil War: cante jondo after, 46; flamenco drag and, 75–76; gender-based dissent and, 4; public establishment regulations after, 46
Spanish Roma (*gitano*). *See* Gitano (Spanish Roma)
Spanish War of Independence, 7
spectators (consumers): amateur spectators, 51; artistic judgment and, 52–55; connoisseurs, 51; erotic judgment and, 52–55; exceptional spectators, 73–75, 80–81; flamenco of exchange (*flamenco de cambio*) and, 15; foreign clients, 47–48; heterosexual spectator mirroring, 58; introduction of, 13; promise of interactions of *bailaoras* with, 64–66; spatial considerations and, 16; voyeurism, 95; women as, 103. *See also* gaze
Spinoza, Baruch, 3, 10, 86
Spivak, Gayatri Chakravorty, xiii

St. Denis, Ruth, 137
streets: Ocaña as street performer, 84–86; as stages, 119–21; street tablaos, 115–19
stripping, 85
Stryker, Susan, 35

tablaos (flamenco nightclubs): archival images of, 39; creation of, 47–50; cuadro and acts in, 50–52; *cuadros*' disappearance in, 108–13; decline of, 98–102; economic issues, 108; emergence of, 4; fundamental types of sets for, 183n64; male prostitution in, 66–70; promise for artists in, 70–73; promise of interactions of *bailaoras* with spectators at, 64–66; solo dancers and, 111–12; tourism and, 48. *See also specific tablaos*
teletouch (*teletacto*), 56
theatrical dance, 13
theatrical spaces, 16
Torres Bermejas (Madrid), 12, 48, 54, 60, 61, 71, 72, 74, 99, 183n64
tourism: *cuadro* and, 51; economics of, 47–48, 108; exceptional spectators and, 73–75, 179n195; gay tourism, 79; sex tourism, 68; *tablaos* as, 94, 108
traditional flamenco: aesthetic reforms/ruptures in, 101–2; as category, 3; intimate spaces of, 4; invention of, 47–50; spectators (consumers) and, 126
transcultural revolution, 133–36
trans folk artists, 88
transformismo (cross-dressing): men dressed as women, 39–42; term usage, 34; two branches of, 34; women dressed as men, 34–38
transformista (cross-dresser/drag queen/king): Canesa, Teresita, 38; defined, xv; development of, 4; Diadema, Carmen, 38; El Chache as, 76; in fairy (*mariquita*) shows, 80; Ferrer, Carmelita, 38; during Franco regime, 76; La Cuenca as, 34–38, 37, 76, 170n34; La Escribana as, 40; La Estrella de Andalucía as, 37; La Fragosa as, 37; La Hija del Ciego as, 37, 76; La Pirula as, 76; Las Argentinas, 38; La Sillera as, 37; male prostitution and, 66–67; Mirco as, 76; Mr. Artur as, 68, 80, 81–82; Pirouletz as, 76
the Transition: arrival in Spain, 78; chronology of, 77–78, 91–93; driving force behind, 93; LGTBIQ movement and, 78. *See also* aesthetic transitions of flamenco; gender transition in flamenco
transition of gender: Carmen de Mairena, 82–83; drag (*travestismo*) in flamenco companies after 1990, 89–91; drag and nostalgia in 2010s, 91–93; during 1970s and 1980s, 4; El Cojo and, 86–88; Mr. Artur, 81–82; Ocaña's cross-dressing in 1970s, 83–86; Paco España, 82; theatrical drag after 1960, 78–81; trans flamenco women, 88–89
transsexuals, 4
travestis: Bella Helen as, 88–89; Carmen de Mairena as, 82–83; defined, xv; El Cojo as, 86–88; Esmeralda de Sevilla (group), 88; Josette as, 89; La del Puente de Triana as, 88; La Otra Pantoja as, 88; Las Folclóricas Gaditanas (group), 88; Law on Social Danger and Rehabilitation and, 78; Margarita as, 79, 83; Mr. Artur as, 80, 81–82; Nacha la Macha, 91–92; Ocaña as, 83–86; Paco España as, 80, 81, 82, 89, 97; spectacularization of, 79; Tamara as, 89; *travestí* dancers, 79; *travestís* act, 80
travestismo/transformismo (cross-dressing): Baras and, 89–90; Carmen duet, 90–91; defined, xv; *farruca* and, 89–90; in flamenco, 3, 89–91; freedom and, 4; Galván and, 129; Liñán and, 90, 129; in "Suite de *La Casa de Bernarda Alba*," 91; term usage, xv, 34; *travestismo masculino* (male drag), 90–91. *See also transformista* (cross-dresser/drag queen/king); *travestis*

Ulrichs, Karl Heinrich, 13–14
UNESCO, 135
Uranians, 13–14
use flamenco (*flamenco de uso*), 15
Usó, Juan Carlos, 39, 45, 69
Utrera, Bernarda de (Bernarda Jiménez Peña), 61
Utrera, Fernanda de (Fernando Jiménez Peña), 61, 164

Valencia Rodríguez, Juana (La Sordita), 150
Vargas Heredia, Juana (La Macarrona), 51
Vargas Jiménez, Miguel (Bambino), 59–60
variety shows, 15, 27, 39–40, 45, 72, 120
Vásquez García, Francisco, 11, 12–13, 25, 169n22
Vilarós, Teresa M., 77–78, 93
Villarrosa (Madrid), 26, 46, 48, 108, 122, 183n64
violence: in demand for bodily beauty/ erotic capital, 103; gender violence, 97–98; love and, 95
voyeurism, couples dances and, 19–20, 95

Washabaugh, William, 64, 169n21, 186n48
Wittgenstein, Ludwig, 10
Wittig, Monique, 19
Woman and Puppet (*La femme et le pantin*) (Louÿs), 22–24, 41
womanly dancing (*baile de mujer*), 136, 151. *See also alegrías*; *bailaoras* (female flamenco dancers); *soleares*; *tientos*
World War I: drug usage in Spain and, 45; music styles after, 7

Zambra (Madrid), 47–48, 51, 61, 71, 76, 100
zapateados, 17, 18, 49, 75, 147, 180n13
zarzuela genre, 15, 38–39
Zorí, Antonio (El Muñeco), 64, 68–69, 71, 72